Organizational Management

WITHDRAWN

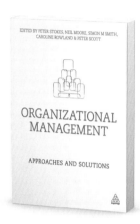

Organizational Management
Approaches and solutions

Peter Stokes, Neil Moore,
Simon M Smith,
Caroline Rowland
and Peter Scott

KoganPage

LONDON PHILADELPHIA NEW DELHI

First published in Great Britain and the United States in 2016 by Kogan Page Limited

2nd Floor, 45 Gee Street	1518 Walnut Street, Suite 900	4737/23 Ansari Road
London EC1V 3RS	Philadelphia PA 19102	Daryaganj
United Kingdom	USA	New Delhi 110002
www.koganpage.com		India

© Peter Stokes, Neil Moore, Simon M Smith, Caroline Rowland and Peter Scott, 2016

The right of each commissioned author of this work to be identified as an author of this work has been asserted by him/her in accordance with the Copyright, Designs and Patents Act 1988.

ISBN   978 0 7494 6836 1
E-ISBN   978 0 7494 6837 8

British Library Cataloguing-in-Publication Data

A CIP record for this book is available from the British Library.

Library of Congress Cataloging-in-Publication Data

Names: Stokes, Peter, 1959- author.
Title: Organizational management : approaches and solutions / Peter Stokes,
    Neil Moore, Simon M Smith, Caroline Rowland and Peter Scott.
Description: London ; Philadelphia : Kogan Page, [2016] | Includes
    bibliographical references and index.
Identifiers: LCCN 2016002987 (print) | LCCN 2016004033 (ebook) | ISBN
    9780749468361 (alk. paper) | ISBN 9780749468378 (ebook)
Subjects: LCSH: Management. | Organizational behavior. | Corporate culture. |
    Organizational effectiveness.
Classification: LCC HD31 .S696135 2016 (print) | LCC HD31 (ebook) | DDC
    658–dc23
LC record available at http://lccn.loc.gov/2016002987

Typeset by Graphicraft Limited, Hong Kong
Print production managed by Jellyfish
Printed and bound by CPI Group (UK) Ltd, Croydon, CR0 4YY

CONTENTS

07   Effective team-working in contemporary organizations   137
Neil Moore

08   Managing internet user behaviour within organizations: Inter- and intra-generational trends   161
Jessica Lichy

09   Arts pedagogy in management development   191
Anne Pässilä and Allan Owens

Supporting resources to accompany this book are available at the following url.
(Please scroll to the bottom of the page and complete the form to access the resources.)

www.koganpage.com/OM

ABOUT THE EDITORS AND CONTRIBUTORS

The editors

Peter Stokes

Peter Stokes is Professor in the University of Chester Business School where, in addition, he successfully completed faculty-wide Deputy Dean (2012–2015) and Acting Executive Dean (2012–2014) assignments. He has taught, researched, published and reviewed extensively in world-class journals in the areas of, among others: management learning and development, human resource management, critical management studies, and research methodology. He is Editor-in-Chief of the *International Journal of Organizational Analysis* and holds senior roles in a range of academic associations. He has applied his work through national and international knowledge transfer and consultancy projects across a range of business sectors.

Neil Moore

Dr Neil Moore (PhD, MA, PgCert, BA (Hons), Cert Ed) is a Senior Lecturer in the Faculty of Business and Management at the University of Chester. He lectures, tutors and consults in a range of business and management areas including international business, management development, contemporary management issues in small and medium-sized enterprises and sport management. His interest in business, management and sport led to his doctoral research into business management practices in the English professional football industry. He has also researched and published in a range of other areas including talent management, organizational behaviour, event management and research methodology. He is currently a visiting lecturer and academic adviser in a number of HE institutions in the UK and overseas. He is also an Associate Editor of the *International Journal of Organizational Analysis*.

Simon M Smith

Dr Simon M Smith joined the University of Winchester in October 2015 as a Senior Lecturer in Leadership and Management. He is currently Programme

Leader for all BA (Hons) Business Management degrees. Simon has expertise and research interests in leadership and management, human resource management, organizational behaviour, organizational analysis and international business. He has recently published in *Human Resource Management*, the *International Journal of Human Resource Management*, *Employee Relations* and the *European Journal of Training and Development*. In addition, Simon is an Associate Editor for the *International Journal of Organizational Analysis*.

Caroline Rowland

Caroline Rowland is Professor of Leadership and Management and Associate Dean at the University of Chester Business School. Her qualifications include an MBA from Henley Management College and a PhD from the University of Manchester. Her research interests are in the areas of leadership, performance management and also organizational culture. She has acted as adviser and consultant to the aerospace industry and to many schools and higher education establishments. She is presently on the advisory board of the Essex and Drake consultancy group based in Silicon Valley.

Peter Scott

Peter Scott is Senior Lecturer in Marketing and Management at Liverpool John Moores University (United Kingdom). He is an MBA and Chartered Marketer who built his career in sales, marketing and general management in the sport and leisure and pharmaceutical sectors before becoming an academic. He has presented at a number of international conferences and has published in the fields of strategic marketing and management. Peter is a regular reviewer of international conference papers and journal articles. His current research interests are in marketing and management and particularly in the marketing of places.

The contributors

Katalin Illes

Katalin Illes is a Principal Lecturer of Leadership and Development at the University of Westminster in London. Previously she held leadership positions in the United Kingdom and China, contributed to international collaborative partnership developments and worked as a consultant. Her research interests include ethical leadership, trust, spirituality in leadership and innovative ways of developing leaders.

Jessica Lichy

Jessica Lichy has a PhD in online consumer behaviour in a cross-cultural context, CEISR (Centre for European & International Studies Research, University of Portsmouth). Employed as *enseignante-chercheuse* (research professor) at IDRAC Research (Lyon), and Erasmus visiting professor at St Petersburg State Polytechnic University (Russia), Satakunta University (Finland), UCLan (United Kingdom), University of Chester Business School (UK), University of Greenwich Business School (UK) and the Cork campus of IDRAC (Ireland). Present research explores business models in internet user behaviour and international consumer behaviour. Member of Academy of Marketing and EDiNEB (Education Innovation in Business & Economics), other fields of interest include social media usage from a cross-cultural perspective, technology-enhanced learning in higher education, and research methodology. A reviewer for *International Journal of Consumer Studies* and *Behaviour & Information Technology*, Jessica teaches e-business, international marketing and research methods.

Martin Mathews

Martin Mathews has extensive business experience notably as export manager for two SMEs in France and as a senior accounts manager in Singapore. His consultancy work includes developing a five-year strategic plan for the defence division of Renault Trucks. He has also worked closely with the Lyon Chamber of Commerce analysing the governance systems of industrial clusters across Europe and formulating recommendations for the governance of clusters in the Lyon region. The results of this work were presented to the 8th International Cluster Conference as keynote speaker. Martin Mathews obtained his PhD in strategy and trust from the University of Chester in 2012. He is also the holder of an MBA from EM Lyon business school in France. He is currently senior Lecturer in Strategy at Westminster Business School. His research interests include trust, both between and inside firms, and he has published articles in major European journals on these subjects.

Allan Owens

Professor Allan Owens, PhD, is Co-Director of the Centre for Research into Education, Creativity and Arts through Practice (RECAP), University of Chester, United Kingdom and a Higher Education Academy National Teaching Fellow. He has led long-term capacity building projects, run intensive short programmes, developed research initiatives and staged pre-text-based interactive performances in collaboration with colleagues locally and internationally. Allan specializes in the use of drama for understanding in the professions and his practice-based research in the use of arts-based initiatives in development processes is informed by extensive experience in creative pedagogy, drama, theatre and the intercultural. Contact: **http://www.allanowens.com**

Anne Pässilä

Anne Pässilä, PhD, is Senior Researcher at LUT, LSI Finland, Visiting Research Fellow of University of Chester, United Kingdom, and partner-entrepreneur in Susinno Ltd. Her expertise is in applying arts-based initiatives to support innovation and organizational development processes. Through her research on the reflexive model of research-based theatre she is contributing to the emergent field of 'arts-based management'. Anne's interests are in investigating a methodological approach in which arts-based initiatives are utilized to involve employees of organizations and networks in development work. She continues to practise internationally and publish widely on the interpretative and intuitive approach to the innovation process. Contact: **http://www.annepassila.com**

Terry Smith

Terry Smith is Senior Lecturer in Marketing at the University of Chester and has taught marketing for over 20 years, specializing in marketing communications, buyer behaviour and services marketing. He has 19 years' experience working in various senior roles in B2B as a marketing practitioner as well as in a consultative capacity. His published work includes papers and chapters on various marketing topics as well as authorship of a key textbook, *Marketing Communications: A brand narrative approach* published by John Wiley. He still classes himself as an enthusiastic student of marketing. His ongoing PhD research covers the broad spectrum of marketing theory and marketing practice.

William Tate

Dr William Tate is a leadership strategist, consultant, writer, researcher, speaker and teacher. He is Director of The Institute for Systemic Leadership, Visiting Fellow at City University's Cass Business School, and Visiting Fellow at London Metropolitan University's Centre for Progressive Leadership. His work draws on principles from systems thinking and the new sciences of complexity and chaos theory to challenge conventional wisdom about how and where to search for leadership improvement in organizations. William is a prolific author, having written over 40 books, articles, papers, case studies and toolkits. Contact: (e-mail) **bill.tate@systemicleadershipinstitute.org**; (website) **www.systemicleadershipinstitute.org**; (tel) 01252 792322

ACKNOWLEDGEMENTS

A book with an editorial team of five knows the meaning of the terms 'teamwork', 'collegiality' and 'friendship'. We also recognize that without the support of our worldwide academic colleagues and associates we and this text would be the poorer. We would like to thank them as contributors to the text, as reviewers, as 'critical friends' and perhaps most important, simply as friends on whom to count in an, at times, challenging world.

We would also like to thank the enthusiastic students who reside at many international faculties and whose insights, points and questions provided much of the inspiration for this text.

Last but by no means least we would like to thank the team at Kogan Page who worked with us through the development of the text. We greatly appreciated their patience, good humour, understanding and professionalism.

The editors:
Peter Stokes, Neil Moore, Simon M Smith, Caroline Rowland, Peter Scott

Introduction

No serious discussion of the subject of organizational management could fail to acknowledge the importance of the external environment. As Jack Welch, former chairman and CEO of General Electric famously said, 'I am convinced that if the rate of change inside an organization is less than the rate of change outside, the end is in sight' (Woods, 2000: 44). Organizations today operate within circumstances of enormous change and the capacity of people – consumers, stakeholders, employees and management – to deal with change is challenged on an almost daily basis. The Western world has recently experienced many years of economic downturn following catastrophic financial collapse. Significant growth is taking place in some major economies but after a long series of spectacular annual increases in economic growth the pace is faltering in China (the world's second largest economy). Moreover, the financial situation in Greece has highlighted chronic issues within the Eurozone. The Eurozone is presently the world's largest single market and it is a very important export destination for, for example, British goods and services but the pressures caused by monetary union without an accompanying settled political union show little sign of resolution. Conflict is raging in Syria and Iraq and is spreading to North Africa and soon Southern Europe may be threatened, and relations between the West and Russia have deteriorated as a result of the situation in Ukraine. Oil prices have dramatically reduced and this is inducing significant effects on the world's economy. In brief and broad macro terms, such is the current global backdrop which forms the contemporary organizational external environment. What will be the shape and condition of the world in the coming decades?

Technological change is a key feature of the environment. This change is currently proceeding at an exponential rate and organizations are in danger of being left behind or similarly experiencing major 'disruptions' within their markets. Keeping abreast of these changes must be a preoccupation for organizational management and this has major implications for the way in which leaders and managers think and act. Above all, the rapidity of information exchange has become a central feature of modern work life. There is a well-known saying, 'A lie can be halfway around the world before the truth has got its boots on,' which has been variously attributed to Mark Twain, Winston Churchill, James Callaghan and Terry Pratchett (bbc.com, 2013). If this was a truism in previous decades it is much more the case in the social media environment of today. Given the ubiquity of social media serious reputational damage can occur in a matter of minutes, whether it is deserved or not.

The contemporary internal environment is also the subject of a great deal of change. People are changing their jobs much more frequently and the expectation of a job for life or even the notion of pursuing a singular career path within a defined sector has become a thing of the past. Colleges and universities may well be training students to take up jobs that have not yet been invented. The boundaries between work and leisure are becoming blurred and many people are now pursuing portfolio careers. Organizational management in the future will require a fresh, and constantly refreshed, approach that embraces these and other changes.

This book aims to address many of the challenges that are currently facing organizational management. The content is equally applicable to small and large-scale enterprises as well as to both the public and private sectors. The editors all have significant private sector business experience outside academia including but not limited to manufacturing, business consultancy, the aerospace industry, pharmaceuticals, financial services, sport and leisure and the music industry. Furthermore, much of the framework and ideas for the book emerged in discussions among the editors at international EuroMed Business Research Institute conferences. These valuable conferences proved to be the catalyst for much thought, collaborative activity, scholarly discussion and the productive interchange of ideas.

The book contains a collection of chapters, each of which concerns current and leading-edge issues in organizational management. Novel and innovative approaches are utilized to bring fresh perspective to historical and contemporary management issues and contexts. Each chapter begins by stating its objectives; the issue is then discussed in full from several different perspectives and many examples are cited. In most chapters there are activities and exercises that can be undertaken either individually or in groups to reinforce learning. Where pertinent, key points are provided for many of the chapters.

The content is therefore presented in a highly readable manner and scope is provided to test the ideas that are presented through the use of exercises. In addition to full referencing, a majority of the chapters contain suggested further reading.

This book will appeal to the 'thinking' student or manager by not adopting a prescriptive approach but rather offering original insights designed to stimulate further thought. The work is the product of careful research, leadership and management experience combined with substantive international business school teaching at undergraduate, postgraduate and research doctorate levels. This teaching includes the doctoral supervision of, and seminars delivered to, managers practising at the highest levels in public and private organizations. A wide range of authors have contributed chapters to this book from a number of academic institutions located in several different countries. This has enabled the book to offer an international perspective and deal with issues and topics that present contemporary management challenges that span and traverse international borders. Thus, they have relevance in many international contexts; this is an important consideration because, in the 21st century, technological developments enable even the smallest companies to compete in international markets. Indeed many organizations today are said to be 'born global'. Each of the chapter authors has particular expertise in the topics discussed in their chapters and has published extensively in those fields. Key issues are identified and explained and these are commented upon with reference to seminal readings, latest research, relevant supplementary literature and current management practice. The book will have relevance for students of business and management at undergraduate and postgraduate levels, as well as practitioners engaged in training and consultancy and leadership. The ideas and discussions in the book will also have great resonance with practising middle and senior managers. We, the editors, hope that you will value and enjoy the book.

References

British Broadcasting Corporation (2013) *Home truths for online falsehoods*, available at: http://www.bbc.com/future/story/20130426-home-truths-for-online-falsehoods

Woods, J (2000) *The Quotable Executive: Words of wisdom from Warren Buffet, Jack Welch, Shelley Lazarus, Bill Gates, Lou Gerstner, and More*, McGraw-Hill, New York

Management and organization
The 21st-century global and international context

SIMON M SMITH

01

OBJECTIVES

- Outlining some traditional and normative stances regarding leadership, organization and the management of talent.

- Introducing and offering alternative perspectives for addressing challenges within leadership, organization and the management of talent.

- Introduction and exploration of organizational ambidexterity – a theory that embraces complexity and contradiction.

- Introducing and outlining challenges and perspectives within global talent management.

Introduction – traditions and normative stances

Within many aspects of organization and management, there is often a desire to find the ultimate answer, to find the one truth behind developing and running a business that will lead to significant rewards. However, as this book will highlight, we firmly believe in embracing the complexities, the chaos and the subjectivity involved when engaging in global business. The former outlook could be considered linear, positivistic and arguably limited (see Chapter 2), but it is not without its merits. Simplicity and a narrowed focus can lead to great rewards – there are many global examples (McDonald's, Amazon and IKEA, to name a few). But what if, as the cliché suggests, 'knowledge is power'? What more could we do if we could understand, interpret and learn from the complex nature of realities? This chapter will consider and explore a number of modern examples in this regard. Importantly, the ideas presented offer an alternative way of looking at global business – they are disputed, a little argumentative, but hopefully thought provoking.

Examples of linear outlooks: normative leadership

The transformational leader

Hater and Bass (1988) provide a traditional definition whereby a transformational leader is seen as someone who can instil pride, faith, respect and a sense of mission. It is suggested such leaders have an ability to delegate, teach and coach employees while treating them as individuals. In addition, these leaders can encourage employees to think and act in new and creative ways.

The transactional leader

Another traditional definition from Hater and Bass (1988) is that of the transactional leader who rewards employees in accordance to their contracts and the efforts they exert. It is argued he or she avoids giving new direction if old practices are fulfilling the performance goals.

Thus, two generic approaches to leadership – the classic polar opposites. In essence, the often autocratic, reward and punishment (carrot and stick) focused transactional leader is considered to be a mirror opposite of the more democratic, caring and nurturing focused transformational leader. These are two leadership styles that have existed within the literature for decades and are still taught as the foundation building blocks of the leadership area. To get into the frame of mind of this book, consider one question at this point.

Activity – Initial task

Spend 5–10 minutes brainstorming leaders who could fit into the transactional and transformational leadership definitions.

Can any 21st-century leader be described accurately by either definition offered? Why or why not?

If you have named even one that is a 100 per cent match, we would be very surprised. Nevertheless, we use such definitions to begin understanding how leaders operate within organizations. They are a good starting point to begin potentially useful classifications. Also, we can start to contemplate how we may want to lead people if we become managers.

Charismatic leadership is a natural extension of the discussion above. Firmly established by Weber (1947) and House (1977), and with some overlap into transformational leadership (theoretically at least), this outlook considers an influence over the perceptions of followers (ie employees and/or customers) leading to a belief that the leader is endowed with exceptional qualities. We know it exists and we know it is potentially important – just consider Steve Jobs, Richard Branson, Anita Roddick and the many other examples that could be inserted here. (*Note:* The examples here are of famous entrepreneurial leaders who are well-known because of their personalities, vision or outlooks. Remember that there is much more to leadership beyond these particular entrepreneurial traits.) However – and remembering the principle of embracing complexity, chaos and subjectivity – read, contemplate and discuss with classmates the following questions (see Chapter 4 for an extended discussion on leadership and management).

Activity – Transactional and transformational leadership

1   How do we know which leadership approach is best?

2   Are these outlooks out of date?

3   Are these definitions an oversimplification of what leaders do?

4   How do we define 'faith'?

5   How can we effectively measure 'pride, faith, respect and charisma'?

6   Can a transactional leader not support creativity?

7   Is it possible for a leader to exhibit traits from both leadership styles (eg traits related to an ability to direct (an autocratic approach) and get tasks completed through standardization and conformity versus traits related to areas like coaching and supporting (a democratic approach) underpinned with innovation and leadership inspiration)?

8   Are there traits missing?

9   Is it possible for a leader to interchange approaches to meet the circumstantial needs of the organization, the situation or even the state of the economy?

10   Can a leader learn to behave with certain traits, or are they fixed?

11   How can we embrace multicultural variation whereby different traits are valued and considered differently within different contexts?

12   How can we understand global leadership variations?

Taking the leadership discussion one step further within this example, Blake and Mouton's (1969, Figure 1.1) *Leadership Grid* consists of five general styles, each with a different concern level for people and production (ranging from low to high). We could argue that transactional leadership fits fairly well into the high level of concern for production, and transformational leadership fits fairly well into the high level of concern for people. The model helps us to consider the performance of individual leaders and gives us a potential framework to possibly measure them against. However, many of the previous questions are still relevant here and we are yet to embrace real complexity, chaos and subjectivity. Remember, many great leaders have failed

FIGURE 1.1   The leadership grid

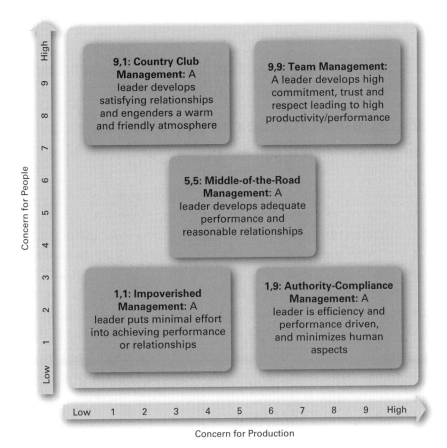

Adapted from Coaching Cosmos (2014)

(eg DeLorean – ever wondered why so few of these cars are left?; Jordan Belfort – the Wolf of Wall Street – although ultimately unethical and criminal in his business approaches, he was a charismatic and galvanizing leader for his employees; Richard Branson and his failing brands like Virgin Records and Virgin Cola; the many leaders of countries who cannot save their people from recession; and the many successful football managers who then find their team relegated).

Thus, Blake and Mouton (1969) begin to recognize that performance is crucial to leadership. This starts to add some complexity when we consider that some managers may be exceptional with people *and* tasks, and that also some managers may completely underperform in both areas. Yet this is still fairly normative, rationally structured and missing many competing factors. The following section will start to highlight how leadership and management can be viewed with much more complexity, and offer an outlook to contemplate and effectively deal with such complexity.

Organizational ambidexterity: opening Pandora's paradox

Within this time of economic uncertainty, organizations are met with an extensive range of external issues including shrinking markets, saturated markets, unstable growth, etc. Internally, human resources and management have to deal with the potential knock-on impacts related to downsizing, job security, motivation, commitment and so on. To use another well-known cliché, an organization could be left with two overarching choices to face this uncertainty: whether to 'stick or twist' (ie whether to consolidate or speculate). However, is it possible to simultaneously stick *and* twist, consolidate *and* speculate? This consideration presents a simplified metaphor for the concept of organizational ambidexterity. The following sections introduce and explore this paradoxical possibility and highlight some potential implications for managers using the traditional leadership theory and well-established organizational concepts. This will help to embrace some of the 21st-century business complexities that exist within the global context.

What is organizational ambidexterity?

Organizational ambidexterity is generally considered within the literature, in principle, to involve and embrace two polar opposites, ie exploitation versus exploration (Birkinshaw and Gupta, 2013; O'Reilly and Tushman, 2004, 2008, 2013; Raisch and Tushman, 2011).

Exploitative approaches focus upon existing customers and/or markets. Other key words related to these approaches include efficiency, refinement and expanding what is generally *known* to the organization. Comparisons can be made here to transactional leadership and McDonaldization theory. Ritzer (2008: 1) refers to McDonaldization as 'the process by which the principles of the fast-food restaurant are coming to dominate more and more sectors of American society as well as the rest of the world'. Here is a simplified breakdown of Ritzer's theory based on McDonald's very successful approaches:

- *Efficiency* – selecting optimum methods of production and service to drive down cost and increase speed.

- *Calculability* – emphasizing quantitative aspects, eg fast service (over high quality), is good. With a relatively low level of quality reached (compared to any high-end restaurants), the emphasis is on selling as many units as possible.

- *Predictability* – products and services are similar all over the world. This helps to keep costs low through standardized approaches and this has an extended benefit in terms of regulated customer expectation when the food is similar all over the world. (*Note:* There are actual variations across the world, but it could be argued that this principle still fits the general cultural context it exists within.)

- *Control* – limited skills required within the workforce leading to cost savings on wages. Customers are controlled by fixed menus and procedures, and low expectation of variety; the classic example being: could we dare ask for a burger cooked in a different way?

The McDonaldization theory appears to fit nicely with transactional leadership as we would perhaps expect a fairly autocratic approach to management in terms of basic monetary rewards and fixed practices. For example, front-line employees within McDonald's are given relatively simple tasks leading to limited skill developments; thus, in terms of motivation (and therefore 'control'), you may expect that concentrating on monetary rewards (primarily a transactional leader's focus) would work effectively for motivation rather than using transformational leader techniques that may emphasize higher skills related to job variety and job richness. We shall return to this example.

Explorative approaches focus on new knowledge and movements away from existing knowledge. Other key words within these approaches relate to experimentation, flexibility, innovation and divergent thinking. Apple, BMW, Google, Netflix, Toyota and many others provide a rich background of organizational examples in this regard. Comparisons can be made here to transformational leadership as aspects of, for example, coaching, mentoring and teaching become essential to achieving such an explorative approach successfully.

In essence, organizational ambidexterity is a metaphor for these two polar opposites working 'paradoxically in tandem', ie exploitation versus exploration, efficiency versus flexibility, stability versus adaptation, and the short-term approach versus the long-term. The challenge, if possible, is to take advantage of the benefits of both these extreme approaches at the same time. But is this feasible, or even realistic? Significantly, there is a growing body of literature that suggests that not only is this approach possible, it is becoming increasingly necessary for short-term survival *and* sustained success (Jansen *et al*, 2008; Kang and Snell, 2009; Kyriakopoulos and Moorman, 2004; O'Reilly and Tushmann, 2008, 2011; Raisch and Birkinshaw, 2008; Raisch *et al*, 2009; Simsek, 2009).

The overview of organizational ambidexterity above is a relatively simplified one to offer access to the subject matter, and there are numerous aspects of complexity and subjectivity to contemplate (see, for example, Stadler *et al*, 2014; Stokes *et al*, 2015).

Organizational ambidexterity versus normative theory

From the above, we can begin to contemplate and explore a new level of complexity. Normative theory could, arguably, be regarded as doing something one way or another – organizational ambidexterity enables us to consider alternative, and often contradicting, approaches. For example, if we look at the very well-known 'generic strategies' from Michael Porter (1980, 1985, 2004), the theory advocates approaching a marketplace either through 'cost leadership' or 'differentiation' within a broad or focused approach (see Figure 1.2).

Porter has argued that a company should focus on either of the extremes – cost leadership or differentiation – to avoid becoming 'stuck in the middle'. An attempt to do both, he would suggest, could lead to doing neither effectively and thus becoming ineffective at being competitive. However, when the theory was widely introduced and popularized in the 1980s, the global economy was less advanced and quite clearly a different playing field. As an extended example, the emerging superpower that is China has grown far beyond the cost leadership capabilities it was once renowned for (eg Wang and Rafiq, 2014). Many Chinese companies have grown, learnt and developed, and perhaps become great examples of modern organizational

FIGURE 1.2   Porter's generic strategies

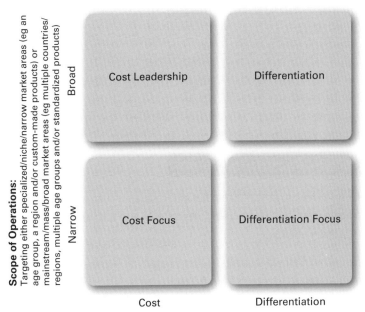

Scope of Operations:
Targeting either specialized/niche/narrow market areas (eg an age group, a region and/or custom-made products) or mainstream/mass/broad market areas (eg multiple countries/regions, multiple age groups and/or standardized products)

Broad

Narrow

Cost Leadership

Differentiation

Cost Focus

Differentiation Focus

Cost   Differentiation

Source of Competitive Advantage:
Targeting economies of scale versus valued and unique differentiation

Adapted from Mind Tools (2015)

ambidexterity. As other emerging nations potentially offer cheaper labour (materials, etc) and thus greater leadership in cost stakes, many Chinese companies have focused on the quality aspects of business to align themselves very effectively in the 'middle' (eg Xiaomi, Phantom, Geak and Tencent), as per Porter's outlook. Add to this complexity the full variety of cultural differences and business approaches applied and adopted throughout the world, and it is perhaps understandable to see how and why paradox can exist within such complicated business climates – the key is effectively understanding and managing such potential chaos. The Chinese perspective provided a simplified example to introduce complexity and contradiction, but it demonstrates that there is always a different way to look at aspects of business. If we applied Porter's theory in its rawest form, we would strongly criticize organizational approaches like this. However, through the organizational ambidexterity lens, we not only embrace the conflicting and contradictory approaches to business, we believe they are potentially essential for business.

The following activity enables us to contemplate the 21st-century challenge surrounding these theoretical outlooks. Try to discuss these questions/scenarios in groups to assist in becoming immersed in this way of thinking. *Note:* There are no right answers to these questions as so much depends on context, individual perspectives, cultural orientation and many other influential factors – embrace the complexity and subjectivity in your discussions.

Activity – Contemplate these scenarios

1   How do we drive down staff costs but embrace employee innovation? (The dispute over touchscreens between Apple and Samsung could be a good starting point.)

2   How do we build ethical business practices but not at the expense of profits? (Consider Marks & Spencer's Plan A approach.)

3   How do we reduce costs *and* increase quality? (Consider McDonaldization theory and the evolvement of Starbuckization*, and the production of TVs, eg Samsung, a company that ensures low prices for high-quality materials and parts by strategically sourcing from different countries. (*Ritzer (2008) suggests that Starbuckization could, in some ways, be argued to have replaced McDonaldization. This is because, for example, the coffee culture enables even more repeat purchases per day, even greater mark-up potentials and also sells 'a great experience'.)

4   How do we maintain predictability but provide a unique customer experience? (Consider how online trading has evolved, and organizations like Netflix, Amazon and IKEA.)

Dealing with organizational complexity

This chapter has so far introduced normative leadership styles, provided a brief overview of organizational ambidexterity and started to make some links between traditional theory and more complex considerations. Thus, how do we begin to deal with such complexities? How do we start to move our thinking into actual management and organizational practice? Here are three overarching possibilities.

1. The mixed leadership approach

In essence, managers need to balance and shift their leadership approaches to get the best of exploitation and exploration. They would apply transactional and transformational approaches, as necessary, to ensure performance results. But how easy is it to get beyond a dominant style of leadership? Indeed, normative theories demonstrate a clear distinction between styles. However, we would argue that in reality and within modern global business, this mixed leadership style not only exists, it is being developed and practiced (eg Stokes *et al*, 2015), and it is reaping rewards.

Consider this – how often are managers expected to reduce costs year on year, but at the same time improve productivity, motivation and commitment? Many of these managers are successful in their mixed approach, but it is perhaps difficult to contextualize these approaches. This is because managers can have very differing styles of leadership between the realms of normative theories, and these styles would expect to change to the needs of the organization and the market it operates there in. Thus, it is hard to measure when everything around you is constantly fluid and changeable.

As emerging markets continue to evolve, and many of their organizations are competing on both cost and differentiation, it has become a reality that ambidextrous approaches exist in abundance. It is a distinct challenge for organizations in developed economies to react and compete directly and effectively. Nevertheless, many organizations are successfully making the transition – Amazon and Netflix are two powerful examples. Amazon has provided an online arena whereby we can gain access to high-quality products at some of the lowest prices available. Netflix, through its relatively low-cost subscription service, allows unlimited access to its entire film and TV product portfolio through high-quality streaming. Both of these companies have clearly taken advantage of technology to achieve economies of scale while maintaining quality.

Crucially, this somewhat paradoxical approach to leadership does not fit within Blake and Mouton's (1969) theory. Their theory suggests that a 'team management' approach effectively addresses production and people – otherwise known as the 'high–high leader', a leader endowed with the (rare) ability to develop and care for his or her staff, as well as meeting demands for high levels of productivity (Yukl, 2002). This type of leader is perhaps considered to be the most effective of transformational leaders, a leader who achieves success without the opposing traits of transactional leadership being applied. Yet the ambidextrous approach above is perhaps a hybrid of their 'country management', 'team management' and 'authority-compliance management' styles. In essence, this ambidextrous leader is trying to meta-phorically get the best of McDonaldization theory and the high–high leader simultaneously. This is incredibly challenging and it is important to note that the suggestions outlined here are open to quite considerable criticism. However, remember two considerations: a) the outlooks here are designed to embrace the complexity and chaos eluded to earlier within the chapter – we are trying to get you to start thinking in a different way; and b) to reiterate, managers and indeed organizations have already, successfully, been wrestling with these contradictions as the economy shifts and changes (see Gibson and Birkinshaw, 2004; and consider the theoretical movement from McDonaldization to Starbuckization – Ritzer, 2008) – technology and the ever-expanding global economy have seen to that.

2. Recruiting different leadership styles

To address many of the challenges above, an organization could be more strategic within its ambidexterity approach. A recruitment policy, for example, that factors in a balance of exploitative and explorative mindsets could be integrated. In other words, when a greater emphasis on exploitative approaches is needed, an organization could employ a manager closely aligned to related attributes (ie transactional style of leadership), and vice versa (ie transformational style of leadership for explorative approaches). There are challenges in how such approaches can work effectively in tandem, but strategically, an organization has started by hiring relevant talent to embrace what they are good at, as opposed to trying to get managers to struggle with the balance of contradicting approaches.

3. Different department, different approach

Another approach to organizational ambidexterity, which has been long established within literature (He and Wong, 2004; Jansen *et al*, 2008; Stadler *et al*, 2014; Tushman and O'Reilly, 1996), is the spatial separation of exploit-ative and explorative approaches. In other words, you could have particular departments working to exploitative approaches and other departments working to explorative approaches. Of course, how such units or departments work together presents potential tensions and difficulties. This particular approach has existed quite extensively in the global economy. For example, how many organizations have moved operations (and thus departments) into emerging markets to gain the benefits of lower labour costs and materials (Nike, Gap, etc, although heavily criticized, are very good examples of early movers), yet their quality and innovation within the actual products and services are maintained within the developed markets (eg Nike is well-known for engineering and launching newly developed shoes and clothing)? Thus, organizational ambidexterity has existed across borders for decades, it has just not been contextualized in this way. However, perhaps organizational ambidexterity provides an ideal theoretical underpinning of such approaches.

Global talent management

In the 21st century, as the world of business continues to develop and expand, it is perhaps essential to refer to the management of global talent. As the 'world becomes smaller' in terms of the ease of movement, technology advances and heightened emigration, the recruitment, selection, development and management of talent have definitely become more complicated. Thus, unsurprisingly, it has also become a crucial area of consideration within businesses and the literature (Agrawal, 2010; Collings and Mellahi, 2009; Collings *et al*, 2007; Farndale *et al*, 2010; Minbaeva and Collings, 2013).

Expatriates: the search for 'Spock'

In terms of finding the perfect talent from a global pool of candidates, Spock, the famous character from the TV series and films *Star Trek*, embodies the perfect expatriate. He works as a senior manager aboard the *Starship Enterprise* and represents a culture of which he is (for the most part) the sole existing member within that working environment. Most important, he is exceptional within his role – he is a wonderful talent. Of course, this is a character from fiction, but he does metaphorically represent many of the ideals that organizations strive to integrate:

- Extensive cultural and market knowledge, including multiple languages and customs.
- Unique skills and attributes different from competitors', including a distinctive leadership style.

- Problem solving and decision making outlooks that provide more potential alternatives to dealing with global issues.

Within the TV series in particular, Spock had numerous issues to deal with as he became more and more integrated into the different cultural setting. This also reflects quite well the realities within organizations and, with the complexities of the existing world cultures, it is perhaps not a surprise to hear there are no concrete methods for tackling such potentially unique issues. Thus, how do we search for Spock? Perhaps more important, once we have found him, how do we keep him?

Traditional conventions of recruitment and selection

Finding and attracting high-quality global talent continue to be problematic for organizations (Farndale *et al*, 2010; Hartmann *et al*, 2010). For example, Collings (2014) suggests there is much work to be done integrating the global mobility of employees and global talent management. This may come as a surprise to many studying human resources when there is such a wealth of knowledge regarding areas such as recruitment and selection. Indeed, these particular processes can fall under a number of traditional conventions that have been tried and tested:

- Recruitment:
  - job analysis;
  - job descriptions, person specifications and competency frameworks;
  - internal recruitment;
  - external recruitment, including educational sources, employment agencies, industry contacts, newsprint sources, social media, and so on.
- Selection:
  - application forms;
  - shortlisting;
  - interviewing;
  - assessment centres;
  - psychometric testing;
  - references.

However, these somewhat normative approaches are not without their criticisms. It is fairly straightforward to find limitations regarding every aspect of these traditional approaches. For example, application forms could inspire CV fraud through the presentation of false information to attain an interview (Smethurst, 2004), and interviews have been long known for their various subjective connotations (Taylor, 2005). In addition, how such human resource processes are applied within small–medium sized organizations versus multinational corporations could be considerably different, due to, for example, resource capability and the application of informal training (eg Valverde *et al*, 2013). Yet, as with many aspects of organizational management, there is comfort and a degree of reliability to take from having traditional conventions like these. And this, perhaps, is where a great challenge lies regarding a global perspective. The management of global talent struggles to fit with these conventions. Indeed, recruitment and selection within a global arena are vastly more complicated due to factors like politics, economic structures and differing business norms, the individual nature of cultural identities, and so on.

Global talent possibilities

When focusing on international operations, we should consider the potential purpose of our global talent venture, as this will have a distinct bearing on the recruitment and selection process. In essence, the type of international operation is an important factor.

Activity – Consider the following scenario

Your organization opens a subsidiary in another country (consider a move from Europe to Asia). This is your first direct step into this country (ie operationally) and your knowledge base is limited to indirect experiences from outside the marketplace thus far (eg selling online to customers, conducting business-to-business activities through importing and exporting). Considering early parts of this chapter, your organization may wish to take advantage of economies of scale and thus this may require a slightly different strategic approach towards the management of staff.

- Choose a European country of origin and an Asian country of destination. Choose a sector of business that you operate in (eg clothing, supermarkets, mobile phones, TVs, banking, and so on). What factors will potentially exist in terms of doing business between these countries?

● What kind of talent is required for success? Look at the following section for ideas.

● Where might we locate such talent?

● Depending on your choices, what will be the strengths and issues related to your talent suggestions?

● When we have found our talent, how can we ensure we retain them?

Below are three general approaches to tackling the recruitment of staff within host country operations:

1 *Using an expatriate to undertake an international assignment – a parent country national (PCN).* This is often desirable for a company as it knows the person and he or she is familiar with the culture and practices of the parent company – there is a sense of control. However, there could be considerable limitations within the host country in terms of language, culture, business practices, expectations, transition, and so on. Also, this approach could be quite ethnocentric in nature and does not fully exploit the potential of the new market strengths. Finally, expatriate assignments do not historically have fantastic results as families struggle to adapt and employees do not desire long stays in unfamiliar cultures.

2 *Recruiting a foreign national from the country whereby the international assignment will take place – host country national (HCN).* This is considered a riskier approach, as the employee is unknown and his or her approach to business could be considerably different from that of the parent country. Yet he or she could have considerable knowledge of the new market, have relevant networks, can speak the language, can understand local practices and customs, and so on. Thus, the potential benefits are large. HCNs are also often difficult to retain as offers from companies within their own culture are desirable for long-term career stability – a somewhat mirror issue to that of PCNs.

3 *Recruiting a foreign national to work in the parent country – an 'inpatriate'.* Perhaps not initially obvious, inpatriates can offer a different solution to the scenario above, but it requires a considerably different approach to recruitment and selection. The general concept of inpatriates refers to drawing international talent into your parent country. However, taken further, finding talent with predispositions to working in different cultures, and then provided with considerable training and developing in the post company, could, in theory, be repatriated into their original country to work in the subsidiary. This dual knowledge of host and parent countries is both rare and desirable. Thus, perhaps the real challenge for the 21st century is learning how to find, develop and harness such talent.

It could be argued that to attain a high level of success within global talent management and find a highly effective employee like 'Spock', organizations need to free themselves from the shackles of traditional convention – also consider the normative versus ambidextrous stances regarding leadership and organizations discussed earlier in this chapter. The complexities and variations in approaches advocate that organizations should perhaps take an individualistic approach towards global recruitment and selection to suit the needs of their organization, as well defying those tried and tested approaches of old. Perhaps organizations need to be brave in this regard to truly reap the benefits they seek from a world of talent.

Job hopping

As an extension of the discussion above, another 21st-century issue for managers potentially relates to 'job hopping'. This is the phenomenon of moving jobs and even careers, which has seen that, according to one study in 2009, employees did not stay in an organization longer than a 3.3 year average (cited in Hamori, 2010). Indeed, the last few decades have seen significant increases in job and career movements due to distinctly higher levels of competition (Yamamoto, 2011). Replacing an employee with a new one can cost approximately 100 to 125 per cent of his or her annual salary (Taylor and Stern, 2009). With global talent being potentially more complicated than traditional aspects of recruitment and selection, the emphasis and importance of staff retention are exacerbated even further.

Activity – Understanding and overcoming job hopping

- Why do people job hop?

- What global factors could exist to further encourage people to job hop?

- What can an organization do to retain staff locally or globally?

- Returning to the idea of organizational ambidexterity, how can an organization retain staff through exploitative and explorative means? In other words, how does it keep the costs of retention down, but at the same increase commitment to the organization?

Concluding thoughts

This chapter has introduced and explored some specific examples of challenges for management and organization in the 21st century. Specifically, there has been a focus on normative approaches to leadership followed by an overview and integration of the more complicated theoretical outlook of organizational ambidexterity. The discussion was designed to encourage thinking in more unique, complicated, subjective and chaotic ways, which we would argue better represent the realities of everyday work. Organizational context was built into the discussion to further enhance the context of ambidexterity. Following this, global talent management provided an essential discussion area to reflect on the modern-day world of working. All areas were designed to provoke thoughts within a more complicated global dimension. The intention was to outline a unique context through creative theoretical connections to offer a genuine alternative outlook, which could then be debated and even criticized by learning scholars. The following chapters within this book will tackle and explore areas at greater length. However, this chapter should give students some essential tools for questioning and contemplating various aspects of management and organization from differing perspectives. One last aspect to remember is that the discussion here provides just some examples of the challenges to be faced by 21st-century managers and organizations; there are many other examples, eg political fluctuations (including the implications of the Trans Pacific Partnership, and discussion of the UK leaving the EU), economic instability (after all, much of the world is still recovering from the banking crisis of 2008), and the continual development of technology, to name a few.

Key points

- Normative stances quite often dominate theoretical perspectives. These are useful, but have their limitations.

- Within leadership, organization and global talent management, it is very difficult to find a 'one size fits all' approach for success.

- Organizational ambidexterity offers a more complicated view of management and organization to provide a distinct set of tools to view the realities of work.

- Modern global businesses are capable of simultaneously competing on cost and differentiation.

- There is a variety of possibilities when recruiting and selecting talent within a global business arena. Non-traditional approaches can potentially offer new strategic approaches for competing on a global scale.

Revision questions

1 What traditional and non-traditional approaches to leadership, organization and global talent management are presented within this chapter?

2 What benefits and limitations do the traditional approaches present?

3 What benefits and limitations do the non-traditional approaches present?

4 How can the mixture of ideas and approaches assist a manager working within an international organization?

Further study

Adamsen, B (2015) *Demystifying Talent Management: A critical approach to the realities of talent*, Palgrave, London

Mowles, C (2015) *Managing in Uncertainty: Complexity and the paradoxes of everyday life*, Routledge, London

References

Agrawal, S (2010) Talent management model for business schools: factor analysis, *The Indian Journal of Industrial Relations*, **45** (3), pp 481–91

Birkinshaw, J and Gupta, K (2013) Clarifying the distinctive contribution of ambidexterity to the field of organization studies, *Academy of Management Perspectives*, **27** (4), pp 287–98

Blake, R R and Mouton, J S (1969) *Building a Dynamic Corporation Through Grid Organizational Development*, Addison-Wesley, Reading, MA

Coaching Cosmos (2014) *Blake Mouton Managerial Grid Balancing Task- and People-oriented Leadership*, http://coachingcosmos.com/34.html (accessed 20 June 2015)

Collings, D G (2014) Integrating global mobility and global talent management: Exploring the challenges and strategic opportunities, *Journal of World Business*, **49**, pp 253–61

Collings, D G and Mellahi, K (2009) Strategic talent management: What is it and how does it matter? *Human Resource Management Review*, **19**, pp 304–13

Collings, D G, Scullion, H and Morley, M J (2007) Changing patterns of global staffing in the multinational enterprise: Challenges to the conventional expatriate assignment and emerging alternatives, *Journal of World Business*, **42** (2), pp 198–213

Farndale, E, Scullion, H and Sparrow, P (2010) The role of the corporate HR function in global talent management, *Journal of World Business*, **45** (2), pp 161–8

Gibson, C B and Birkinshaw, J (2004) The antecedents, consequences and mediating role of organizational ambidexterity, *Academy of Management Journal*, **47** (2), pp 209–26

Hamori, M (2010) Job-hopping to the top and other career fallacies, *Harvard Business Review*, July/August, pp 154–7

Hartmann, E, Feisel, E and Schober, H (2010) Talent management of western MNCs in China: Balancing global integration and local responsiveness, *Journal of World Business*, **45** (2), pp 169–78

Hater, J J and Bass, B M (1988) Superior's evaluations and subordinate's perceptions of transformational and transactional leadership, *Journal of Applied Psychology*, **73** (4), pp 695–702

He, Z and Wong, P (2004) Exploration vs exploitation: An empirical test of the ambidexterity hypothesis, *Organization Science*, **15** (4), pp 481–94

House, R J (1977) A 1976 theory of charismatic leadership, in (eds) J G Hunt and L L Larson, *Leadership: The cutting edge*, Southern Illinois Press, Carbondale, IL, pp 189–207

Jansen, J J P, George, G, Van den Bosch, F A J and Volberda, H W (2008) Senior team attributes and organizational ambidexterity: The moderating role of transformational leadership, *Journal of Management Studies*, **45** (5), pp 982–1007

Kang, S C and Snell, S A (2009) Intellectual capital architectures and ambidextrous learning: A framework for human resource management, *Journal of Management Studies*, **46** (1), pp 65–92

Kyriakopoulos, K and Moorman, C (2004) Tradeoffs in marketing exploitation and exploration strategies: The over-looked role of market orientation, *International Journal of Research in Marketing*, **21** (3), pp 219–40

Minbaeva, D and Collings, D G (2013) Seven myths of global talent management, *The International Journal of Human Resource Management*, **24** (9), pp 1762–76

Mind Tools (2015) *Porter's Generic Strategies*, http://www.mindtools.com/pages/article/newSTR_82.htm (accessed 20 June 2015)

O'Reilly, C A, III, and Tushman, M L (2004) Ambidexterity as a dynamic capability: Resolving the innovator's dilemma, *Research in Organizational Behavior*, **28**, pp 185–206

O'Reilly, C A, III and Tushman, M L (2008) The ambidextrous organization, *Harvard Business Review*, **82** (4), pp 74–81

O'Reilly, C A, III and Tushman, M L (2011) Organizational ambidexterity in action: How managers explore and exploit, *California Management Review*, **53** (4), pp 5–22

O'Reilly, C A, III and Tushman, M L (2013) Organizational ambidexterity: Past, present, and future, *Academy of Management Perspectives*, **27** (4), pp 324–38

Porter, M E (1980) *Competitive Strategy: Techniques for analyzing industries and competitors*, Free Press, New York

Porter, M E (1985) *The Competitive Advantage: Creating and sustaining superior performance*, Free Press, New York

Porter, M E (2004) *Competitive Strategy*, Free Press, New York

Raisch, J and Tushman, M (2011) A dynamic perspective on ambidexterity: Structural differentiation and boundary activities, *Harvard Business School Working Paper*

Raisch, S and Birkinshaw, J (2008) Organizational ambidexterity: Antecedents, outcomes, and moderators, *Journal of Management*, **34** (3), pp 375–409

Raisch, S, Birkinshaw, J, Probst, G and Tushman, M L (2009) Organizational ambidexterity: Balancing exploitation and exploration for sustained performance, *Organization Science*, **20** (4), pp 685–95

Ritzer, G (2008) *The McDonaldization of Society*, Sage, London

Simsek, Z (2009) Organizational ambidexterity: Towards a multilevel understanding, *Journal of Management Studies*, **46** (4), pp 597–624

Smethurst, S (2004) The allure of online, *People Management*, **10** (15), 29 July, pp 38–40

Stadler, C, Rajwani, T and Karaba, F (2014) Solutions to the exploration/exploitation dilemma: Networks as a new level of analysis, *International Journal of Management Reviews*, **16**, pp 172–93

Stokes, P, Moore, N, Moss, D, Mathews, M, Smith, S M and Liu, Yi-Peng (2015) The micro-dynamics of intra-organizational and individual behaviour and their role in organizational ambidexterity boundaries, *Human Resource Management*, DOI: 10.1002/hrm.21690

Taylor, J and Stern, G (2009) *Trouble with HR: An insider's guide to finding and keeping the best people*, AMACOM Books, New York

Taylor, S (2005) *People Resourcing*, CIPD, London

Tushman, M L and O'Reilly, C A (1996) Ambidextrous organizations: Managing evolutionary and revolutionary change, *California Management Review*, **38** (4), pp 8–30

Valverde, M, Scullion, H and Ryan, G (2013) Talent management in Spanish medium-sized organizations, *The International Journal of Human Resource Management*, **24** (9), pp 1832–52

Wang, C L and Rafiq, M (2014) Ambidextrous organizational culture, contextual ambidexterity and new product innovation: A comparative study of UK and Chinese high-tech firms, *British Journal of Management*, **25**, pp 58–76

Weber, M (1947) *The Theory of Social and Economic Organization*, Free Press, Glencoe, IL

Yamamoto, H (2011) The relationship between employee benefit management and employee retention, *The International Journal of Human Resource Management*, **22** (17), pp 3550–64

Yukl, G (2002) *Leadership in Organizations*, 5th edn, Prentice-Hall, Upper Saddle River, NJ

Historical and contemporary contexts

The representation and character of 'modern' organizations

02

PETER STOKES

OBJECTIVES

This chapter aims to outline the modernistic and positivistic philosophies and paradigms that underpin contemporary markets, management and organizations by:

- Elaborating the historical context of the role of the Enlightenment and the emergence of science.

- Explaining the development of the Industrial Revolution, the development of positivism and the recognition of modernism and its powerful implications for the shape and nature of organizations and management.

- Elaborating the nature and role of Taylorism and Fordism as consequences of the general modernistic movement and events.

- Contextualizing modernism and positivism by developing a conceptual understanding of epistemology and frames of reference.

- Providing examples of modernistic effects in organizations such as hard and soft management and corporate cultures, key performance indicators and metrics, audit cultures, managerialism, McDonaldization and the role of fashions and fads in management thinking and ideas.

Introduction

Chapter 1 mapped out the contemporary nature of work, organizations and their environments, in local and global terms, and underlined the contexts and issues that have become important for organizations. This chapter now proceeds to examine modernism and the phenomena of, for example, managerialism, Taylorism and McDonaldization and how they have endured as powerful influences on contemporary work settings.

The management of change and evolution has been a recurrent experience in business and organizations generally. It has become common to read in texts that, in the contemporary era, change is happening at an unprecedented rate and on a global scale. However, organizations and societies have always undergone change. At times this change has seemed radical and unpredictable while at other times there have been periods that have provided a semblance of stability and continuity (Linstead *et al*, 2009: 619). Historically, it is possible to cite many major events that have caused severe and extensive disruption to established society processes and structures that have in turn caused companies and organizations to go bankrupt and disappear forever. Changes may be relatively small or on a continental scale. These may include major tragedies such as, for example, plagues and illnesses (the Black Death and the post-World War I influenza outbreak in 1918–19, both of which killed hundreds of thousands of people and brought about significant transformations in social hierarchies, land and wealth distributions); conflicts (such as World War I and II – 1914–18 and 1939–1945) and economic collapses and depressions (the Wall Street crash of 1929 and the 'credit crunch' recession of 2008). Moreover, whatever changes are taking place, different periods of history are characterized by particular values and beliefs regarding the drivers that shape the epoch. Such beliefs are likely to change over time and acknowledging this is important for contemporary managers and organizations because this will facilitate a better understanding of the energies and forces at play in the contemporary world and workplace.

A key philosophy that has shaped the 20th and 21st centuries has been that of modernism, which can be considered to have followed on from pre-modernism. Modernism can be considered to have exerted influence from the mid-1600s until the contemporary era, whilst pre-modernism embraces Ancient History (that is, for example, Ancient Greek, Roman and other civilizations of the surrounding eras) leading up towards the early

Medieval period (Cummings, 2002). Modernism is important to understand because the values it embodies are very different from those that prevailed in the preceding pre-modern and Medieval eras.

Activity – The centrality of organizations in everyday life

Organizations play an unavoidable central role in everyone's life. It is almost impossible to pass through daily existence without connecting, or having to deal with, in some way or other, many different forms of organization.

Think about the organizations that you encounter during the course of your average day. Start with the time you wake up, the beginning of your day, your activities and movements during the day and your return home and finally to bed again. Ask yourself the following questions:

1 How many organizations did I connect with before I left the house for work?

2 How many organizations did I encounter, notice or was involved with on my way to work?

3 At my place of work or daytime activity how many organizations again did I connect with?

4 Finally, during the period of returning back to my house and my evening at home how many organizations crossed my path?

Each of these organizations potentially has a structure, aims and objectives, a legal framework for its set-up and operation, markets and customer bases, a history of its past, a particular set of employees and managers, all of whom are experiencing the joys, pleasures, stresses, tensions and pressures of the contemporary workplace. An organization is thus a complex amalgam of many things and dimensions that produce and reproduce how individuals and groups behave and conduct their work. In other words, organizations as entities or artefacts are not neutral, innate objects; rather they are created by the actions of people and take particular forms and actions based on individuals' choices and actions. In turn, the organizations so formed and shaped influence the behaviour of people and the overall dynamic is interactive and osmotic.

Modernism – a key shaping force of the contemporary world

'Modernism' is not a word often mentioned in everyday life; however, it is a term widely in operation in societies and which points at, and represents, a wide range of effects on managers and organizations (Dereli and Stokes, 2007; Lyotard, 1979; Peci, 2009; Stokes, 2011b; Townley, 2002). In order to gain insight into the nature and impact of modernism it will be useful to take an historical perspective. History may on occasion seem rather dry and what has already happened may not always seem as exciting as the contemporary period or the prospect of what may be likely to happen in the future. However, if it is possible to develop a basic understanding of how a contemporary event, a current situation or phenomenon was produced by a series of historical events, this enables us to understand the likely future trajectory of developments. Moreover, this allows us to see more clearly why things are the way we see and experience them. This is the case with the influence of modernism on management and organization. Modernism arose from a period that has been labelled the Enlightenment (Watson, 2006). It will be useful to understand more about why that period is significant as it has had an enduring and widespread impact on the manner in which management and organizations are shaped; this is addressed below.

The Enlightenment and its significance for modern management

The Enlightenment occurred between approximately the 1640s and the late 1700s/early 1800s in Western Europe. It was a period in which many philosophers, artists and writers were developing new and challenging ways of thinking about and organizing society and its institutions. This led to many new ideas about governance, values, beliefs and the rights and responsibilities of the individual (Pagden, 2015). Today, many of the ideas that were introduced, argued and even battled over during the Enlightenment period are considered as normal and usual in many contemporary societal contexts. These include democracy itself, the right to vote, human rights, the rule of law (ie everyone is equal before the law and nobody is above the law) and many more rights and responsibilities. Above all, the Enlightenment sought to bring logic and rationale to bear on the challenges and issues confronting society.

In addition, the emergence and formalization of the field of science came into being during this period. Science and the scientific method for the determination of knowledge provided a method for developing knowledge that could be seen as logical and rational, offering objectivity, cause–effect and empiricism. The overall approach, ideas and spirit of the Enlightenment and its embodiment of the scientific method challenged many of the long-standing ideas of privilege and power. This contrasted substantially with the status quo, which had vested power in the monarchy, aristocracy, landed gentry, formal state religion, folklore and custom and superstition. This led to many major upheavals and changes in society, not least the French Revolution and also, vitally for management and organization, the Industrial Revolution (Mokyr, 2012).

The Industrial Revolution, which took place in the 18th and 19th centuries in the United Kingdom and wider Europe caused major reorganization of agricultural methods and production, a rural exodus to new and growing cities and urban conurbations (Trinder, 2013). In tandem with this, new factory systems of production became prevalent in which there was specialization of task (each stage of the task being undertaken by a particular skill, or group of skilled workers and therefore accomplished faster and more efficiently). This contrasted sharply with the cottage and subsistence forms of production that had existed previously. In those earlier processes it was commonly the case that many of the different tasks and processes to make products or outputs would be undertaken by the same person, or small group of people. Within these new structures, managers came into being as a recognized and powerful set of figures within the production processes and, in many ways, a new social class (*ibid*).

As an integral part of this wide set of changes, new organizational structures emerged as firms and markets for commodities, money (capital), and business grew larger and larger (Prak, 2014). This was the emergence of the capitalist free market system that operates across the globe today and what is generally referred to as 'capitalism'. The overall period has been labelled 'modernism'. Science and the scientific technique are central to that world, and the research methodology that is employed to use this technique is called positivism (Kuhn, 2012).

Positivism and its role in modern business

Modernism is a product of, and underpinned and informed by, the Enlightenment. Positivism is the most frequent methodological approach used to conduct research within this modernist environment. It is a methodology that prizes rationalism and objectivity and employs the scientific experimentationalist technique. Kindred with the historical development of the

Enlightenment and modernism, positivism was developed in the first half of the 19th century (at the height of what would be considered the modernistic era) and led most notably by a Frenchman, Auguste Comte (1798–1857). Like so many philosophers and writers of his time, Comte was keen to see evolving scientific principles applied to a wide range of social issues such as poverty, crime, urbanization and a society that was industrializing. He and his adherents saw these scientific approaches contrasting with preceding and competing religious, societal authority-based and folklore-based ways of making sense of, and decisions on, issues.

Many students encounter positivism when they come to do a major piece of research in their course of study. Therein, they may develop the belief that they have a choice between positivism and interpretivism (an approach that acknowledges and works with a subjective, rather than uniquely objective, view of the world) (Stokes and Wall, 2015). Of course, the choice of methodological approaches is, in reality, much wider, but the lived experience of many dissertations is that students hover between the choice of these two approaches. Many students choose to adopt a positivistic methodological approach. Often this will attempt to measure phenomena, events or situations and employ some figures/numbers or statistical data to make its arguments in line with the categorization, quantification and attempt to objectify the issues in the problem under examination. When students are using positivism in their research it is a direct product of and consequence that stems from the Enlightenment and positivism. Moreover, and very important, because modernism and positivism have been a powerful influence for a number of centuries, many institutions and their processes have evolved grounded in the scientific principles and approaches. These institutions encompass not only corporate companies and their structures and processes but also wider societal organizations including health care providers, educational establishments and military organizations to name but a few. For example, the manner in which a hospital is structured into specialist wards and departments, the specialized training career routes of doctors, the appointment system, the waiting list and waiting targets (**www.aihw.gov.au/australias-health; www.nhs.uk**, 2015) are just a few examples of modernistic structuring. Equally, in a school, the structuring of forms, the rotational session change and timetable, the specialisms of the teachers, the system of placing learning in different stages of achievement, the setting of predicted and target grades are useful examples of modernistic structuring in everyday settings. Individuals grow up in, are surrounded by and immersed in these modernistically shaped atmospheres and environments.

Modernism also infuses styles of art, creative writing, music and architecture (Wolfe *et al*, 2010; Wood, 2004).

Modernism and its affects are everywhere around us. Much of business, organization and management studies and the various disciplinary and subject fields they embrace are equally heavily influenced by modernistic constructs. Because modernism is so profoundly imbued in the fabric of contemporary society it is often the case that individuals do not realize that they are thinking, behaving and making choices under scientific-method-informed modernistic and positivistic principles.

Frederick Winslow Taylor

Frederick Winslow Taylor is a well-known and early illustration of modernistic approaches and applied positivism in action. Whenever students undertake a module on, for example, topics such as human resource management, performance management or organizational behaviour it is highly probable that the content includes a discussion of Frederick Winslow Taylor (1856–1915) and his approach to creating efficient work processes for organizations. His thoughts and proposals were embodied in his book *The Principles of Scientific Management,* originally published in 1911 (Clegg *et al*, 2011).

Based on his experiences of working in factories and industrial settings at the turn of the 20th century, Taylor began to design what he considered to be the principles on which industrial production could be made more efficient and ultimately optimized. These included organizing work processes by the *scientific study* and breakdown of tasks and replacing custom and practice and local methods; ensuring that management was in charge of structuring work and removing power from the (often unionized) workforce; standardization of process and identification of the 'one best way' to complete the task (Watson, 2006). The categorization, measurement and identification of Taylor's quest for an optimum 'one best way' echoes positivism, scientific experimentationalist approaches and an overall atmosphere of modernism. In this way it can be seen that Taylor and his work were very much imbued by, embrace and encapsulate the spirit of modernistic thinking.

Taylorism was applied to some degree in Henry Ford's car manufacturing factories to increase efficiency and outputs. Ford's manner of organizing car production led to the introduction of the term 'Fordism', which points at the large-scale mass-production manufacturing operations organized and run as efficiently as possible. However, in modernistic and Fordist settings, the conditions for employees and the attention paid to their physical and mental wellbeing were not always paramount (Knights and Willmott, 2012). The essential principles of Fordism, albeit modified to a greater or lesser extent by new ideas and approaches (for example, lean manufacturing, just-in-time, Kaizen) are still in operation in many manufacturing operations and factories in the contemporary era, but increasingly flexible specialization and customization have come to the fore. Within Fordism the production facilities often tend to be fixed and not easy to reconfigure. Flexible specialization allows the processes and stages of manufacturing to be organized so that the core product can be constructed with all its common features and then can be adapted and customized for specific customer needs and requirements (Worthington, 2012). Thus, for example, in the case of car manufacture, while the basic model of a vehicle may essentially be the same across the range of cars within a model type, at the point of order and purchase the client can indicate a range of options and accessories (sunroof, gear-change mechanism options, wheel types, etc) depending on their preference. All of this can be readily achieved in the factory when the order arrives because the assembly track has flexible specialization built into its layout.

Activity – Do a Tayloristic experiment for yourself

An integral part of Taylor's work was the observation and measurement of every aspect of each task or work role that made up a part of the industrial or manufacturing process, and ultimately would be connected to, and interlinked with, many other similarly measured and assessed activities. As mentioned earlier, his objective was to make each task and the overall process and outputs as efficient as possible.

Think about your routine in the morning from waking up to leaving the house. Reflect and make notes on the following points:

Thought prompt: How would you divide up the experience and process into a series of tasks? What would be the dividing lines that separated out those tasks?

Ideas for thought prompt: Think about waking up, getting out of bed, picking up your dressing gown, walking from the bedroom to the shower, showering, exiting the shower, drying off, getting dressed, going to the kitchen, etc.

You will see that what at first sight seems like a relatively straightforward matter of getting up and getting ready to leave the house for the day's activities is in fact a complex series of tasks. Each task can be studied and further broken down into sub-tasks and each one of these can be measured and gauged so that it can be performed as efficiently as possible. For example, when the alarm goes off, where and how is the alarm positioned so that it can be reached easily? Is the device itself easy to switch off? Should 'snooze five minutes' be allowed as part of the standard process? Then, following the Taylorist approach, you would think about getting out of bed as swiftly and efficiently as possible. What would be the best body position to achieve this? What series of movements, and in which order, would achieve this task most quickly? How long would each take? What are the alternatives? You will need to double-check that these alternatives are not faster. This separating out of activities to the smallest level goes on through every aspect of the various stages of your morning right up to leaving the house. In effect you would end up with a work-flow time-motion plan and table indicating each task within each stage of the morning, its sub-stage and a timing for each stage/action.

Imagine, therefore, how this approach and thinking can be applied to the management of business and industrial processes. While this illustration does not represent every detail of Tayloristic thinking, it does provide an insight into the broad approach.

Frame of reference and epistemology – contextualizing modernism and positivism

When we state that we need to 'put something into context' it means setting the item or event in the time, space and circumstances in which it occurred. Things or events are often more fully understood when we learn about what was happening around, or in relation to, them. For example we may witness a heated exchange at work which, on the face of it, looks unreasonable and inappropriate. However, when we learn about the circumstances and events leading up to it then it may become easier to understand and appreciate actions and reactions and also motives, emotions and thinking that brought it about.

How individuals think about a situation in context is very much dependent on the mindset that has built up over the years of their life and through the many contacts and experiences they have had. Within these processes, powerful environmental and historical legacies such as modernism and positivism – which it was established above, heavily imbue and shape many organizational practices in the contemporary world – play a significant and unavoidable role. A person's mindset, thus formed, can be said to be operating in line with a given frame of reference as a consequence of a wide range of influences over time (Stokes, 2011b: 49).

Linking frame of reference and epistemology to modernism and positivism

Frame of reference and epistemology play a role in the formation of context and assist in facilitating a better understanding of the ideas that make and drive organizational life. 'Frame of reference' means the typical and habitual way in which a person thinks about the world and the people, things and events within it. Such approaches are instrumental in developing the knowledge and understanding a person has about the world. This might be expressed as their personal philosophy towards the world or, more colloquially, how they make sense of their experiences and the experiences of others. A person's frame of reference is developed and constructed over their life. It may be based on, for example, experiences directly lived or read about. The environment and setting in which actions and thoughts occur will also have a major impact.

A further, perhaps more technical term linked to, and often operating as part of, frame of reference is 'epistemology'. Epistemology concerns analysis and understanding of the philosophies through which knowledge is created. In other words, knowledge is not something that 'just happens' or 'just comes into being' (Stokes, 2011b: 41–3; Stokes and Wall, 2015: 94–5). Knowledge *is made* by the frames of reference people employ and the choices they make about what they consider valid or invalid. Epistemology works to understand the thinking and philosophical processes that produce a given knowledge or perspective on knowledge. Modernism and positivism are two such philosophical approaches that have particular epistemological stances. We saw above that these approaches are underpinned by scientific experimentationalist principles such as objectivity, categorization/representation, measurement and causality. When applied to business management and organizations these approaches tend to seek heightened and optimized efficiency and effectiveness as a priority. Thus modernism and positivism prevail as very dominant and pervasive frames of reference in many individual managers' and employees' operational frames of reference.

So, to summarize, epistemology is any system of thought that people use to develop and justify the knowledge and ideas that they believe. Thus, for example, a scientist, or a person adopting a scientific approach, will use a positivistic approach operating in relation to the requirements and traditions of their field (physics, chemistry, biology, etc). Alternatively, someone might use knowledge based on the traditions of a particular religion. For example, someone might state that they make decisions and sense of the world through

Christianity, Islam or Buddhism and the principles and ideas from these respective religions inform what they believe, say and how they act. In a more everyday, parochial sense it might be possible to see how the customs, traditions and accumulated knowledge of a given settlement, village or human environment support and influence the way people think and behave. Some of these examples offer recognized and clearly defined epistemologies whereas others are more evolving and iterative.

Modernism and positivism, through their prevailing objectivity, can appear clinical in nature. The application of these principles to work settings also risks alienating individuals and dehumanizing work, which can impact negatively on work atmospheres and environments and indeed, ultimately, performance and productivity. During the course of the 20th century, many philosophies and approaches which are different from, and challenge or offer alternatives to, modernism and positivism have emerged. These too have been applied to organizations and management. There is a wide range of philosophies, including human relations school, critical theory, deconstructionism, postmodernism, and poststructuralism developed and discussed in relation to organizations (Knights and Willmott, 2011). The nature of these and how they have influenced organizations and management, and provided a response to modernism and positivism, are addressed in Chapter 3.

The enduring legacy and impact of modernism and positivism

It is perhaps no accident that many organizations appear very similar in terms of function and appearance. While there is a constant stream of novel and innovative ideas about organizing and conducting business organization and management, there are, nevertheless, often some recurrent principles that are underlying them. Many of these principles stem from the general influence of the approach and underpinning philosophy of modernism and its kindred positivism.

How do modernism and positivism manifest themselves in relation to management and organization? Their influence is more pervasive than might at first appear to be the case. For example, the general push to achieve enhanced profit, or enhanced return on capital, measured by key performance indicators (KPIs) is a preoccupation (not to say an obsession) for many organizations

(Wilson, 2010: 95). Moreover, in many business settings everyday conversations turn towards a focus on 'effectiveness', 'efficiency' and outputs, especially metrics such as profits and various turnover rates (sales, labour, stock). It is commonly felt that by adopting or establishing KPIs a manager will be able to monitor and manage an organization appropriately (Marr, 2012). Thus, these are seen as comprising 'what should be talked about' and what is 'important' in a usual business context. Through repetition and reinforcement talking about management and organizations in this way becomes what is considered 'normal' and 'normative'. In other words, it becomes what is expected 'to be' and anticipated 'to happen' and if it does not then it may be felt that something is not quite right and probably needs to be corrected.

Modernism and positivism have become such an integral part of our work lives that it is very easy to accept them and move through environments without noticing them or seeing their effects. An example can be found in the plethora of targets and goals that reign across public and private sectors alike, including:

- *Accounting metrics and ratios:* Return on capital; Current ratio; Debtors ratio; Net profit; Gross profit.

- *Human resource ratios:* Labour turnover; Wellbeing index; Employee stability.

- *Marketing ratios:* Market share; Customer loyalty; Customer (market).

These are just a few examples of the tendency to try to measure performance and productivity in organizations' penetration (for further illustrations see Marr, 2012). The establishment and use of KPIs of this nature lead to the commonplace retorts and sayings of the ilk: 'What gets measured gets managed/what isn't measurable doesn't get managed'; 'He or she knows the price or cost of everything and the value of nothing'. Such sayings are, in some ways, criticisms of a particular mindset – one that makes sense (Weick, 1995) of the world by quantification, numbers, measurements and managing through these forms of metrics. Based on the discussion above, it will be apparent that this is a view that has been influenced and nurtured by the predominant modernistic environment in structured academic subject areas and knowledge bases, and has infused education at all ages. Thus, it is perhaps little surprise that it is dominant in contemporary organization and management.

Many people working in contemporary organizations and environments find that there is an ever-increasing pressure to respond to the need to audit, report on and document their work activities. This may take the form of monthly sales, productivity and performance reports. Equally, it could be a need to respond to some information request by a governmental or quasi-governmental body for statistics, figures on some aspect of the business – data protection, Inland Revenue and taxation, quality assurance institutes, health and safety agencies or equality and diversity bodies to name but a few (Strathern, 2000). While auditing and monitoring of course play a role in gathering potentially valuable data they also create extra work and tasks that need to be accomplished. It can also be argued that they echo Tayloristic and modernistic approaches that seek to improve performance and outputs through measurement and assessment.

It is often said that each organization and workplace is unique. While this may be the case, because modernism has been so dominant there may also be many commonalities between them. Examples of such shared features include:

- The broad ways in which the organization is structured into departments, teams, hierarchies and so on, or at the very least the sorts of ideas on structure that it adopts and implements.

- The types of role and positions that exist in an organization – for example, managers, assistant managers, directors and other organizational staff members such as marketing, production and accounting staff.

- The types of procedures and processes it creates and follows: committees, legal arrangements, accounting procedures and business development operations.

Many of these will be predicated and constructed on modernistic and positivistic assumptions of categorization, measuring and the belief in the possibility of optimizing performance, believing in and implementing notions such as 'best practice', and finding the 'one best way' (to echo Taylor) to achieve the task.

Activity – Structure and communication

Think about an organization where you have worked or with which you have had some form of contact, or have read or heard about.
How is the organization structured?

- What are the layers (or hierarchy) of the organization like?

- How many are there?

- Are there large perceived distances between the layers? Is there a great distance between what are seen as the top and the bottom?

- Is the organization split up into different departments or sections?

- Are the divisions between these sections clearly delineated?

- How do managers behave towards the colleagues they manage?

Communication and information exchanges between different sorts of the organization:

- Does information flow with difficulty between the different sections?

- If no, why does the information flow freely?

- If yes, what is blocking the information? Politics? Defensive behaviour around the area?

- Is e-mail used to communicate with employees who are seated not far from the sender (eg just down the corridor)?

- Do individuals, and particularly managerial staff, talk in a way that seems to describe work as being separate from emotional input and as if it were disembodied and disconnected from human opinion or perception? In other words, is it treated as if it has a free-standing identity and presence of its own, rather than being created by the frames of reference and actions of people interacting in the workplace?

'Hard' and 'soft' management

Modernistic and positivistic approaches, and the types of measure and KPIs they employ are commonly seen as 'hard' management. Hard management is particularly concerned with KPIs based on measurements using numbers and statistics. Here, the direct link to a scientific approach with its use of mathematics can be seen. Alternatively, soft management, or soft factors in corporate cultures, is seen as focusing on issues such as motivation, leadership, coaching and so on (Connors and Smith, 2000; Weber and Tarba, 2012). Some managers and employees think that 'hard' management techniques are the only ones that matter in organizations. They may have the view that the 'soft' factors are all very well but that they are difficult to categorize and measure and, therefore, it is challenging to define them and manage them to any performative or productive end. Commencing in the latter half of the 20th century there has been increasing attention paid to 'soft' dimensions including many new perspectives on organizational study and innovative training and development approaches such as emotional intelligence, organizational learning, knowledge management, coaching, and neuro-linguistic programming to name but a few (Crossan and Easterby-Smith, 2000; Goleman, 1996; Knight, 2009; Schein, 1985). This does not mean that 'hard' management approaches have been put aside; however 'soft' and 'hard' approaches tend to interact in sometimes a competing and at other times a complementary manner.

Managerialism

Managerialism is a phenomenon that has emerged over the last century (Kitchener, 2002; O'Reilly and Reed, 2011). Managerialism is generally used as a pejorative term by those who wish to criticize particular styles of managerial behaviour. However, those managers behaving in a manner that might attract such criticism may often believe that they are behaving in a useful and highly appropriate manner. Typical managerialist behaviour could include regularly using buzzwords and talking in organizational jargon rather than plain and clear language. The typical behaviour will also have a tendency to be focused on achievement of task and targets. Processes and relationships will be addressed in a mechanistic, tokenistic and clichéd manner. Managerialist behaviour more often than not treats employees as units of (human) resource that need to be configured and directed to ensure maximum efficiency, effectiveness, outputs, productivity and, wherever possible, optimum solutions. Within managerialist behaviour, managers consider themselves the most important people in the organization and critical to the organization's success – managers have the right and duty to manage and they will be in total control at all times (Anderson, 2008).

However, it can be envisaged that such behaviour might cause upset and discontent among many employees who do not like to be treated in a managerialist manner. Critics of managerialist conduct point to its robotic and machine-like nature. It seems dehumanized and disembodied from a sense of social relations within the workplace. In general, it is a common product of the overall modernistic and positivistic environments discussed above and is linked, although not exclusively, to 'hard' approaches to directing companies and organizations. Managerialism is but one questionable effect of modernistic environments. A further effect is the emergence of what has been termed 'McDonaldization'.

McDonaldization

McDonald's, and the fast food it sells, is a world-renowned brand. The burgers and other products sold by McDonald's are known for their economic pricing, consistent presentation of its retail outlets and the consistent level of quality. These characteristics are carried across a range of different locations and countries. While some customization may take place in particular national markets (for example, the ability to purchase wine in French McDonald's) one of the benefits of the approach to having homogeneous products and services is that the company can achieve economies of scale. This in turn assists in keeping operating costs low and consequently increases profit levels.

Within the retail outlets, this is achieved by organizing the work and activities of the outlets through specialization of tasks, which involves dividing up the work and allocating the tasks and work to be accomplished among employees. Efficiency is a central ethos within these processes. Within this way of working, it is possible to see the influence of Taylorism and modernism, which are both adherents of categorization of (work) environments, delineation, seeking to identify cause-and-effect and believing in the possibility of an optimal solution.

The focus on standardization, cost reduction and an apparent rational efficiency is of course a useful and important thing in any organization. However, if pursued in isolation from other factors such as employee engagement, motivation and ensuring things are done effectively as well as efficiently, then undesirable side effects and dysfunctional aspects may occur. These issues were captured by Ritzer (1993). Ritzer studied the types of work organization used and developed by companies like McDonald's and also noticed that similar work organization processes were being implemented in other domains of society including health care, education and the wider public sector. What he saw as the McDonaldization of large swathes of commercial and public life was a response to the prevailing economic and financial conditions and the limited resources available to deliver outputs and services.

It has even been noted that the employees' behaviour can be 'McDonaldized'. In wanting to ensure that the product and service offering are consistently and efficiently offered it is possible companies may insist that employees speak to customers using pre-prepared scripts. These might direct employees to use statements such as, 'Would you like to go large on that order?' or at the end of the service, 'Have a nice day!' Equally, a company may insist that employees wear a uniform or maintain a particular appearance. These dimensions of the workplace have become a significant feature of the modern organization.

However, there are many sides to McDonaldization that have been criticized (Taylor and Lyon, 1995). One of these aspects is 'emotional labour' (Hochschild, 1983). Hochschild studied air stewards and stewardesses and the way in which they are obliged to remain smiling and pleasant to passengers even in the most challenging and demanding, perhaps unreasonable, circumstances. Equally, staff might be obliged to wear particular clothes, uniforms or have a particular appearance. There is a range of further reasons why McDonaldization of society may not be necessarily a desirable thing:

- While it seems a good idea to organize work in an efficient manner, often this may not result in very interesting tasks or work roles for workers. A worker may find that he or she has to carry out a repetitive and monotonous task day after day in a consistent and uniform manner and this is often not very interesting.

- Achieving economies of scale by organizing workflow and making or buying in goods at the cheapest price, etc is a logical idea. However, goods and materials purchased at the lowest cost may not always be of the best or most appropriate quality. Moreover, this means that a firm or producer has to be making the goods at a very low cost. Firms may feel forced to produce and sell at a very low cost because major retail outlets, operating on McDonaldized principles, require or even demand very low prices which the suppliers are cornered into accepting.

- When a business McDonaldizes its processes and employees it may be felt that the organization does not respect its employees but rather sees them as a unit, resource or a factor of production to be used and possibly exploited. In this sense, the question might be asked – does the organization really respect its employees?

If we think about McDonaldization in a reflexive manner (meaning that we look back inwards on the very conceptualization of the worlds and processes that formed Ritzer's work) could it be suggested that Ritzer was in fact McDonaldizing knowledge about work processes by coining the term and writing his bestselling book (Roberts, 2005)? In other words, was he merely creating yet another commodity for a consumerist world to consume and then gradually discard and move on to the next idea? We can perhaps see an echoed attempt of this in work on Disneyization (Bryman, 2004; Dey and Steyaert, 2007; Hochschild, 1983; Kociatkiewicz and Kostera, 2010). This reflexive point in relation to Ritzer's ideas and concept underlines the pervasive and complex nature of McDonaldization – where the concept itself is subject to the same effects of the very characteristics it critiques. In addition, McDonaldization is in the process of transforming itself to adapt to changing organizational processes and consumer and stakeholder demands and tastes. Illustrations here include the ways in which consumers purchasing through internet sites are able, through site options and choices, to customize standardized products and services yet are still following a given process to access products in a rapid and efficient manner (often without direct human interaction).

Modernism, fads and fashions in organizational life and literature

Management literature is prone to coming up with an idea, concept or approach that is 'the best thing ever' in terms of management practice and performance. Of course, all of these ideas have potential value and contributions to make to various organizational contexts or aspects of managing organizations. Moreover, it is perhaps to be expected that in a world of global dynamic change and a commensurate academic field of study it is inevitable that fresh thinking will emerge and filter into practice. Nevertheless, it should also be noted that there may be a more sceptical element of producing new ideas for the sake of having something new to talk about as academics, or to reorganize around as managers or to sell as consultants – having already sold pre-existing ideas widely and needing to re-energize sales (Newell *et al*, 2001).

Understanding the role of modernism (and indeed other philosophical and paradigmatic approaches to management) helps in appreciating the originality and novelty of new ideas as they come along. Although new management ideas and approaches may look new, quite often they have the same assumptions and principles underlying them. Because of the dominance of modernistic approaches to managing and organizing over decades, more often than not it is capitalistic, modernistic and positivistic values and characteristics that are driving and underpinning the thinking behind many new fashions (Whittle, 2008). In essence, this involves the categorizing of complex environments into more simplified and reduced models, the notion that by doing action 'X' reaction or outcome 'Y' will be achieved in a linear manner, that measurement and performance enhancement are imperative and that, ultimately, it will lead to a 'bottom line' (ie profit) improvement. Quite often, discussions of employees and individuals are embraced in these ideas but, in effect, are important only in so much as they fit in with the initiative and contribute to the desired outcomes. For instance, any notion of resistance is deemed as something that will have to be addressed and may ultimately lead to the individual(s) being removed from the organization.

Concluding thoughts

Modernism and positivism have been, and remain, very powerful shaping and influencing forces in producing management and organizations as we witness and experience them in the contemporary era. However, perhaps surprisingly, this is not widely recognized or acknowledged by many people who work in organizational life. It is as if there is an omnipotent but invisible effect in operation in the world of work – as if a trance is operating over wide realms and domains. Nevertheless, an ability to recognize the presence, nature and role of modernism and positivism in the contemporary work arena will enable you to be a more astute and aware observer of modern work life. This perceptiveness will enable you to make choices and take actions that do not simply recycle old ideas and processes but rather will provide you with a freedom of thinking and contribution that hopefully will complement the dominant approaches.

Key points

- The Enlightenment and the Industrial Revolution were key turning points in the shaping of work, markets, organizations and management.

- Modernism and the scientific method of positivism emerged as the key principles, philosophies and approaches with which to shape management and organizations.

- While modernistic approaches such as Taylorism and Fordism sought worthy objectives such as optimized efficiency and productivity they nevertheless created and raised serious issues around their lack of attention to human and social aspects of work.

- Modernistic approaches have produced a range of questionable effects in the contemporary workplace including managerialism, McDonaldization, 'hard' factors and cultures in management, KPIs and audit cultures to name but a few.

- Many apparently novel fads and fashions in management and organizations may be 'old wine served in new bottles' in that they are often offered as 'Holy Grail' responses to organizational challenges when in fact the assumptions and concepts underpinning them are essentially the same as what has preceded them.

Revision questions

1 What is the Enlightenment and why was it so important in the development of the Industrial Revolution and modern management?

2 Try to provide a brief and simple explanation of modernism and positivism. What are the key principles that underpin them? How do they play a role in shaping and influencing the character of contemporary work environments?

3 How can managerialism create difficulties in a work environment? Are there any benefits to managerialism?

4 Think about Fordism and McDonaldization – can you think of situations in contemporary organizations (schools, colleges, universities, offices, hospitals, military forces, government departments, etc) where it is possible to find evidence of Fordist and McDonaldized processes?

5 As a manager, what could you do to work within a dominant modernistic environment in order to avoid some of the negative aspects that have a tendency to occur?

Further study

There is a plethora of texts and articles that can assist in understanding the topics and issues discussed in this chapter. These books may help in the development of your thinking:

Fineman, S, Gabriel, Y and Sims, D (2009) *Organizations and Organizing*, Sage, London

Hatch, M-J and Cunliffe, A (2006*) Organization Theory: Modern, symbolic, and postmodern perspectives*, OUP, Oxford

McAuley, J, Johnson, P and Duberley, J (2013) *Organization Theory: Challenges and perspectives*, Pearson, London

References

Anderson, G (2008) Mapping academic resistance in the managerial university, *Organization*, **15** (2), pp 251–70

Bryman, A (2004) *The Disneyization of Society*, Sage, London

Clegg, S, Kornberger, M and Pitsis, T (2011) *Managing and Organizations: An introduction to theory and practice*, Sage, London

Connors, R and Smith, T (2000) Corporate culture: Benchmarking cultural transition, *Journal of Business Strategy*, **21** (3), pp 10–12

Crossan, D and Easterby-Smith, M (2000) Organizational learning: debates past, present and future, *Journal of Management Studies*, **37** (6), pp 783–96

Cummings, S (2002) *Recreating Strategy*, Sage, London

Dereli, C and Stokes, P (2007) Reconceptualizing modernity for management studies: Exploring the tension between the scientific and the spiritual in the age of modernism, *Philosophy of Management*, **6** (2), pp 131–9

Dey, P and Steyaert, C (2007) The troubadours of knowledge: Passion and invention in management education, *Organization*, **14** (3), pp 437–61

Goleman, D (1996) *Emotional Intelligence and Why it can Matter More Than IQ*, Bloomsbury, London

Hochschild, A (1983) *The Managed Heart: The commercialization of human feeling*, University of California Press, Berkeley, CA

Kitchener, M (2002) Mobilizing the logic of managerialism in professional fields: The case of academic health centre managers, *Organization Studies*, **23** (3), pp 391–420

Knight, S (2009) *NLP At Work: The essence of excellence*, Nicholas Brearly, London

Knights, D and Willmott, H (2011) *Organizational Analysis: Essential readings*, Cengage Learning, Andover

Knights, D and Willmott, H (2012) *Introducing Organizational Behaviour and Management*, Cengage Learning, Andover

Kociatkiewicz, J and Kostera, M (2010) Exclusion and denial within experience economy, *Organization*, **17** (2), pp 257–82

Kuhn, T (2012) *The Structure of Scientific Revolutions*, 50th anniversary edn, Chicago University Press, Chicago, IL

Linstead, S, Fulop, L and Lilley, S (2009) *Management and Organization: A critical text*, Palgrave Macmillan, Basingstoke

Lyotard, F (1979) *The Postmodern Condition: A report on knowledge*, Editions de Minuit, Paris

Marr, B (2012) *Key Performance Indicators (KPI): The 75 measures every manager needs to know*, Financial Times/Prentice Hall, London

Mokyr, J (2012) *The Enlightened Economy: An economic history of Britain 1700–1850*, Yale University Press, New Haven, CT

Newell, S, Swan, J and Kautz, K (2001) The role of funding bodies in the creation and diffusion of management fads and fashions, *Organization*, **8** (1), pp 97–120

O'Reilly, D and Reed, M (2011) The grit in the oyster: managerialism and leaderism as discourses of public services modernization, *Organization Studies*, **32**, pp 1079–101

Pagden, A (2015) *The Enlightenment: And why it still matters*, OUP, Oxford

Peci, A (2009) Taylorism in the socialism that really existed, *Organization*, **16** (2), pp 289–301

Prak, M (2014) *Early Modern Capitalism: Economic and social change in Europe 1400–1800*, Routledge, London

Ritzer, G (1993) *McDonaldization of Society: An investigation into the changing character of contemporary social life*, Pineforge, New York

Roberts, J (2005) The Ritzerization of knowledge, *Critical Perspectives on International Business*, **1** (1), pp 56–63

Schein, E (1985) *Organizational Culture and Leadership*, Jossey-Bass, San Francisco, CA

Stokes, P (2011a) *Key Concepts in Business and Management Research Methods*, Palgrave Macmillan, Basingstoke

Stokes, P (2011b) *Critical Concepts in Management and Organization Studies*, Palgrave Macmillan, Basingstoke

Stokes, P and Wall, T (2015) *Business Briefings – Research Methods*, Palgrave Macmillan, Basingstoke

Strathern, M (2000) *Audit Cultures: Anthropological studies in accountability, ethics and the academy*, Routledge, London

Taylor, S and Lyon, P (1995) Paradigm lost: The rise and fall of McDonaldization, *International Journal of Contemporary Hospitality Management*, **7** (2/3), pp 64–8

Townley, B (2002) Managing in modernity, *Organization*, **9** (4), pp 549–74

Trinder, B (2013) *Britain's Industrial Revolution: The making of a manufacturing people, 1700–1870*, Carnegie Publishing, London

Watson, T (2006) *Organizing and Managing Work*, Financial Times/Prentice Hall, London

Weber, Y and Tarba, S (2012) Mergers and acquisitions process: The use of corporate culture analysis, *Cross Cultural Management: An International Journal*, **19** (3), pp 288–303

Weick, K (1995) *Sensemaking in Organizations*, Sage, Thousand Oaks, CA

Whittle, A (2008) From flexibility to work–life balance: Exploring the changing discourses on management consultants, *Organization*, **15** (4), pp 513–34

Wilson, F (2010) *Organizational Behaviour and Work*, OUP, Oxford

Wolfe, M, Bush, D and Parsons, J (2010) *Hill Country Deco: Modernistic architecture of central Texas*, Texas Christian University Press, Houston, TX

Wood, D (2004) *Varieties of Modernism (Art of the Twentieth Century)*, Yale University Press, New Haven, CT

Worthington, F (2012) Change and innovation: new organizational forms', in Knights, D and Willmott, H, *Introducing Organizational Behaviour and Management*, Cengage Learning, Andover, pp 410–47

www.aihw.gov.au (2015) 'Australia's Health 2014', http://www.aihw.gov.au/australias-health/2014/health-system (accessed 26 June 2015)

www.nhs.uk (2015) http://www.nhs.uk/choiceintheNHS/Rightsandpledges/Waitingtimes/Pages/Guide%20to%20waiting%20timesaspx

Using critical management approaches in managing people and organizations

03

PETER STOKES

OBJECTIVES

- Providing an outline and understanding of the approaches to organization and management that have emerged and been developed during the last century and presenting a number of ongoing theoretical developments.

- Providing introductions to philosophical stances such as postmodernism, poststructuralism, critical realism and related approaches such as discourse analysis and social constructionism.

- Providing a counterpoint and alternative perspective on managing and organizing to the predominant modernistic casting and view of these areas.

- Offering ideas and techniques to facilitate better understanding of issues such as organizational relationships, interpersonal and team dynamics, identity and power and their impact on work and practice.

Introduction

Chapter 2 outlined modernistic and positivistic outlooks that have represented the dominant manner of approaching and understanding organizational and managerial situations in many contexts during the 20th century and into the 21st. The discussion also indicated the limitations that may exist with such approaches and, in particular, how they might not always reflect or respond to the complexities of the human conditions and situations in which people often create and find themselves in work and other contexts.

Critical management studies and critical perspectives are approaches that have developed over recent decades and, in many ways, have challenged and provided a response to modernistic constructions and representations of the workplace. Knowledge of critical perspectives provides people with alternative and deeper insights and understanding of the complex dynamics and operation of work settings. It may even be postulated that such knowledge assists in enabling people to become more rounded managers.

Thinking about positivistic and modernistic views of management as mainstream

We can think of the term 'mainstream' as the dominant or the principal way things are done or, alternatively, the recurrent way in which a topic is discussed or viewed (Stokes, 2011). For example, in the medical field, there will be a view on how to approach particular illnesses and conditions. Clearly, there may also exist alternative, even radical approaches in the treatment of the given illness or condition and these are likely to run counter to a greater of lesser extent to mainstream medical approaches. Homeopathy may be a case in point. Homeopathy draws on herbal and organic/plant materials to propose medical cures. However, a number of practitioners in mainstream medicine question the efficacy of these approaches. One of the reasons commonly cited is that such applications and treatments have not been subjected to extended scientific testing (Masoodi, 2015).

The tensions between mainstream and alternative approaches are an important dynamic and critique and, drawing on the discussion in Chapter 2, link back to the very core of modernism. As you will recall, modernistic and positivistic approaches are based on the scientific paradigm and philosophy.

In other words, they use scientific methods and paradigms to build, test and prove the knowledge that underpins their approach. Referring back to the example above, mainstream medicine is very much a scientifically, positivistically and modernistically informed and underpinned domain whereas homeopathy does not have such an established tradition in this regard (Schmacke *et al*, 2014). This is not to say that homeopathy has any less worth in its own right but it does mean that many medical practitioners will not be convinced by its claims because they are not scientifically founded and proven.

It will be valuable to look at how a similar situation has arisen in relation to mainstream and critical management approaches.

Critical management studies

Critical management studies (CMS) evolved in the 1990s, although the ideas from which it derives the paradigm it espouses can be identified in a range of philosophies. A key early influence was critical theory (see below). In particular, Alvesson and Willmott (1992, 1996) wrote two initial texts that applied critical theory ideas to different functional areas and bodies of writing. Around this time, other writers were also seeing the potential of applying ideas and systems of thought other than positivism and modernism to organization and management issues. This led writers to move on to apply philosophical approaches such as, inter alia, existentialism, postmodernism, poststructuralism, critical realism and deconstructionism (Appignanesi *et al*, 2004; Lips-Wiersma and Mills, 2014; Liyan and Yuguo, 2014).

Writers engaged with CMS were typically dissatisfied with the manner in which modernism and positivism had portrayed many aspects of organization and management. In broad terms, CMS generally believes that research and commentaries underpinned by positivism and modernism tend to talk about management and organization in a simplistic manner. For example, events and interactions are often talked about in simple cause-and-effect ways, and complex issues and situations are represented in oversimplified manners and married with equally simplistic responses (Fournier and Smith, 2012; Stokes, 2011; Wickert and Schaefer, 2015) As noted in Chapter 2, modernistic management leads on to create the world in particular ways, producing managerialism, McDonaldization and so forth.

CMS introduces issues overlooked by positivistic and modernistic approaches. Such issues include (among many others): a concern for how identity, voice, resistance, power and oppression might operate. Above all, CMS and the philosophies it employs to develop its ideas, introduce the idea of different and varying perspectives and the role that they may have on people and work within organizations.

Where to find and engage with the CMS community and debates

There are a number of key ways in which you can find and explore CMS ideas and communities.

Journals

It would be incorrect to say that certain journals are 'CMS journals'. Nevertheless, a number of journals do tend to have a leaning towards or heightened interest in CMS-related ideas. This means that they will be using, for example, postmodern, poststructural, critical theory, critical realist or deconstructionist frames of references through which to make their arguments. Examples of journals include:

Culture and Organization

Ephemera

Human Relations

Management Learning

Organization

Organization Studies

Tamara: Journal of Critical Postmodern Organization Science

It is worth looking through recent issues of these journals to obtain a sense of the type and range of topics addressed and the way in which they approach and construct their arguments in relation to these topics. Also, as with all literature, some writers have very much shaped the CMS field and these too are worth study; some authors are:

Paul Adler

Mats Alvesson

Joanna Brewis

David Boje

Nick Butler

Rick Delbridge

Tara Fenwick

Yiannis Gabriel

Chris Grey

Campbell Jones

Mihaela Kelemen

Stephen Linstead

Martin Parker

Carl Rhodes

Andre Spicer

Mark Tadajewski

Hugh Willmott

Clearly, many more commentators are involved in working in the CMS domain than the few listed above; the intention here is to provide an initial introduction.

Books

Several years ago there was a dearth of texts examining management and organization through CMS frames of reference. This has now changed; here is a small sample of the many books on these approaches:

Alvesson, M (2002) *Understanding Organizational Culture*, Sage Publications, London
Alvesson, M and Bridgeman, T (2011) *The Oxford Handbook of Critical Management Studies*, Oxford University Press, Oxford
Carroll, B, Ford, J and Taylor, S (2015) *Leadership: Contemporary critical perspectives*, Sage, London
Clegg, S, Kornberger, M and Pitsis, T (2011) *Managing and Organizations: An introduction to theory and Practice*, Sage, London
Knights, D and Willmott, H (2012) *Introducing Organizational Behaviour and Management*, Cengage Learning, Andover
Pullen, A and Rhodes, C (eds) (2014) *The Routledge Companion to Ethics, Politics and Organizations*, Routledge, London
Stokes, P (2011) *Critical Concepts in Management and Organization Studies: Key terms and concepts*, Palgrave-Macmillan, Basingstoke
Tadajewski, M, Maclaren, P, Parsons, E and Parker, M (2011) *Key Concepts in Critical Management Studies*, Sage, London

Conferences and websites

Standing Conference on Organizational Symbolism (SCOS) (**http://www.scos.org**)

European Group on Organizational Studies (EGOS) (**http://www.egosnet.org**)

International Critical Management Studies Conference (CMS) is usually hosted at various universities, and their websites.

Underpinning philosophies of CMS

Here are three key underpinning philosophies of CMS and their influence on organization and management.

1. Critical theory

Critical theory is a body of thought primarily associated with the Frankfurt School at the Institute of Social Research in Frankfurt. The initial period of the Frankfurt School occurred during the 1920s and 1930s (however, its work and legacy endured post-WWII) and the names of philosophers most associated with the development of its work are Max Horkheimer (1895–1973), Herbert Marcuse (1898–1979), Eric Fromm (1900–1980) Theodor Adorno (1903–1969) and Jurgen Habermas (1929–).

Critical theory played an important role in the gestation and early development of CMS. Important ground-breaking work for CMS, using critical theory, was conducted by Alvesson and Willmott (1992, 1996). Critical theory is connected with, and built upon, the work and analysis of capitalism and workers' conditions conducted by Marx and the psycho-analytic work conducted by Freud (see also Yiannis Gabriel's work in this regard: Gabriel, 2000).

A key theme emerging from critical theory was the presence and significance of the notion of alienation within various aspects of society, organizations and institutions and a need to challenge existing paradigms and knowledge bases. A core objective for critical theory is the achievement of 'emancipation' or freedom from the constraints imposed by societal structures and power relations and particularly the 'artificial' divisions between subject and disciplinary areas. This desire for emancipation encompassed all spheres of human endeavour and experience including moral, artistic, aesthetic, contractual, commercial and intellectual notions.

In terms of impact on organization and management, critical theory has not tended to be used or referred to extensively in management and organizational writing. Nevertheless, it is important to note that it did play an important role in launching CMS, and its ideas and ambitions (ie emancipation) remain a central tenet of much thinking in CMS. Moreover, emancipation has endured as an important idea in contemporary organizational life. This is whether or not, for example, managers are supposed to be empowering employees, people are striving for work–life balance and freedom from too much stress or having the possibility of negotiating and realizing a career plan and portfolio activities rather than being constrained to a particular work trajectory.

2. Postmodernism

Postmodernism is a complex set of philosophical ideas that have emerged in the latter part of the 20th century from a range of sources. Importantly, although not exclusively, modern French philosophy has been a generator and influencer of thinking in this area. In terms of general principles, postmodernism contrasts with modernism in a radical manner; a comparison of modernism and postmodernism views on various facets of organizations is shown in Table 3.1.

Postmodernism does not recognize or accept the manner in which modernism represents and constructs organizational and management life and events. Postmodernism aims to question, for example, what constitutes an employee's identity and how it is constructed and evolves. Such things are not taken as given or taken for granted. This also has implications for managerial identity and the complexities of what 'managing' might actually involve rather than accepting some of the rather mono-dimensional representations modernism offers based on hierarchies, key performance indicators, targets and senior management generated and disseminated mission statements.

Managing with a postmodernist mindset means not accepting things and events at face value but rather trying to understand the issues of identity, power and social construction that may be at play at any given moment. For example, an organization may have an organizational structure chart placed on the wall but this may not actually capture the dynamics that take place within the organization. Equally, the organization chart suggests a 'boundary' around particular departments and the overall organization but this is in many ways a notional 'wall' or limitation and the entire environment and its multiple interactions and complexities can enter the organizational or individual's space at any time. In fact, such interactions take place as a rhizome, or in a rhizomatic manner (Blaug, 1999; Santana and Carpentier, 2009). Rhizomes include plants such as ivy or in mangrove swamps. These plants grow, interconnect and intertwine in what seems a chaotic and unpredictable manner. One node or branch of the plant suddenly emerges from the mid-point

TABLE 3.1　Modernism and postmodernism

Modernism	Postmodernism
Prone to authoritarian and directive management style.	Power and control are not fixed and tend to move around a network of people and objects within the organization.
The organization is seen as operating in a relatively closed system environment (albeit with acknowledgement of globalization and international trade). In other words 'things' are seen as coming into and out of the organization in a linear, input–output manner.	The organization is merely one location among multiple possibilities in a permeable and osmotic web through which the complex interactions of a range of actors and events occur.
Boundaries around the organization are clear and defined and identify what is inside and what is outside the organization.	All boundaries are at best blurred and are viewed as arbitrary and temporary constructions in various groups and individual sense-making.
Structures tend to be based on, and operate through, hierarchies.	The organization may have hierarchies but in fact it operates more as a series of shifting networks, and interconnections are horizontal across the organization as much as vertical.
Centralist planning and control.	Dissipated, fragmented and shifting political coalitions that create actions and effects.
Unitary culture; for example, one mission statement set by senior management.	Pluralistic cultures; many varied and constantly evolving cultures and views of identity and direction.
Technology, buildings and other objects and artefacts shape actions, behaviours.	Behaviour is a consequence of multiple and complex sense-making and social constructionism in relation to the many aspects of environments and human interaction.

Adapted from Boje and Dennehey (1999)

of a given branch and starts to grow and interconnect with another area of the plant. This is used as a metaphor for the manner in which human and organizational interactions seem to be increasingly taking place. Phenomena such as internationalization of trade and capital, globalization and the advent of the internet and social media have accentuated and accelerated these impressions. In the political arena, the emergence and surge of the Arab Spring was, in part, attributed to the extensive use by demonstrators of social media to gather and organize demonstrations (in a rhizomatic manner) without any real central point of organization.

This means that from a postmodern perspective a manager might indeed set out linear plans (moving from A to B to C, etc) and associated targets, but he or she is also strongly mindful of the role of competing and changing perceptions of what those targets actually look like and represent. In tandem with this dynamic there will be an expectation that plans are almost certainly likely to change and extensive adaptability and flexibility will be required.

3. Poststructuralism

Poststructuralism is kindred with postmodernism in many regards. Poststructuralism is seen as challenging the structuralism that modernism so prizes and values. In particular, poststructuralism is interested in the role of language, discourses, signs, semantics and semiotics and how they may operate to create meaning and action. Discourse communicates in multiple and simultaneous manners. For example, we read texts from documents, e-mails and signs; we listen to conversations and meetings and so forth. However, we know that body language is important as are the aesthetics and appearance of objects and situations and what they can signal to different people at various times. Our senses of smell and touch also are important in adding discursive information to our sense-making of situations. Alternatively expressed, any environment and the people within it might, at any given moment, be communicating a vast array of ideas and messages.

For a manager in an organization who is operating with a poststructural awareness and mindset, the meanings operating in communication – in all its forms – will be constantly observed and evaluated into his or her sense-making. This means that, for instance, e-mails may be read as containing signals and coded messages regarding views or organizational politic stances; meetings contain many other agendas than the one on paper in front of everyone. In such an environment, coalitions and sharing meanings with other people to make new meanings and actions become imperative.

Some key ideas from postmodernism and poststructuralism for organization and management

There are many terms and concepts that have emerged from, and are associated with, CMS (see Parker *et al*, 2014; Stokes, 2011; Tadajewski and Maclaren, 2011). A number of these terms have already been mentioned above and an illustration of some recurrent and important terms is discussed below.

Bricolage

'Bricolage' is a French word meaning to improvise, make do with or to tinker with. It also means DIY in French. In an everyday social sense it has a negative connotation because it often implies to botch or to patch things up.

However, within CMS bricolage is used to illustrate the fragmented, agile, flexible, contingent and ever-changing sense-making, planning and actions that lived experience (see below) seems to involve. Bricolage situations describe a postmodern world and environment that contrast sharply with the fixed, linear, positivistic representations of much of normative management (O'Doherty, 2008; Quack, 2007).

Deviance

From a modernistic point of view, deviance is considered to be an act or behaviour that strays from the usual, normative and conventional. In modernistic cultures where unitary perspectives underpinned by authoritarian and autocratic postures dictate that there is one corporate mission and 'way of being' in the firm, anyone not complying with such views is regarded as being deviant. Deviance might quite possibly lead to resistance (see below).

CMS views deviance from differing perspectives, seeing it as a means of resisting managerialism and oppression in workplace settings. Alternatively, deviance from normative behaviour may be a means of dealing with a measure or situation seen as foolish or even boring (Ackroyd and Thompson, 1999; Zhang *et al*, 2008). Furthermore, Gabriel (2000) points at how deviance can fester in the 'unmanageable' spaces in employee minds.

Lived experience

The expression 'lived experience' attempts to capture the everyday micro-moments, events and situations that challenge, and are generally not encompassed in, a normative and modernistic representation of managerial and organizational life (Stokes and Harris, 2012). For example, emotion is an important part of lived experience representations but it is often omitted from modernistic discussions. Also, lived experience-informed accounts of organization and management are often rendered through storytelling and narrative techniques (Eastmond, 2007).

Resistance

Resistance is an action taken to push back or work against something or someone. For modernistic approaches, resistance is nearly always characterized negatively. An employee who displays resistance is not complying with the orthodox unitary culture and some form of sanction or dismissal commonly follows. CMS views resistance differently: it is a signal or a sign of some form of discontent or the expression of a different and alternative viewpoint to that being suggested or offered by the dominant power (usually the modernistic management) (Ackroyd and Thompson, 1999; McCabe, 2010; Spicer *et al*, 2009).

Sometimes resistance will be open and formal, as with trade union action and representation. Often, resistance will be hidden or an undercurrent chipping away at the authority and work of the dominant power(s). Often workers do not have formal authority but they are still able to exercise power. Collinson (1994) suggested that resistance might take place as resistance by distance or, alternatively, resistance through persistence. In the former, the resistors do all they can to not engage with the power centre or a given issue. In the latter, they inundate the power centre or group (for example, senior managers) with endless requests for information and for further clarification.

Silence

Silence points at the absence of noise or other sound. In organization and management it is often linked to the idea of 'voice', which means the capacity of someone to be able to express his or her thoughts or views. The silence imposed can be a form of oppression or even bullying.

On occasion, it may be the case that a manager or other person appropriates the voice of an employee or other person. This effectively silences the person (Park and Keil, 2009; Simpson and Lewis, 2005).

Examples of postmodernism and poststructuralism in action

Ricardo Semler – **Maverick!**

Ricardo Semler is the CEO of Semco, a large Brazilian manufacturing firm. His first book *Maverick!* recorded how he went about revolutionizing the traditional and conventional approaches that were employed in the firm. Typical approaches centring on worker autonomy, independence and responsibility include, for instance:

- Workers are encouraged to set their own production targets.
- Profit sharing throughout the company rather than large bonuses only for senior management.
- The hierarchy was disposed of and three concentric circles replaced it. From the central circle moving out responsibilities were accorded to new roles of 'Counsellors', 'Partners' and 'Coordinators' rather than conventional management and supervisors.
- Flexitime and job rotation are standard.
- No dress codes.
- Reverse evaluation – all new appointees are evaluated by their entire team.
- A percentage of everyone's salary is dependent on the firm's performance.
- Transparency – all data is open (for example, salaries) and available to all.

- Home working is encouraged as it is often more productive than being office based.

- There is no formal organization chart.

The company, Semco Partners, clearly operates in a radical and alternative manner compared to traditional modernistic views of organizations and continues to be highly successfully commercially. Ricardo Semler is now a recognized and sought-after speaker throughout the world (see **http://www.ted.com/speakers/ricardo_semler**).

Lars Kolind – Oticon and the Spaghetti Organization

Oticon is a Danish company in which Lars Kolind adopted an alternative approach to managing work and innovation. Within the company any employee could propose a project on a simple standard form as long as there are a couple of other employees who are prepared to join the project. Employees subsequently self-organize into particular projects and the successful projects become self-evident through their accomplishments. As a consequence, the organization and its structure, such as it is, take an anti-bureaucratic spaghetti style rather than a traditional organizational form (see Kolind, 2006; Kolind and Botter, 2012).

Stephen – Logistics Manager

Managerialism (as discussed in Chapter 2) is the use of key performance indicators or the use and application of fear. Managerialism was brought into the mainstream public and private sector workplaces during the 1980s and 1990s when, among others, a model called 'New public management' or NPM was created (Miller, 2001). This model was a response to the pressure placed on local government to cut costs and improve its efficiency levels. Managers from private sectors, spanning various diverse industries, were drafted into national government to instil their managerialistic culture.

Here is Stephen's account of working within such a culture in a private context. Having first-hand experience of working within an industry where directors actively use the technique of managerialism (and have little insight into CMS approaches or appreciations) the argument below provides insights to its application within a working environment:

'I have worked for a wide range of directors; however, my experiences of managerialism are from within private limited companies where it appeared, and the rules on managing could be in some cases circumvented.

'My initial experience of managerialism was in 2007 when heading a logistical function within a frozen food manufacturing company. As with any business the company encountered a change of director and the incoming director favoured the use of managerialism. Clearly this director's brief was to improve business performance in light of a forthcoming sale of business therefore improving profitability; however, from their arrival the element of fear soon spread throughout the company. (Interestingly enough on reflection given the age of the director, in 2006 he was already in his 50s, which indicated he was managing, or has been managed in previous roles during the 1980s and 1990s – the age of NPM and the rise of managerialism. Therefore, he had become acculturated to that particular set of behaviours.) The director applied the use of fear as a motivator. Many managers were threatened with 'having a tough conversation' and suffering 'some blood being spilt' should they not hit their targets (such targets were rarely achievable). The KPI used on which to base the element of managerialistic fear was to operate within such a budget that success was virtually impossible. The business was highly volatile and sales would spike erratically, yet resource was expected to be on hand to react and all based on a finite budget. Fear was not only instilled when being managed on a line manager one-to-one basis, but also the risk of being ridiculed by the director in senior meetings should targets not have been hit.

'On reflection this method of managerialism was in effect a form of shock management; it was meant to create a culture of fear and to shock a manager into risking his, or her, health to deliver performance in order to keep their jobs, protect their homes and provide for their families. Although this form of management was quick, it was harsh and to a specific timescale. If managers did not perform they would be placed on a performance management plan and ultimately dismissed. Decisions were based on the balance of risk versus reward; managers would be dismissed, however prior to the dismissal the 'commercial' risk was established, this was the cost of a tribunal versus the saving made on the manager's salary and a replacement with a better skilled manager for the same price.

'In light of the approaching business sale and planned exits for the company's owners, the option for using an almost dictatorial like version of managerialism was an effective, if questionable, choice. It brought a hierarchy, a culture of fear and this was used as the ultimate motivator. It stripped out managers' toolboxes and armed them with the ability to threaten jobs and family security, the business became very simple: do or die.

'My second experience of managerialism was working in a sales position within a global freight company, again, privately owned. Sales by its nature is subjective: some view it as a method of hunting and winning new business whilst others view sales as a protector of customers and therefore vital to ensuring the security of a business through relationships. Within this role however, I worked for a director which presented interesting and non-comparable likenesses with my initial experience of managerialism when working for my previous director. The new director tended to favour her staff more if their home life was aligned to hers; for example, she enjoyed yoga and taught lunchtime classes within the depot. People who went to such classes became part of the clique and almost secured their stability by being at arm's length from the managerialistic and fear-instilling dimension. Within my previous experience of managerialism, this was something the director had not operated – there were no cliques, no gangs and no favouritism.

'However, again the age of the director perhaps came into effect as she was in her mid-50s and would also have been managed herself in the managerialism evolution that was the 1980s and 1990s. Was this a factor that underpinned her behaviour?

'There was however a managerialistic tone to her style; this was through the form of high KPI levels, each sales manager (and there were only two in the company) was expected to secure 15 new business meetings per week whilst cold-calling and formatting and delivering business quotations. Failure to deliver on these targets would result in dismissal and the fear factor arose once again. As with the manufacturing business, this experience was also based on almost unachievable and unrealistic targets. The freight business lacked a number of key ingredients to be able to achieve such targets – its purchasing power was low and its ability to offer a full range of logistical services was very poor. This greatly narrowed the sales channels to a number of small sectors, all of which were overrun with larger more extensive freight providers. Through the use of this managerialism the focus soon became clear of making the most phone calls and trying to meet the most amount of people in a week. This can be likened to throwing mud at a wall and hoping some will stick. This is an example of a downfall of managerialism in that the skill of sales and development has been compromised through its application and therefore the skills of winning sustainable business were redundant. The focus was on numbers and by hitting productivity numbers the sales managers could hope to have a weighted argument should a potential dismissal be lurking round the corner.

'On reflection, however, in both experiences the correlation of managerialism being used as a sharp shock tool does work. In the freight business should a sales manager not have delivered within the first three months, their employment is usually over. Of course, commercially this makes sense; the business is paying for an asset that is not making any return. Likewise, in the manufacturing business, the director's brief was to shake the departments and slicken the finances. This had to be done rapidly and therefore managerialism was used. One might say it had its uses. It might also be possible to say that the use of managerialism is well placed in private companies where the risks can be commercially assessed and decisions made by the people ultimately responsible not only for governance but for the purse strings also. But, the stories above point up limitations too.'

Stephen's account provides a striking illustration of the challenges of working in managerialistic settings. CMS helps in understanding such settings and provides ways in which alternative sense and meaning may be derived from them. This is not to say that managerialism can be tackled in a direct manner or that it is diminishing in the workplace. Nevertheless, a deeper understanding helps in providing alternative coping mechanisms and strategies.

Concluding thoughts

CMS is now a well-established and institutionalized field in its own right. In many ways it still remains at odds and in conflict with prevailing modernistic, positivistic perspectives on organizations. However, where managers glean an appreciation of CMS insights on organizations they tend to feel more at ease and able to tackle the excesses of phenomena such as Taylorism, managerialism, McDonaldization and so forth. Chapter 4 picks up issues of leadership and management and raises the topic of performance. As you progress through the material of the chapter (and subsequent chapters) it will be useful to keep CMS ideas, philosophies and concepts in mind and to consider how they relate to, and play out with, the idea and action of performance.

- Critical perspectives in management emerged, in large part, as a response to the predominant mechanistic, functionalistic, Tayloristic and modernistic patterning and shaping of commentary on, and experiences in, organizations and management.

- CMS is concerned with looking in a different and alternative manner at all aspects of social, cultural, political and economic organizational and management life – and especially at the everyday dimensions of, and interactions within, these arenas.

- CMS tends to analyse organizational and managerial issues by considering a range of diverse aspects (on which substantial literatures have now been generated) including, inter alia, discourse, power, identity, gender and meaning.

Revision questions

1 In the cases of managerialistic behaviour outlined above, what approaches and CMS-informed strategies might be possible as an alternative?

2 What do the cases suggest about people's behaviour being produced by particular environments or experiences?

3 How might an understanding of postmodernism or poststructuralism have opened up the minds of the managerialistic directors?

4 What strategies of resistance might have been available to people?

Further study

Clegg, S, Kornberger, M and Pitsis, T (2011) *Managing and Organizations: An introduction to theory and practice*, Sage, London

Linstead, S, Fulop, L and Lilley, S (2009) *Management and Organization: A critical text*, Palgrave-Macmillan, Basingstoke

Mowles, C (2011) *Rethinking Management*, Gower, Aldershot

References

Ackroyd, S and Thompson, P (1999) *Organizational Misbehaviour*, Sage, London

Alvesson, M and Willmott, H (1992) *Critical Management Studies*, Sage, London

Alvesson, M and Willmott, H (1996) *Making Sense of Management: A critical introduction*, Sage, London

Appignanesi, R, Garrett, C, Sardar, Z and Curry, P (2004) *Introducing Postmodernism*, Icon Books, London

Blaug, R (1999) The tyranny of the visible: Problems in the evaluation of anti-institutional radicalism, *Organization*, **6** (1), pp 33–56

Boje, D and Dennehey, R (1999) *Managing in a Postmodern World*, Kendall-Hunt, Dubuque, IA

Collinson, D (1994) Strategies of resistance: Power, knowledge and subjectivity in the workplace; in (eds) J Jermier, D Knights and W Nord, *Resistance and Power in Organizations*, Routledge, New York, pp 25–68

Eastmond, M (2007) Stories as lived experience: Narratives in forced migration research, *Journal of Refugee Studies*, **20** (2), pp 248–64

Fournier, V and Smith, W (2012) Making choice, taking risk: On the coming out of critical management studies, *Ephemera: Theory & Politics in Organization*, **12** (4), pp 464–74

Gabriel, Y (2000) *Storytelling in Organizations: Facts, fictions and fantasies*, Oxford University Press, Oxford

Kolind, L (2006) *The Second Cycle: Winning the war against bureaucracy*, Wharton School Publishing, Old Tappan, NJ

Kolind, L and Botter, J (2012) *Unboss*, Jyllands-Postens Forlag, Copenhagen

Lips-Wiersma, M and Mills, A (2014) Understanding the basic assumptions about human nature in workplace spirituality: Beyond the critical versus positive divide, *Journal of Management Inquiry*, **23** (2), pp 148–61

Liyan, S and Yuguo, H (2014) Derrida's deconstructionism and identity, *Nankai Journal (Philosophy, Literature and Social Science Edition)*, **1**, p 6

McCabe, D (2010) Strategy as power: Ambiguity, contradiction and the exercise of power in a UK building society, *Organization*, **17** (2), pp 151–75

Masoodi, N A (2015) Homeopathy: In God we trust, all others must bring data, *British Journal of Medical Practitioners*, **8** (1)

Miller, D (2001) *Consumption: Critical concepts in the social sciences*, Routledge, London

O'Doherty, D (2008) The blur sensation: Shadows of the future, *Organization*, **15** (4), pp 535–61

Park, C and Keil, M (2009) Organizational silence and whistle-blowing on IT projects: An integrated model, *Decision Sciences*, **40** (4), pp 901–18

Parker, M, Cheney, G, Fournier, V and Land, C (2014) *The Routledge Companion to Alternative Organization*, Routledge, London

Quack, S (2007) Legal professionals and transnational law-making: A case of distributed law agency, *Organization*, **14** (5), pp 643–66

Santana, M and Carpentier, N (2009) Mapping the rhizome. Organizational and informational networks of two Brussels alternative radio stations, *Telematics and Informatics*, **27** (2), pp 162–76

Schmacke, N, Müller, V and Stamer, M (2014) What is it about homeopathy that patients value? And what can family medicine learn from this? *Quality in Primary Care*, **22** (1), pp 17–24

Semler, R (1993) *Maverick!* Random House, New York

Simpson, R and Lewis, P (2005) An investigation of silence and a scrutiny of transparency: Re-examining gender in organization literature through the concepts of voice and visibility, *Human Relations*, **58** (10), pp 1253–75

Spicer, A, Alvesson, M and Kärreman, D (2009) critical performativity: the unfinished business of critical management studies, *Human Relations*, **62** (4), pp 537–60

Stokes, P (2011) *Critical Concepts in Management and Organization Studies*, Palgrave-Macmillan, Basingstoke

Stokes, P and Harris, P (2012) Micro-moments, choice and responsibility in sustainable organizational change and transformation: The Janus dialectic, *Journal of Organizational Change Management*, **25** (4), pp 595–611

Tadajewski, M and Maclaren, P (2014) *Key Concepts in Critical Management Studies*, Sage, London

Wickert, C, and Schaefer, S (2015) Towards a progressive understanding of performativity in critical management studies, *Human Relations*, **68** (1), pp 107–30

Zhang, Z, Spicer, A and Hancock, P (2008) Hyper-organizational space in the work of J G Ballard, *Organization*, **15** (6), pp 889–910

Leadership and management
The challenge of performance

CAROLINE ROWLAND

OBJECTIVES

In the previous chapters we have considered the organization, the context and critical thought; we now turn to the challenges of leading and managing people and getting results. This chapter provides:

- An explication of the differences between leadership and management.

- An historical contextualization of leadership.

- An elaboration of the nature, purpose and operation of performance management systems and tools.

- Models to guide good and useful practice.

04

Views on leadership and management

Warren Bennis (1925–2014) was one of the greatest thinkers and writers about leadership. He first started writing about leadership and management in the 1950s when very little had been reported about business leadership. He subsequently published over 30 books and became a world name for both academics and practitioners. His main belief was that 'Leaders are the ones with vision, who inspire others and cause them to galvanize their efforts and change,' a quote from his book *Managing People is like Herding Cats*, published to great acclaim in 1999.

Leadership is now a central part of any business school's curriculum and is also inevitably mentioned in most corporate plans. Most organizations say that leadership and management are crucial to achieving success but very few show signs of understanding what it takes to make a good manager or leader and how to ensure organizations end up with the right recipe for success. The challenge is that the recipe entails hard work, long-term planning and sometimes difficult conversations.

Since the writings of Bennis the concept of leadership and associated attributes have been explored in considerable detail by many academics and practitioners. Great interest has been shown in context, sociocultural aspects and practice. Leadership has been keenly observed in the public arena along with associated scandals in the business community such as Enron, Royal Bank of Scotland and success stories such as Virgin and Microsoft.

It is not surprising to find many studies and theories relating to leadership models. Many of them include similar themes and attributes. Influential authors include Adair (2002), Bass (2008), Cameron (2011), Blake and Mouton (1964) and Likert (1967), Blake and Mouton focus on the orientation and emphasis leaders and managers place on people and production. Their research concluded that high concern for both production and people results in the most effective leadership. Likert found that the highest producing supervisors were those who trusted their teams but also gave them both training and mentorship. Adair's model of action-centred leadership focused on the inter-relationship and appropriate balance between the needs of the task, group and individual. Bass gives a comprehensive description and review of models of leadership and management practice, while Cameron emphasizes issues such as sustainability, ethics and corporate social responsibility.

Learning from history

Machiavelli versus Frederick the Great

Niccolò Machiavelli (1469–1527) was an Italian diplomat, politician, philosopher, historian and writer based in Florence during the Renaissance. The Renaissance was a period of great cultural change that swept across Europe and was characterized by a passionate interest in all aspects of intellectual pursuits. He was a first-hand observer of the many wars between city and papal states under the Borgias and also invasion from the superpower of the time, France. He wrote many plays and books but is best remembered for *The Prince,* published in 1532. It is still in print and widely read. Many leaders and managers have adopted Machiavellian strategies. He was a firm believer in the divide-and-rule principle. Manipulation often by fear was his preferred model for leadership because he believed that fear was a much more reliable motivator than respect or affection. He stated unequivocally that it was better for a leader to be feared than loved.

Frederick the Great of Prussia (1712–1786) was King of Prussia (now Northern Germany) from 1740 until his death in 1786. He was best known as a highly successful military leader and for his organizational skills in building armies and supporting infrastructure to enable supply chains. He was also a talented musician and philosopher. In 1740 he published his essay, *Anti-Machiavel: A critical essay on The Prince by Machiavelli.* The famous philosopher Voltaire wrote the introduction and commended his insight.

Frederick's standpoint was very different from that of Machiavelli. He argued that expediency was not morally right and that leaders should be both rational and humane. Fredrick was highly critical of Machiavelli's model, which he suggested was leadership based on manipulation and fear and he proposed an alternative model based on kindness and mercy. Although his work is not as well-known as Machiavelli's in terms of modern leadership he provides more insight into the motivation of people and the complexity of behaviours resulting from altruism and belonging rather than pure self-interest. This was reflected in the later work of Kant (1790) and of Cameron (2011) who examines models that focus on virtue, care, compassion, inspiration, respect and integrity.

In the 21st century new views on ethics, emotional intelligence and compassion, sustainability and uncertainty continue to emerge. There is also a willingness to revisit the philosophy of Frederick and his contemporaries and take the lessons of history to ensure better organizational performance. This understanding of emotional intelligence including kindness in leadership promotes other values that may improve the effectiveness of the organization as a whole. These values include shared purposefulness, responsibility, commitment, practicality, participation and an improved understanding of the meanings that underpin leadership strategy. Senge (1999) criticizes heroic and 'macho' leadership approaches as having little lasting value to establishing high-performing organizations. However, there are confusion and misunderstanding regarding emotional intelligence for leadership, with some holding a more Machiavellian view that it is a tool to sustain manipulation of employees rather than the development of others for their benefit (Archer and Cameron, 2009). This debate about leadership requiring an awareness of and reaction towards the feelings of others continues. We shall also consider certain aspects of uncertainty, performance and leadership towards the end of this chapter.

CASE STUDY   Pete Hall's leadership style

Pete Hall is 42 years old. He started work at Riverside Instruments 10 years ago after leaving the army where he was a sergeant major. He has worked as a supervisor responsible for 20 production workers for the past seven years. He has consistently demonstrated high performance. His team has the highest productivity, lowest waste and least absenteeism in the company.

Pete's team work hard and mistakes are rare. He is known to be 'a hard man but fair'; workers often comment that they like his no-nonsense approach and respect his experience as a sergeant who now brings his military approach to the production line. They particularly appreciate his approach to mistakes: he expects people to own up and make good but then for all to move on.

The company promoted Pete to a middle management position six months ago and has since paid for him to attend several management development programmes focusing on strategy and finance. Pete is now responsible for five junior managers. They are all university graduates with several years' experience. They are: two production coordinators, an IT analyst, a quality assurance supervisor and an engineer. All five have voiced informal complaints about Pete, claiming that he is authoritarian, obsessed with deadlines and is always checking their work. One of the coordinators says she is thinking of resigning.

Questions

1 Describe what you see as the problem.

2 What are the options open to Pete's boss?

3 What are your recommendations?

What managers do

We have considered some key issues concerning leadership. Other academics and practitioners have been interested in what makes a good manager and what they do within the organization, the most influential being Mintzberg (1973) and Drucker (1995, 2008).

Mintzberg saw a manager's job as characterized by pace, interruptions and a fragmentation of activities. He described the manager as having three major roles: the interpersonal, the informational and the decisional. The interpersonal comprises acting as a figurehead, a leader and a key liaison facilitator. The informational role comprises acting as a monitor, disseminator and spokesperson. The decisional role comprises being an entrepreneur/risk taker combined with acting as a disturbance handler, resource allocator and negotiator. Essentially he saw the reality of a manager's daily life as ensuring efficiency and effectiveness by using appropriate communication skills combined with decision-making and problem-solving skills.

Drucker saw the role of management as to fulfil the mission of the organization, to make work productive and to manage social responsibilities. His work resulted in the notion of Managing by Objectives (MBO). This involved: setting objectives, organizing, motivating and communicating, target setting and measuring performance and developing the workforce. We shall be considering this approach later on in this chapter.

Differences between leadership and management

The manager maintains; the leader develops.

The manager focuses on systems and structures; the leader focuses on people.

The manager relies on control; the leader inspires trust.

The manager has a short-range view; the leader has a long-range perspective.

The manager asks how and when; the leader asks what and why.

The manager has his or her eye always on the bottom line; the leader's eye is on the horizon.

The manager imitates; the leader originates.

The manager accepts the status quo; the leader challenges it.

The manager does things right; the leader does the right thing.

(After Bennis, 1999)

Historically, some academics believe there was a time when the role of the manager and that of the leader could be separated and remain that way within the organization throughout their careers. A foreman in an industrial-era factory probably didn't have to give much thought to what he was producing or to the people who were producing it. His job was to follow orders, organize the work, assign the right people to the necessary tasks, coordinate the results, and ensure the job got done as ordered. The focus was on efficiency and control and very much grounded in conventional hierarchies, in many cases mirroring the military. However, in the new post-industrial economies, where value comes increasingly from the knowledge of people, and where workers are no longer undifferentiated cogs in an industrial machine, the thinking is focusing more on competitive advantage and the benefits that flexibility and teamwork bring the organization. Leadership and management are no longer seen as mutually exclusive.

Activity – Discussion areas

1 'It is easier for a leader to be a good manager than it is for a manager to be a good leader.' Do you agree?

2 What are the roles you most commonly take on in your everyday work? What role are you most comfortable with and why?

People and performance

History

The first written reference to performance management dates to around 220 AD when it was reported that the emperors of the Wei dynasty had an 'Imperial Rater' whose task it was to evaluate the performance of the official family.

The phrase 'performance management' as part of human resource strategy was first used by Beer and Ruh (1976). Performance management may be viewed as an important component in both human resource strategy and operations management. There is a strong and growing worldwide interest in performance management and organizations use it to add value to their products or services and thereby achieve competitive advantage.

Performance management: a definition

Armstrong and Baron (1998: 38) define performance management as:

A strategic and integrated approach to increasing the effectiveness of organizations by improving the performance of the people who work in them and by developing the capabilities of teams and individual contributors.

Other definitions focus on the contribution of employees to the organization and also the setting of objectives and targets for both individuals and groups. Some definitions also focus on how each employee can contribute to the overall success of the organization by reference to key performance indicators (KPIs) – the setting of individual and group performance objectives that are directly related to specific business goals. Rowland (2013) emphasizes that performance management is a total system effort, involving leaders and managers with the goal of increasing general organizational effectiveness and health. They should help in the accomplishment of specific organization objectives and targets by means of planned interventions in the organization's structure and processes using their knowledge of behavioural and management sciences. It is seen as crucial that the process has to engage employees if it is to be sustainable.

Why organizations use performance management systems

In a turbulent economic climate, characterized by pressures to improve productivity and reduce costs, performance management has a more central role in helping to ensure competitive advantage (CIPD, 2009). Organizations use performance management systems to seek to add value to their product, services and/or efficiency. They use them to feedback on staff performance and set objectives for individual performance. They also seek to increase the productivity of employees by clarifying goals and measuring individual performance (Torrington *et al*, 2002). In general, performance management is used by organizations to:

- help set objectives for individuals and teams;
- review or measure performance against objectives and agree plans for improvement;
- reward employees for good performance;
- develop employees for future roles as an aid to succession planning;
- identify skills gaps and training needs; and
- control cultural change.

Performance systems seem to offer additional benefits to the management process. They can help managers focus on results required and may be used to depersonalize issues by focusing on observable behaviours of individuals and their results (Armstrong and Baron, 2005).

Finally, performance management systems are perceived to be useful in measuring performance for the purpose of benchmarking, comparing or setting standards internally or with competitors. They can provide a consistent basis for comparison during internal change efforts. They can be used to indicate results during improvement efforts such as employee training, management development and quality programmes. Many managers also believe they can ensure equitable and fair treatment of employees based on performance, although this belief is often mistaken. In short, organizations have high expectations of performance management systems. Unfortunately they seldom live up to these expectations. The reasons for this will be explored throughout this chapter.

Activity – Consider

What do you think are the reasons that most performance management systems do not deliver expected outcomes? How can these poor results be improved?

Managing for effectiveness and efficiency

Organizations have a purpose: it might be to maximize profits for shareholders or to offer a service to stakeholders. All organizations strive to perform effectively and efficiently. Effectiveness is the achievement of a goal; efficiency is the low cost of resources. Success in implementing the management process requires a capability to make decisions, solve problems and take action to use resources effectively and efficiently in the management of change and productivity improvement. It is essential that leaders and managers understand how to assemble and use the appropriate tools to ensure optimum performance. This is no easy task and requires a good balance of concern for task and concern for relationships combined with both leadership and management skills.

Motivation is inextricably linked to effectiveness and efficiency. To achieve efficiency/productivity and effectiveness/quality, people have to be motivated (Neely, 1998; Torrington *et al*, 2002). Performance is seen to be determined primarily by ability and motivation. Environmental factors including the activities managers and leaders engage in to improve employee performance also have an impact on the ability and motivation of the individual; as do the tools and systems they design and implement.

Tools and systems

Performance management and measurement systems

Drucker's extensive work on management theory and practice resulted in Management by Objectives (MBO) becoming a widely recognized tool in the management armoury. It has become firmly established in many organizations around the world. It has developed into schemes known by many other names but the principle remains. In the 1990s work by Fowler recognized other versions of MBO that had evolved into different forms, most noticeably Performance Management Systems (PMS). He compared the MBO and PMS approaches; you can see from Table 4.1 that the main differences are those of appraisal and links to cultural issues – MBO is a package bought off the shelf, PMS tends to be tailor made and grounded in vision and values. MBO tends to be generally limited in application to managers whereas PMS is usually extended to include all staff. Therefore, PMS is owned by line management, MBO by specialists. Fowler (1990) emphasized the importance of cultural congruence to the success of either system and stated that both would fail unless compatible with the style, beliefs and values of the organization or unless they are an integral part of a planned programme of cultural change. He gave examples of highly structured schemes being imposed upon organizations whose style was informal and flexible and also examples of attempts made to induce collaborative working into highly controlled and status-conscious environments. More discussion about the importance of culture will follow later in this chapter and throughout the book.

Since Fowler's work, PMS in the workplace is more widely used than MBO (CIPD, 2009) but the risk of failure is high when schemes place almost total emphasis on statistically measured task performance to the exclusion of broader, people-based issues of personal competence and development. This is exacerbated by the tendency for schemes to become administratively complex such as a myriad of KPIs, resulting in cynicism and the failure to convert good ideas into action and practice. Target setting is also fraught with inconsistencies such as hard targets set for some individuals/departments and more achievable targets set for others. The results of this can often be divisive and can leave workers feeling aggrieved and alienated. Target setting may also place emphasis on short-term tasks at the expense of long-term strategy. This approach and the resulting inefficiency and low morale may be seen in a wide raft of performance measurement systems imposed on the public sector such as police response times, hospital bed occupancy and GCSE pass rates.

The balanced scorecard

The majority of organizations use some form of measurement to gauge their performance. Such measures often include customer satisfaction surveys, quality surveys, productivity scores, shareholder feedback, stakeholder feedback,

TABLE 4.1   A comparison of MBO and performance management
systems

MBO	PMS
Packaged systems	Tailor-made systems
Applied to managers	Applied to all staff
Emphasis on individual objectives	Emphasis on corporate goals and values
Emphasis on quantified performance measures	Inclusion of qualitative performance indicators
Jobs divided into key results areas (KRAs)	Jobs divided into principal accountabilities
Objectives set for each KRA	Objectives set for each accountability
Performance measures	Performance indicators (including KPIs)
Task and personal goals	Task and personal goals
Annual appraisal including discussion of new goals	Annual appraisal including discussion of new goals
Most schemes use complex paperwork	Some schemes have complex paperwork
Schemes 'owned' by specialists	Schemes 'owned' by line management

After Fowler (1990)

supplier performance scores, customer loyalty feedback cards and financial scorecards. Many organizations use a combination of such measures but few seem to achieve the required blend of meaningful data and its effective use in sustaining competitive advantage.

The traditional view of measurement as a means of control may be naïve. Certainly the human relations view rather than the managerialist one (see preceding chapters) believe this to be the case. As soon as performance measures are used as a management control tool, the people who are measured begin to manage the measures rather than the performance. Data is manipulated, incidents are reported selectively and information is presented in a way to make the people look good. Research by Neely (1998) argues that when individuals and groups are linked to performance figures the pressure to manipulate information is even stronger. There is also a danger in having numerous KPIs. This may be counterproductive because if people are rewarded for returning good figures they are bound to pursue courses of action that will make the figures look good even if this damages the performance of the business as a whole.

Kaplan and Norton (2000) proposed a tool to measure performance that uses and builds upon the traditional financial measurements but also balances these out with the measurement of both quantitative and qualitative reviews of customer relationships, internal business processes and learning and growth. The aim of their balanced scorecard framework was to give organizations a comprehensive view of the business and to allow them to drive both strategy and improvement forward (see Figure 4.1). They recognized the need to include hard and soft measures, that is to say the measurement of

FIGURE 4.1   The balanced scorecard

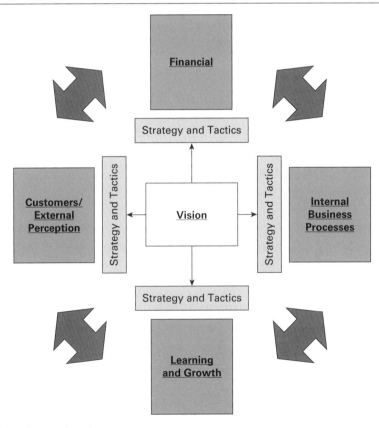

After Kaplan and Norton (2000)

both tangible and intangible products including internal and external relationships. They recognized that no single measure can be used to assess or control performance. Organizations that have used versions of the balanced scorecard include UK public sector agencies and private sector companies such as Skandia, Coca-Cola, British Airways and General Electric.

A suggested model for good practice: a mixture of measurement and management

The real value of measurement comes from the actions that follow it. Organizations need to understand:

- why they want to measure their performance;
- what they currently measure and what they *should* measure;
- how they should measure these things; and
- what they should do with the data once they have it.

If organizations can answer these questions they may benefit in the following ways:

- by establishing a means of ensuring compliance against non-negotiable performance parameters;
- by establishing a means to challenge the assumptions that underpin organizational strategy and as a result understand the key areas critical to success; and
- by being able to check the all-round health of the organization.

Activity – Consider

- Why bother to measure performance; wouldn't it be better to channel effort directly into improving performance rather than just measuring it?

- What things are measured in an organization known to you and how does it use the data?

You may find it helpful to discuss your thoughts on this issue with other colleagues and/or students.

Performance appraisals and reviews

As organizations have developed more structured approaches to strategic management, there has been some movement towards the integration of these processes with the management of human resources. This has involved many organizations in the introduction of formal performance systems, frequently characterized by appraisals or performance reviews. In the United States and the United Kingdom most large organizations employ some kind of systematic appraisal and review (CIPD, 2009).

The purposes of appraisal are seen as being for the maintenance of organizational control and for the measurement of the efficiency with which the organization's human resources are being utilized, and the improvement of these resources. Appraisal applied to organizational control is the wider context of administration, inputs of human, physical, technological and financial resources and the outputs or performance of the organization itself. Appraisal applied to the efficiency and improvement of human resources is the context of measuring the output of individuals and teams in terms of their own contribution to organizational efficiency and effectiveness. The most common way of attempting to measure this contribution is by use of performance assessments usually called 'appraisals' or 'staff reviews', although in some public sector organizations they are called 'supervisions', rather confusingly. These may take place annually or at set times throughout the year. Most appraisals take place with line managers and are recorded for future reference. They are viewed by the organization as a way of reviewing employee progress and as an aid to succession planning.

The review of progress to date requires the appraiser to take on a judgemental role that focuses on past performance. It often has the objective of improving performance by extrinsic means such as rewards, both monetary or promotion. The appraisee often takes a passive or defensive role in this encounter. The succession planning approach requires the appraiser to take on a counselling role that focuses on improvement in future performance. It often has the objective of improving performance through self-learning and growth. The appraisee often takes on an active role in their learning. It is the use of appraisal systems that combine these two approaches that results in conflicting roles and mixed messages being sent out to employees. This practice ensures the unpopularity of this all too common type of appraisal or performance review with both managers and employees alike.

Other difficulties with appraisal often cited by managers and employees are: targets being hard to establish, no money for merit, no objective measurement, no support from the organizational culture and poor training of appraisers with inconsistency and subjectivity being seen as the main problems (CIPD, 2009). The research showed that appraisal was also seen as reinforcing power relationships and regularly perceived as being open to abuse; another issue was that most individuals have to work with their appraisers after the appraisal. This hostility towards appraisal came from those carrying out appraisals as well as those being appraised. Many organizations have more than one system for different groups of employees, which caused confusion and frustration. Many employees were unhappy about pay for performance and few could see a clear link between pay increases and performance. There were also issues of equity and justice that result from appraisals when workers all too often believe that managers are reluctant to recognize and act on poor performance and that many of them do not have sufficient knowledge of the subordinate's job. Ensuring quality and equity was seen to be a major problem that was related to the different degrees of commitment line managers gave to the process.

Employee appraisal/review systems are seen by many as being like seatbelts. Most people believe they are necessary but they do not like to use them. As a result, appraisal systems are often used reluctantly to satisfy organizational policy or legal requirements but managers are ingenious at finding ways to bypass them. Appraisers and appraisees often show marked antipathy to what they see as form filling and bureaucracy and an often voiced belief that no actions result from the process. The appraisal interview is still widely regarded as a nuisance at worst and as a necessary evil at best.

Appraisals can serve a number of useful purposes such as scheduled communication; they can also enhance planning. If they are carried out in a climate of trust and are used positively to enhance development they can be an effective tool enabling continuous improvement. Some organizations operate 360 degree feedback appraisals where employees are able to feedback their assessments of line managers. This approach carries some risk and has proved not to be popular; trust is often fragile in working relationships where power and politics coexist.

There are clear indications that both managers and employees see a potential for appraisal that is rarely achieved in practice. If the sole purpose of appraisal is to encourage personal and professional development, then the appraiser will act as counsellor, adviser and coach. This is almost universally seen as desirable and effective in gaining commitment. If, at the same time, the appraiser also acts as a judge or evaluator, then commitment degenerates into resigned compliance, with widespread resentment and perceptions of inequity.

Research confirms that most people are able to assess their past performance and predict their future performance accurately if supported by a 'no blame' culture. It also confirms that those who are involved in actually setting their targets tend to perform better. However, the real issue is whether in the prevailing managerialist culture they are willing to do so. Development planning and performance measurement do not sit easily within one appraisal framework. People are uncomfortable revealing weaknesses in a climate of downsizing and diminishing career progression opportunities.

Performance-related pay

The conundrum of performance-related pay is which comes first: paying for performance or performing for pay? There is a need to understand clearly why incentive and bonus schemes can work in some situations and not in others. We also need to understand what other strategies we can adopt to create improved performance and productivity and use these strategies when appropriate.

The question that managers often ask is, 'How do we link performance to pay for a wide range of employees?' This is probably the wrong question because it focuses on rewarding performance and not creating it. The question is based on three faulty assumptions. The first is that by creating a link between reward and performance standards, performance will take place naturally. The second assumption is that other factors that create performance already exist and are just waiting for pay to trigger them. The third assumption is that performance is already there; the only problem is how to pay for it. These approaches assume that it is the management of pay rather than performance that is the biggest challenge. This belief is further reinforced by many organizations having created separate compensation and benefit departments, and understandably these departments have a clear pay agenda rather than a performance one. Research from many sources concludes that findings on pay as a motivator and as an agent for change have never been impressive. The implications of these findings are that pay as the motivating and energizing strategy has severe limitations. These are:

- it has relatively short-term effects;
- it diminishes in value the more it is used;
- it produces more satisfaction than motivation;
- it is unlikely to convince employees that it is a fairer method of reward;
- it will not in itself convince employees that the performance management process is improving performance; and
- it causes bad feelings amongst and between teams.

Widespread difficulties are prevalent in traditional systems in the assessment of efficiency and effectiveness. This is because there are many jobs that have no readily identifiable units of output. Payment by results is seen as fraught with problems such as bias, inaccuracy and variables outside the control of the individual. Demotivation is also a major issue. Appraisal-related pay and/or performance-related pay impairs the chances of securing the commitment of poor performers and may damage the motivation of unrecognized good performers. Financial constraints also often thwart worker expectations when rewards are perceived as insultingly small in comparison to outstanding achievement. Cynicism is also generated and may become pervasive and affect morale, motivation and subsequent performance. The potential for ratings drift is also a concern in appraisals that are quantified and may be linked to pay and bonuses. Systematic overrating of staff may become an ongoing problem because of linkages to the performance appraisal form and salary increases. There is always the temptation for line managers to manipulate the system to their advantage, particularly if they wish to remain popular with their workers.

Substantial empirical research, from the time of Herzberg (1966) onwards, has shown that in many contexts employees are not motivated to perform better by the prospect of receiving monetary reward. Performance-related pay has provided many high-profile examples of failed schemes, criticism by many practitioners and a plethora of research studies questioning its effectiveness. A focus on teamwork has become an almost universal feature of performance management in modern organizations. Organizations are saying that teamwork is an essential component in the achievement of organizational objectives. However, the emphasis of appraisal, development and pay continues to be on the individual (Armstrong and Baron, 2005). The challenge for organizations is to bring about commitment to discretionary effort, which is increasingly a key feature in gaining competitive advantage. As the prevalence of performance appraisal has grown so has its influence in shaping employee perceptions of justice. Outcomes and processes that are perceived as unfair in an organization will result in a workforce whose contribution through enthusiasm and 'going the extra mile' is not fully achieved (Rowland and Hall, 2012). The fact that rewards and progress may be in the hands of a single 'superordinate' or appraiser and that they are not always trusted to be fair is a common assumption and experience within workforces. One way of ameliorating this situation is to separate appraisal and reviews from salary considerations.

The adoption of the mechanisms of employee appraisal and remuneration do not solve management's problems, but in many ways generate new ones. The weakness of performance-related pay is that it sets a pay agenda rather than a performance agenda. The big challenge for organizations is the management of performance, not pay.

Culture and organizational effectiveness

The central argument supporting the use of performance management is that it will improve the organization's effectiveness. Thus, it is the aim of performance management to modify employee behaviour to achieve set objectives such as increased efficiency, enhanced job performance, improved motivation and better-quality product or service. There is a convincing raft of evidence from research that confirms that performance management may have a positive or negative effect depending on its congruence with prevailing cultures.

The issue of Total Quality Management with its central philosophy of self-checking versus the control aspect of appraisal and performance-related pay needs addressing in many organizations. One of the prime objectives of performance management is to motivate employees. There is a rapid growth in the UK of companies that use appraisal as a method to rate contribution to the organization and reward the contribution by performance-related pay. Many continue to experiment with various permutations of appraisal, bonus and individual and group performance-related pay. However, prevailing employee cultures at many organizations show a marked negative reaction to such systems, with a widespread cynicism. It may be that if the powerful subculture of senior management expects people to be indifferent and mainly motivated by money, resulting strategies can be expected to train them to behave in this way. Money is recognized by workers as being important and is a satisfier but in most circumstances their culture does not value it as a motivator (Rowland, 2013). In a quality culture, emphasis on rating individuals is seen as unreliable as differences in performance may largely be due to uncontrolled variables. Targets and objectives for individuals may also run counter to teamwork. However, formal reviews are seen to be valuable in terms of giving the individual the right to obtain feedback. This feedback signals acknowledgement for individual contribution and allows opportunities for dialogue and development. Feedback is regarded as a powerful reinforcement tool and also as a crucial stimulus that affects motivation and thus performance. In a culture that values quality the appropriate type of feedback would be developmental and in the form of a continuous improvement initiative. Employees at organizations that strive for quality cultures may accept the need for constant evaluation and often reject appraisal-related pay. It is condemned as it is seen counter to the self-checking and empowerment expected in a quality culture.

A central issue at the heart of the performance management debate is team versus individual contribution. One side believes that emphasis on the individual stretches targets and increases personal productivity for those who have significant discretion over their own output. The other side believes that individual targets are counterproductive because they create individual competition at the expense of the collaboration so important to team success.

The notion that appraisal 'is a bad idea and doesn't work', held by many academics, is not always echoed by those who apply it. There are two distinct yet closely related reasons why appraisal is not successful in practice. First there are the problems associated with the measurement of performance, and secondly there are tensions between cultures of development and control. Managerialistic cultures of control see appraisal and performance-related pay as legitimate tools to reinforce authority and ensure compliance. Most employee cultures place a high value on trust, equity and development. Unless there is cultural congruence compatible with the style, beliefs and values of the stakeholders the system will fail. It is essential that leaders and managers have this knowledge and work together to devise and implement systems that are appropriate to need.

Most organizations tend to be good at managing good performance and very bad at managing poor performance. Change driven from the top down stands little chance of long-term success. Until new behaviours encouraged by performance management systems are rooted in the shared values of the organization's culture they will be diluted or circumvented as soon as any weakening of the driving forces occurs. The performance management system will never be better than the stakeholders choose to make it.

Although there are fundamental weaknesses in many performance management systems, they may well have an important role to play in improving organizational culture and promoting organizational effectiveness. There is still a place for performance management at the heart of the organization's strategy if the reasons for its use and its limitations are well understood by those using it. The performance management system itself is crucial. If it is to have a positive influence it must be reliable, valid, feasible and perceived as fair. In this way it will be congruent with both explicit and implicit cultures. A badly constructed system will have a negative influence by encouraging an emphasis on the wrong activities and engendering resentment and demotivation. Many systems become overly complex and bureaucratic. They attempt to measure all measurable tasks and processes without focusing on the cost benefits of such an approach. Many organizations have shifted from hier-archical structures to more complex, team-based and democratic systems and the appropriateness of traditional judgemental appraisal reviews and performance-related pay to manage performance is increasingly questionable. Nevertheless, performance management can be a valuable strategic tool and is now more likely to be part of an integrated management strategy than it was a decade ago (CIPD, 2009).

Activity – Consider

1   What can you do as a leader, manager or team member to improve efficiency and effectiveness in your own organization?

2   To what extent does congruence between performance management systems and organizational culture influence contribution to organizational effectiveness? Try to give examples of cases you know.

3   The use of traditional methods of appraisal and performance-related pay is a questionable practice in organizations that are moving away from hierarchical structures to more complex democratic systems. What can you suggest might be a better approach?

Leading performance now and in the future

This chapter has explored the way that leadership can enable people and organizations to achieve targets and perform effectively. It has also reviewed the history of management theory and practice with regards to both leadership and performance. Finally, some aspects of current management thought are worth consideration.

In the past decade, academics led by business practitioners have started to focus more on leadership agility as a prerequisite for success in the turbulent 21st-century world of expanding global markets and the exponential rise of the digital technology and communication. The emphasis for the agile leader (Bennett and Lemoine, 2014; Horney *et al*, 2010) is grounded in the world of VUCA, a term first coined by the US Army College to explain the dynamic nature of the world. The acronym VUCA stands for Volatility, Uncertainty, Complexity and Ambiguity. Agile leaders are responsive, innovative and flexible but above all can anticipate change and are able to initiate action in work situations that feature rapid change and or ambiguity.

A 'Nine box' model for reviewing performance and leadership agility is shown in Figure 4.2. The 'Nine box' review method assesses individuals on performance and leadership agility. All those considered as Strategic Agility Asset, Agile High Performer and Rising Star would be considered as high contributors and potential leaders who should be given special access to developmental assignments, projects and training.

Concluding thoughts

Organizations are operating in a world of rapidly changing scenarios. They are under constant pressure to improve productivity and reduce costs. Effective leadership is a crucial component of helping to ensure competitive advantage by ensuring high performance. Current management thought emphasizes a clear need for strategy that recognizes important linkages between leadership and performance in flexible and responsive actions that reflect the context of volatile political, economic and technological circumstances.

There are strong indications to suggest that many organizations favour pragmatic, short-term approaches to performance management. Research is all too often discounted in favour of quick-fix solutions.

FIGURE 4.2   Leadership agility and performance

	High Professional/Master Contributor	Agile High Performer/High Professional	Strategic Agility Asset
High Performance	Consistently produces exceptional results. High performer. Knows job extremely well. May not effectively adapt to new situation.	Consistently produces exceptional results. Knows job extremely well. High performer. Demonstrates ability to adapt to new situations.	Outstanding results and performance. Demonstrates agility. Ability to take on major stretch assignments to new areas. Anticipates and acts proactively on changing trends that will impact on the organization.
	Key Performer/Solid Professional	**Adaptable Key Performer**	**Rising Star**
	Consistently meets expectations. Knows job well. Has not demonstrated ability to adapt to new situations.	Consistently meets expectations. Knows job well and enhances skills as appropriate. Can adapt to new situations as necessary.	Consistently meets expectations. Knows job well. Demonstrates ability to anticipate change and initiate action.
Low Performance	**Low Performer/Low Agility**	**Inconsistent Performer**	**Diamond in the Rough**
	Not delivering on results as expected. Does not adapt to change well.	Delivers results inconsistently. Knows the job and may be a passive learner. May adapt to new situations if necessary.	Delivers results erratically. Has demonstrated agility potential but is not living up to it.

Low Agility ——————————————————————————→ High Agility

After Horney, Pasmore and O'Shea (2010)

As mentioned at the start of this chapter, organizations are purposive entities. They have goals and need to measure the achievement of those goals. But, according to Rowland and Hall (2012: 290), 'weighing the calf does not fatten it'. Indeed, the trauma of the measurement process may hamper development. Creating an environment where individuals can grow and develop is enhanced by appraisals designed for that purpose. Measurement of individual performance is of dubious relevance in team-working environments. Judgements about how individuals contribute to teams are perhaps best made by teams themselves. Individual appraisal interviews are best suited to counselling and identification of development needs. Certainly, the inclusion of performance measurement clouds the process and leads to cynical beliefs about organizational value systems. If performance management is to contribute to the achievement of an organization's goals, then the organization needs to be clear about why appraisal is in place and how it fits with strategy, culture and philosophy.

Performance management should ultimately be about performance enhancement. We need to understand the difference between leadership and management. This will enable us to take on either role (or both) to facilitate conditions that ensure people can achieve their best and remain motivated to do so. Herzberg (1966) recognized that by treating people the way they are rather than the way we want them to be, we have a chance to motivate them. There are many tools that can be used to support efficiency and effectiveness but to achieve lasting success we have to show knowledge, understanding, tolerance, respect and above all fairness. In this way organizations will be able to develop strategies that are suitable, feasible and successful.

Revision question

Examine the model shown in Figure 4.2 and rate yourself, explaining the reasons for this rating and giving examples from your own practice within a workplace or social situation.

Further study

Harvard Business Review (2007) The tests of a leader, January
Haslam, S A, Reicher, S D and Platow, M J (2011) *The New Psychology of Leadership*, Psychology Press, New York

References

Adair, J (2002) *Effective Strategic Leadership*, Pan MacMillan, London
Archer, D and Cameron, A (2009) *Collaborative Leadership: How to succeed in an interconnected world*, Elsevier, Oxford
Armstrong, M and Baron, A (1998) *Performance Management: The new realities*, Institute of Personnel and Development, London
Armstrong, M and Baron, A (2005) *Managing Performance: Performance management in action*, Chartered Institute of Personnel and Development, London
Bass, B and Bass, R (2008) *The Bass Handbook of Leadership*, 4th revised edn, The Free Press, London
Beer, M and Ruh, R (1976) Employee growth through performance management, *Harvard Business Review*, July–August, pp 59–66
Bennett, N and Lemoine, G J (2014) What a difference a word makes. Understanding threats to performance in a VUCA world, *Business Horizons*, 57 (3), pp 311–17

Bennis, W G (1999) *Managing People is Like Herding Cats*, Executive Excellence Publishing, Provo, UT

Blake, R R and Mouton, J S (1964) *The Managerial Grid*, Gulf Publishing, Houston, TX

Cameron, K (2011) Responsible leadership as virtuous leadership, *Journal of Business Ethics*, **98**, pp 25–35

CIPD (2009) *Performance Management in Action: Current trends and practice*, Hot Topics Report No 5040, November, Chartered Institute of Personnel and Development, London

Drucker, P (1995) *People and Performance: The best of Peter Drucker on management*, Routledge, London

Drucker, P (2008) *The Five Most Important Questions*, Jossey-Bass, San Francisco, CA

Fowler, A (1990) Performance management: The MBO of the 90s, *Personnel Management*, July, pp 47–51

Herzberg, F (1966) *Work and the Nature of Man*, Staples Press, New York

Horney, N, Pasmore, B and O'Shea, T (2010) Leadership agility: A business imperative for a VUCA world, *People and Strategy*, **33** (4), pp 32–8

Kant, I (1790) *Critique of Judgement* (J C Meredith, 2007, trans) Oxford University Press, Oxford

Kaplan, R S and Norton, D P (2000) *The Strategy Focused Organization: How balanced score card companies thrive in the new business environment*, Harvard Business Press, Boston, MA

Likert, R (1967) *The Human Organization: Its management and values*, McGraw-Hill, New York

Mintzberg, H (1973) *The Nature of Managerial Work*, Harper and Row, New York

Neely, A (1998) *Measuring Business Performance*, Economist Books/Profile, London

Rowland, C (2013) Managing team performance; Saying and paying, *International Journal of Organizational Analysis*, **21** (1), pp 38–52

Rowland, C and Hall, R (2012) Perceived unfairness in appraisal: Engagement and sustainable organizational performance, *EuroMed Journal of Business*, 7 (3), pp 280–93

Senge, P (1999) The leadership of profound change, in (eds) Senge, Kleiner, Roberts Ross and Smith, *The Dance of Change*, Nicholas Brearley, London, pp 3–34

Torrington, D, Hall, L and Taylor, S (2002) *Human Resource Management*, 5th edn, Financial Times Management, London

Employee engagement through effective communications

05

TERRY SMITH

OBJECTIVES

This chapter aims to outline why and how employee engagement is a pivotal strategic corporate imperative in creating and sustaining competitive advantage by:

- Examining what we mean by 'employee engagement'.

- Explaining how the concept of 'the internal market' is a practice, a process and an independent domain.

- Presenting evidence to demonstrate how internal corporate culture is central to an organization's form, function and philosophy and how this informs external marketing.

- Contextualizing marketing communications as an integrative force in business, management, corporate and organizational communication.

- Examining the interdependence of communication *format* and *content* with particular reference to the impact of digital communications media.

Introduction

In today's dynamic, global markets, effective employee communications, as part of fully developed corporate communications, is becoming a strategic imperative (Dolphin, 2005). To sustain a competitive advantage, it is increasingly acknowledged that a workforce that is engaged, complicit with corporate strategy and aware of its critical contribution to customer orientation can have a pivotal role to play in the interface between company and customer. Wellins and Concelman's definition, 'an amalgamation of commitment, loyalty, productivity and ownership' (2005: 1) perfectly captures the essence of employee engagement.

A UK government report in 2009 – the *MacLeod Review* (MacLeod and Clarke, 2009) – confirmed an earlier CIPD report (Gatenby *et al*, 2009) which highlighted internal connectivity and communication as key internal and external customer drivers. Academics have been less inclined to theorize the practice of internal communications from a marketing perspective; organizations have equally been reticent to enact theory. As Verčič *et al* (2012: 223) suggest: 'internal communications, as a practice and an independent domain, is in its infancy'. Although employee engagement through effective communications is still a relatively underdeveloped element of management strategy, it is an essential part of organizational function and philosophy. As Grönroos (2007: 383) asserts: 'Without good and well-functioning internal relationships, external customer relationships will not develop successfully. Managing employees – on all levels – is a true test of managing an organization.'

Discussions over the loci of communication objectives and the foci of target markets would suggest that a good starting point for evaluating approaches to employee engagement might be to reconsider the word 'employee' and to redefine the word 'engagement'. The former implies a contractual arrangement, a physical or human resource, a commitment to linear, transmitted communications; the latter often suggests a restricted internalized work-oriented arrangement. Effective, symbiotic relationships between management and employee will underpin effective, symbiotic relationships between employee and customer. There are different perspectives, of course: while HRM research frames communication as a managerial control mechanism (Lachotzki and Noteboom, 2005), marketing research views interaction with employees as 'customers' (Ahmed and Rafiq, 2002; Dunmore, 2002). 'Leadership communication' (Windsor-Lewis, 2002) and 'the internal market' set the binary parameters for this debate on internal communications; they also signpost the content of this chapter.

The meaning of employee engagement

A precursor to any strategy or discussion on the 'internal' aspects of marketing strategy must be an examination of how market-oriented an organization is. Indeed, Gounaris (2006) considered this to be the philosophical base of internal marketing. Kohli and Javoski (1999) describe this as 'the organization-wide generation of market intelligence and information on customer's current and future needs and... the organization-wide response to it'. Internal marketing, when linked to a philosophy of continuous improvement, aligns employee behaviour with corporate objectives by affecting service attitude through communication to sustain a positive customer experience. It is essentially about attitude management and communications management. Robinson *et al* (2004: 2) describe engagement as 'a positive attitude held by the employee towards the organization and its values... aware of the business context'.

Macey and Schneider (2008) present a complex nomological network encompassing trait, state and behavioural engagement but draw a conceptual difference with levels of psychological company connection. *State* engagement – passion, enthusiasm, energy and activation – precedes *behavioural* engagement, often referred to as 'adaptive behaviour'. *Trait* engagement is prescribed and covers positive affectivity, conscientiousness, proactive and autoletic (selfish) personality. Perhaps the difficulty here is viewing employees as an 'operand' resource – just an ingredient or factor in the production process – rather than an 'operant' resource crucial to the act of value co-creation and an integral customer relationship pivot. Skills and knowledge, as well as attitude and commitment, are seen as the most important type of resource (Vargo and Lusch, 2004).

The internal market

It is on this essential philosophical point – that the production of value is a co-creative act – that a paradigm shift has taken place in our marketing discussions involving the role of employees in the 'exchange relationship' value proposition. In other words, employees are not just instrumental but integral to the 'value chain' (Porter, 1985). They are co-creative partners in the production of value, and their impact on customer satisfaction and the achievement of strategic corporate objectives is now fully recognized. Ravald and Grönroos (1996) argue that the ability to provide superior value to customers is a prerequisite of creating and maintaining successful relationships with customers. Levitt (1960) argued that a purely internal focus was myopic; Gummesson (1994) similarly criticized a dominant external focus as being singularly restrictive.

What is required is an *integrative* approach, strategically interlinking the external marketing efforts with an internal one. Rafiq and Ahmed (1993: 230) recognize this by identifying the internal market as key in aligning and integrating cross-functional and corporate objectives and improving the critical link between internal customers and external suppliers in creating value. Dunne and Barnes (2000: 190) extol the virtues of integration as a 'continuing process of transforming the whole organization into a customer-focused entity'. But managing the creative and intellectual assets of its people is instrumental to this process (Quirke, 2000: 21) in order to produce behaviour change and enhanced performance at the customer interface (Piercy *et al*, 2002). This suggests a hybridity of employee with a dual perspective. To these ambidextrous participants, marketing communications must be targeted. At the core of this process is the notion of the 'internal market': a focus on employees as customers or recipients of internal service in order to fully integrate all marketing activities.

As a new management perspective, the concept of employees being seen as an internal market captured the attention of marketing academics (Albrecht, 1990; Berry and Parasuraman, 1991; Grönroos, 1985; Gummesson, 1987), although internal marketing of one sort or another had been practised long before. Antecedents of this internal focus (Gounaris, 2006) claim that employee satisfaction and behaviour change precede any implementation of external marketing efforts to enhance customer value. An early observer of this phenomenon, (Berry, 1984: 272) comments on the perspective that views employees as internal customers integral in the achievement of corporate goals but essential as communication targets. There were obvious internally focused precursors under the auspices of Taylorism (Grönroos, 1994), but an active, market-oriented perspective linked to the external environment instilled a less insular, wider strategic purpose. A broadened concept of internal marketing relating to management strategic issues is listed by Lambert

(1995): retention of employees through engagement; enhanced management and employee relationships; the understanding of the need for competitive service; building a corporate brand with internal as well as external relevance; and coordination and commitment of all stakeholders. In many businesses, particularly those with an enlightened service orientation, the first customers are the company's own staff (Ambler, 2001). Employees should be seen as co-creators of value and 'partnerships must be built with internal stakeholders' (Sowa, 2005: 433).

The notion of an internal market is not restricted by the limitations of function; rather it is the convergence of a number of previously separate management technologies such as HRM, employee relations, strategic management, quality management, corporate communications and macro-marketing; it is an integrative framework (Varey and Lewis, 1999: 938). At its heart is the promotion of continuously improving service quality and the maintenance of co-creative company/customer relationships. Christopher *et al* (1991) point out that 'Internal marketing is an important activity in developing a customer-focused organization... developing internal and external customer awareness and remove functional barriers to organizational effectiveness.'

Figure 5.1 shows the relationship of internal marketing to the external communications strategy and the connection to the customer. *External* marketing, the communications aimed at outside stakeholders, is very much about what the firm *says* it will do – essentially the company's promise to the marketplace. *Internal* marketing is what the firm *does* – enabling those promises. *Interactive* marketing is the delivery of that promise and what others say about the organization's value proposition.

Varey and Lewis (1999: 926) observed that 'explicit discussion of the marketing concept in use in the internal operations of the organization entered the marketing and service management literature in the late 1970s'. Day and Wensley (1983) articulated the role of marketing as being the management of all exchange relationships between the internal and external constituencies of the organization. George's (1990: 63) definition still resonates: 'the process for achieving internal exchanges between the organization and its employee groups as a prerequisite for successful exchanges with external markets'.

In the 1990s, academic interest in the internal market concept focused on a relationship-oriented, network-based perspective. The initial perception and evaluation of company value propositions were seen as paramount to outward-facing strategy. The key role of internal personnel engaged in the

FIGURE 5.1   The internal in relation to the external environment

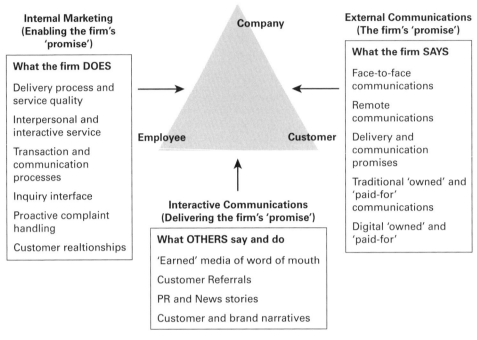

Adapted from Grönroos (2000a)

interface between company and customer was to be extended beyond the written contract: the psychological, moral and customer-facing unwritten contract of customer engagement:

> Internal marketing has been proposed variously as a structured approach to strategy implementation, to the diffusion of innovations, to recruiting and retaining service-minded staff, to creating a service culture, or to increasing internal service productivity. (Varey and Lewis, 1999: 926)

The acknowledgement of the importance of the interface between company and customer is perfectly illustrated in this from Gremler *et al* (1993: 34): 'an internal service encounter is the dyadic interaction between an internal customer and an internal service provider.'

Ballantyne (2003) develops a relationship-mediated theory of internal marketing which has 'knowledge renewal as its purpose and market orientation and improved market based performance as its end goal'. He suggests a four-phase internal marketing cycle (see Table 5.1) that reflects these knowledge

TABLE 5.1   Four phases of the internal marketing cycle

	Energizing	Codebreaking	Authorizing	Diffusing
Learning activity (planned)	Learning how to work on useful goals that are outside the bounds of any individual job description.	Learning how to apply personal 'know-how' in working together to solve customer problems, create new opportunities and change internal procedures.	Learning how to review choices between options on a cost–benefit basis and get policy decisions from the appropriate line authority.	Learning how to circulate and share knowledge across managerial domains in new ways.
Spontaneous community (emergent)	Two-way value propositions. Trust in fellow participants.	Creative dialogue. Obligation to stick at it.	Knowledge application. Trust in management.	'Customer consciousness' confirmed in actions.
Knowledge renewal (emergent)	Common knowledge of the complexity of the task emerges between community members in open exchanges about their own work experiences. These interactions are understood as a movement from tacit to explicit levels of knowing.	New ideas relevant to the task are discovered and a range of customer-oriented internal change proposals are developed. This phase is understood as raising tacit knowledge to explicit levels with the added input of market-based customer research.	Cost–benefit knowledge is used to evaluate and rank the policy proposals for discussion with the line and specialist management. These decision-making intersections are understood as a movement from explicit levels of knowing.	Knowledge is codified into new design, procedures and training programmes then tested in action and integrated into the working ways of the organization. This final phase of the cycle is understood as a diffusion of knowledge from explicit to tacit.

SOURCE: Ballantyne (2003)

exchange patterns. The four phases of this cycle feature: *energizing*, which is to do with workforce education that might include 'market-orientation' induction for example; *codebreaking*, which is turning 'tacit' knowledge ('know-how') into cohesive procedures and innovative practices; *authorizing* is reviewing choices between options establishing authorized policy decisions; and *diffusing* where knowledge and expertise are disseminated.

An internal market orientation can provide 'an easily accessible and user-friendly mechanism for executives to analyse the organizational issues which need to be addressed in implementing marketing strategies' (Piercy and Morgan, 1991: 936). As Gounaris *et al* (2010: 1671) point out: 'internal market orientation has a clear objective – to improve value for the customer – but is different from "market-orientation" because it seeks to do so by catering for the needs of the company's employees'.

Corporate culture

Corporate culture is central to an organization's form, function and philosophy. An interpretive perspective focuses on the communal generation of narratives and symbolic expression, the interpretation of beliefs and values. It is about learnt behaviour, the lived experience, the social construction of meanings. Wilson *et al* (2008: 269) describe culture as a framework for 'shared beliefs and values that give members of an organization meaning and provide them with rules for behaviour'. For the purposes of our discussion here, perhaps the most appropriate definition of culture (of a group) is from Schein (1990: 58): 'the collective or shared learning of that unit as it develops its capacity to survive in its external environment and to manage its own internal affairs'. But of course interpretivists would argue that there can be multiple realities in this shared, collective 'meaning'; it is a strategic imperative to unify this as much as possible.

Corporate culture isn't the same as *service* culture. Grönroos (2000a: 220) described this as 'a culture where an appreciation for good service exists and where giving good service to internal as well as external customers is considered a natural way of life'. A prerequisite of employee engagement needs to work on cognitive, affective and conative levels. Kahn (1990) described these factors as physical, cognitive and emotional work. Engaged employees, with a pro-company attitude, will spread positive word of mouth and act as true company advocates; Gallup (2003; cited in Melcrum, 2005) claim that 67 per cent of engaged employees externally recommend their company.

For company culture to foster internal value creation, communication has to be a social system of relationships not solely focused on economic transactions. As Varey and Lewis (1999: 942) state: 'whilst communication can occur without an economic transaction, any economic transaction cannot occur without communication'. Christensen (2011: 199) describes marketing as 'a system of auto-communication, a set of self-referential communication practices... in short, its own culture'.

Internal marketing communications

The role of internal marketing communications is to affect three key strategic areas: the *management of change* such as new strategy, policies, infrastructure, technology; the creation and maintenance of *corporate and brand image* in line with corporate objectives and competitive market positioning; and the application of *strategic internal marketing* by developing internal coherence in order to allow external marketing to be successfully implemented. Internal marketing is fundamentally a 'brand social system which is the interface between company, customer and media, [where] all points of contact with the brand "talk" to existing and potential customers and help constitute brand meaning' (Dahlen *et al*, 2010: 31). Below is a list of the key features of internal marketing:

- A socially constructionist perspective and experiential process where company values, ethos and culture are internally aligned to the external competitive and social environment.

- Hybrid philosophy and function of HRM and marketing in order to affect employee attitude and engagement.

- Discrete activities and embedded practices in service marketing philosophy, marketing initiatives, customer service frameworks and broader business strategies.

- Structured activities are accompanied by a range of less formal ad hoc initiatives.

- Appreciate the valuable contribution of employees in co-creating value.

- Internal marketing communication is critical to the external application of marketing communications.

- Affects external market positioning and competitive differentiation.

- Needs commitment from highest levels with employee cooperation vital to success.

Integrating a cohesive internal marketing strategy has a number of benefits:

- Encourages the internal market to function better by empowering employees and extending personal responsibility and accountability.

- Helps promote internal cohesion and cooperation by creating better common understanding and customer orientation in order to reduce conflict between functional areas and reduce barriers between departments and functions.

- Integrates business strategy, vision, culture, structure and management of physical and intellectual resources with employee professional and social needs and market requirements.

- Recognizes the notion that everything communicates and everyone is a customer.

- Improves employee retention and in turn enhances customer loyalty.

- Fosters an atmosphere and a spirit of creativity conducive with the implementation of innovative practices and introduction of continuously improved products and services.

The relationship between the implementation of internal marketing communications and employee engagement – the internal market – is to maintain information flows to allow connection with, and understanding of, the *strategic narrative*. It can facilitate an informed *employee voice* which, in turn, promotes employee advocacy and helps complicity and commitment to the implementation of strategy and policy.

Christensen (2011: 197) argues that 'although marketing-oriented organizations are heavily engaged in external communication activities, they often communicate primarily with themselves'. However, while his claim that marketing can be self-referential – auto-communication as he calls it – it is a *sine qua non* of successful marketing that internal marketing communications have to have simpatico with external marketing communications. As Ahmed and Rafiq (2002: 60) suggest, 'internal marketing is a planned effort using a marketing-like approach directed at motivating employees for implementing and integrating organizational strategies towards customer orientation'. While 'everything communicates something about a firm and its goods and services – regardless of whether the marketer accepts this and acts upon it or not' (Grönroos, 2010a: 303), communication must be seen, as Drucker (1973) stated, not just as the *means* but as the *mode* of organization. Welch (2012) notes the positive/negative paradox between good internal communications that promote solid internal relationships, and poor communications that can be counterproductive in creating gaps between perception and expectation.

Welch and Jackson (2007) devised an internal communications matrix model (see Figure 5.2) linking the company to the external environment, combining line management, team, project peer and internal corporate communications with goals of environmental awareness, commitment to the organization, its evolving aims and challenges and individual sense of belonging.

FIGURE 5.2   Internal communication matrix

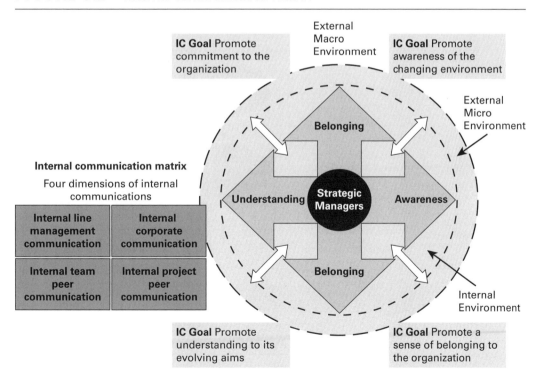

Adapted from Welch and Jackson (2007)

The key elements of this internal marketing framework are awareness, understanding, belonging and commitment. Kalla (2005) offers a similar demarcation, all absorbed under the heading of 'integrated marketing communications': *business communication* focusing on employee skills; *management communication* focusing on management capabilities; *corporate communication* focusing on formal communications; and *organizational communication* addressing more philosophical and theoretical aspects of strategy. Grunig (2009) points to recent approaches based more on *bridging* rather than *buffering*: building relationships with stakeholders rather than activities designed to separate organization from employee.

Figure 5.3 is a model adapted from Ahmed and Rafiq's (2002) framework for engaging employees through the use of marketing communications. (Note: the original describes a framework for implementing a CSR programme into an organization.) There are four 'strategic levels':

1 *Direction*, which infers a 'top-down' agenda and strategy to be deployed.

FIGURE 5.3 Model of internal communication for employee engagement

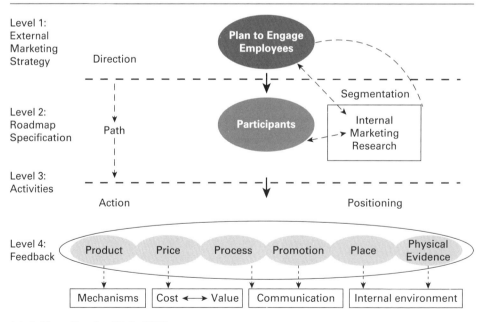

Adapted from Ahmed and Rafiq (2002)

2 *Path,* which covers the suggested specification of possible routes to take, highlighting barriers and mechanisms to overcome those barriers. Programmes are selected for specific employee groups and the use of planning (segmentation and positioning) as a result of marketing research is utilized to aid implementation.

3 *Action* is the plan and decisions translated into activities.

4 *Feedback* represents the employee's contribution.

The 'extended marketing mix' has been incorporated as the traditional tools applied to a service-oriented or market-facing organization. In this instance, because the emphasis is on *people* (employees), 'participants' have been separated from the other elements of the mix. For the purpose of this application, a brief explanation of the application of this is as follows:

- *Product* refers to job design and content, reward mechanisms, learning opportunities and creating a smart working environment including ambassadors, steering groups and even the creation of 'intrapreneurs' (see Kistruck and Beamish, 2010) as champions of innovation within the organization.

- *Price* is not just wages and other costs of employment but the value created in engagement, the acknowledgement of 'psychological contracts'.

- *Promotion* covers all aspects of the internal marketing communications programme that supports the external marketing communications strategy.

- *Place* is concerned with the work environment and includes the organizational culture, values, assumptions, artefacts and every symbolic aspect of the organization (Ahmed and Rafiq, 2003). (Organizational culture is covered separately above.)

- *Physical evidence* describes the tangible elements that make the intangible elements seem more concrete such as office layout, décor, uniforms, office or factory grounds.

- *Process* is the methods of operation, intranet/extranet connections, remote working, meetings and other methods or frameworks for enactment of strategy or policies.

Not all employees are customer-facing or have contact with the *external* customer and have influence over the provision of service. Judd (1987) devised a matrix to examine the relative level of influence and frequency of contact that various internal employees have (see Figure 5.4).

FIGURE 5.4 Employees and their influence on customers

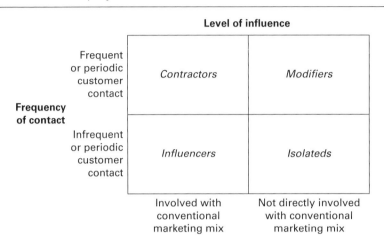

SOURCE: Judd (1987)

Here employees are segmented into the following types:

- *Contractors:* frequent or regular customer; involved with marketing mix and hold positions like selling or customer service. Customer-facing personnel. Marketing/customer interface.

- *Modifiers:* receptionists, credit departments, switchboard personnel, not directly involved with mix but have frequent customer contact. Need to develop customer skills.

- *Influencers:* product development, research. Customer responsiveness rather than face-to-face skills.

- *Isolateds:* Purchase department, data processing.

Ruck and Welch (2012) point to the focus on channels and explanations instead of on understanding of content. In 2010, the growing importance of internal communications was such that UK practitioners set up the Institute of Internal Communications, a dedicated body separate from the CIPR.

The influence of new communications media

Internal efforts must take a holistic strategic approach combining elements of HRM, marketing (including service and PR), information management and sales. The successful application of marketing communication should integrate both traditional and digital media. While the 'principles that govern behaviour, interaction and support remain constant' (Solis, 2011: 19), the significant impact of a digital landscape that has 24/7 connectivity, more democratic communication and the availability of 'real-time' information has been neither fully recognized nor reconciled. There has always been an element of interactivity with internal communications, but in a multimedia, computer-mediated environment, the feedback loops are shortened and the nature of the discourse becomes less transmissive and more dialogic (as illustrated in Figure 5.5). The content is often shared and recycled and the sender–receiver relationship is less permanent than transmission models of communication. From an organizational point of view, the 'social' element of digital communications offers perhaps the best opportunity as it has the ability to connect people and ideas and allow interactivity and ownership to facilitate successful internal communications.

FIGURE 5.5   Computer-mediated communications

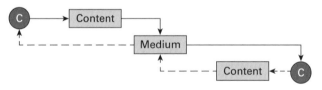

SOURCE: Hoffman and Novak (1996)

There is a growing range of digital tools that facilitate a different type of 'social' communication:

- Real-time information sharing enhances communication dissemination.
- Social media platforms like Twitter, LinkedIn and Facebook allow engagement.
- Corporate and employee narratives allow 'voice' and buy-in.
- Mobile technology platforms extend communication network.

- Digital publishing of pdfs instead of printed newsletters.

- Creative company apps for internal communication.

- Customization of messaging provides more personal communications.

- Video training and PR heighten impact and improve corporate image.

- Analytics, including employee engagement metrics, allow accurate segmentation and targeting of key stakeholders.

- Intranet, extranet, e-mail and social networks aid control and dissemination.

- Visual representation including infographics aid explanation and communication of strategy and policies.

- Gamification of standard communications, training, etc enhances use and effectiveness.

- Traditional media such as print, poster and face-to-face communications.

- BYOD (companies have relaxed the use of non-organizational technology by allowing a 'bring your own device' to work).

The use of key opinion leaders and company ambassadors within an organization can help internal adoption of change and policies and act as *de facto* sales force and help to spread word of mouth externally. The effectiveness of internal communications is dependent upon the communications preferences – message and media – of the internal market. These may not be uniform; employees should not be considered a homogeneous group (L'Etang, 2005; Welch and Jackson, 2007). Drawing on 'medium theory', Hallahan (2010) examines the interdependence of communication *format* and communication *content* and the influences and consequences of communication. Key elements of internal communications are:

- how information is disseminated and the reach of that communication;

- understanding and interpretation of communication; and

- the effects of communication.

With echoes of Marshall McLuhan, a lot of recent research suggests that 'the medium is the message' inside organizations (White *et al*, 2010) since there is a symbolic, psychological role as well as a practical one. Evidence of preference for electronic media has been well documented (eg, Woodall, 2006), but increasingly digital communications, with the ability to facilitate instant dialogical Business-to-Customer (B2C) as well as Customer-to-Customer (C2C) direct communications, are the conduit for the creation and maintenance of the company/customer interface. However, as digital becomes progressively embedded in the corporate communications toolkit, a recent report from internal marketing communications specialists newsweaver.com revealed some surprising results showing traditional methods of communication were still most widely deployed internally. Figure 5.6 ranks the most effective internal marketing communications channels, with established mechanisms like e-mail, intranet, leadership communications and team briefings still featuring high in the list.

FIGURE 5.6 Most effective internal marketing communications channels, 2014

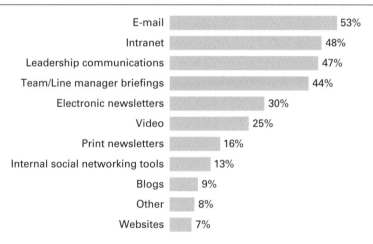

SOURCE: www.newsweaver.com (2015)

This is evidence that while digital connects, face-to-face communications still drive engagement in ways that digital can't. E-mail, a forerunner for this digitalization of communication media, still represents a sophisticated technological facilitator with the ability to send high-impact interactive messaging embedding 'rich' content such as video, commenting, networking, multi-channel conversation, and now used with insightful segmentation and metrics for deep 'real-time dashboard' analysis of use. Trends for the coming years suggest less reliance on traditional media but with greater development of social networking tools such as Twitter, LinkedIn and Facebook and expansion of intranet and mobile app usage.

Extending their research, what emerged were trends for how practitioners saw internal communications developing. The emphasis is switching to the 'social' elements of communication with internal social networking tools and controlled communication channels such as intranet very prominent (see Figure 5.7).

FIGURE 5.7   Trends for internal marketing communications channels, 2015

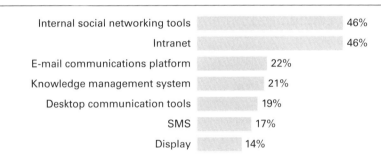

Internal social networking tools   46%
Intranet   46%
E-mail communications platform   22%
Knowledge management system   21%
Desktop communication tools   19%
SMS   17%
Display   14%

SOURCE: www.newsweaver.com (2015)

Communication may have become more immediate, but it becomes infinitely more complex (De Bussy *et al*, 2000). The internal (and external) media landscape is an audio-visual multimedia environment and a multidimensional construct (Smidts *et al*, 2001) in which an organization is seen as a social business. Corporate communications start with an internal focus, aimed towards internal publics (Hollensen, 2010) that are both 'digital natives' and 'digital immigrants' (Plowman *et al*, 2014).

The impact of digital communications, generally speaking, has changed the connections of parties in the communication process and the way those parties think and relate to each other. Littlejohn and Foss (2008) conceptualize the age of broadcast media as essentially a *social interaction* approach and the new interactive digital age as a *social integration* approach. There is now less emphasis on media and more on the communal element of communication. It is critical to evaluate the impact and role that all internal marketing communications as well as digital have. Another extract (Figure 5.8) from the www.newsweaver.com internal marketing survey indicates what practitioner metrics are used to evaluate effectiveness.

FIGURE 5.8 Internal marketing communications metrics 2015

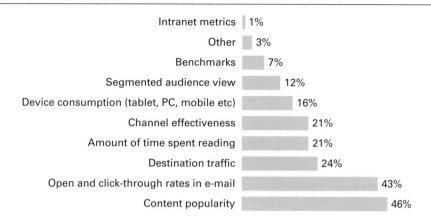

Intranet metrics 1%
Other 3%
Benchmarks 7%
Segmented audience view 12%
Device consumption (tablet, PC, mobile etc) 16%
Channel effectiveness 21%
Amount of time spent reading 21%
Destination traffic 24%
Open and click-through rates in e-mail 43%
Content popularity 46%

SOURCE: www.newsweaver.com (2015)

Concluding thoughts

Employees are the primary marketing interface with key influential organizational stakeholders. Using internal communications to achieve employee complicity and enhance effective stakeholder relationships is an increasingly important imperative of corporate strategy. Effective internal communications can help embed organizational vision, mission, strategy, values and overall company culture. At its best, it can promote a mutually beneficial conversation between company and employee.

This chapter has described how effective employee engagement can achieve sustainable competitive advantage through well executed strategic internal communications. The concept of 'the internal market' as a practice, a process and an independent domain was discussed and evidence was presented to demonstrate how internal corporate culture is central to an organization's form, function and philosophy and how this informs external marketing. Using both academic and practitioner research, marketing communications were contextualized as an integrative force in business, management, corporate and organizational communication. A range of models was incorporated and provided a conceptual framework within which internal and external communications were planned and executed. With particular reference to the impact of digital communications media, the interdependence of communication format and content was examined. This newer form of internal communications is still in its infancy and its impacts – particularly in respect of the democratization of communications, the undermining of traditional transmitted 'top-down' corporate communications – are yet to be reconciled as a management communication tool and employee engagement mechanism. Future research in this area will clarify its effectiveness.

References

Ahmed, P K and Rafiq, M (2002) *Internal Marketing: Tools and concepts for customer-focused management*, Butterworth Heinemann, Oxford

Ahmed, P K and Rafiq, M (2003) Commentary: Internal marketing issues and challenges, *European Journal of Marketing*, 37 (9), pp 1177–86

Albrecht, K (1990) *Service Within*, Dow-Jones-Irwin, Homewood, IL

Ambler, T (2001) What does marketing success look like? *Marketing Management*, 10 (1), pp 12–18

Ballantyne, D (2003) A relationship-mediated theory of internal marketing, *European Journal of Marketing*, 37 (9), pp 1242–60

Berry, L (1984) The employee as customer, in *Services Marketing*, American Marketing Organization, Chicago, IL, p 242

Berry, L and Parasuraman, A (1991) *Marketing Services: Competing through quality*, Free Press, New York

Christensen, L T (2011) Marketing as auto-communication, *Consumption Markets and Culture*, 1 (3), pp 109–227

Christopher, M, Payne, A and Ballantyne, D (1991) *Relationship Marketing: Bringing quality together*, Butterworth Heinemann, Oxford

Dahlen, M, Lange, F and Smith, T (2010) *Marketing Communications: A brand narrative approach*, John Wiley & Sons, Chichester

Day, G and Wensley, R (1983) Marketing theory with a strategic orientation, *Journal of Marketing*, 47 (4), pp 79–89

De Bussy, N M, Watson, R T, Pitt, L F and Ewing, M T (2000) Stakeholder communication management on the Internet: an integrated matrix for opportunities, *Journal of Communication Management*, 5 (2), pp 138–46

Dolphin, R R (2005) Internal communications: Today's strategic imperative, *Journal of Marketing Communications*, 11 (3), pp 171–90

Drucker, P F (1973) Managerial communications, in *Management, Tasks, Responsibilities*, Heinemann, Oxford, pp 481–93

Dunne, P A and Barnes, J G (2000) Internal marketing: a relationship and value creation view, in (eds) R Varey and B Lewis, *Internal Directions for Management*, Routledge, London

Dunmore, M (2002) *Inside-out Marketing: How to create an internal marketing strategy*, Kogan Page, London

Gatenby, M, Rees, C, Soane, E C and Truss, K (2009) *Employee Engagement in Context*, Chartered Institute of Personnel Development, London

George, W R (1990) Internal marketing and organizational behaviour: A partnership in developing customer conscious employees at every level, *Journal of Business Research*, **20** (1), pp 63–70

Gounaris, S (2006) Measuring internal market orientation in services: Some empirical evidence, *Journal of Business Research*, **22** (1), pp 68–90

Gounaris, S, Vassilkopoulou, A and Chatzipanagiotou, K C (2010) Internal-market orientation: A misconceived aspect of marketing theory, *European Journal of Marketing*, **44** (11/12), pp 1667–99

Gremler, D D, Bitner, M J and Evans, K R (1993) The internal service encounter, *International Journal of Service Industry Management*, **5** (2), pp 34–56

Grönroos, C (1985) Internal marketing – Theory and practice, in (eds) T Bloch, G Upah and V Zeithaml, *Services Marketing in a Changing Environment*, American Marketing Association, Chicago, IL, pp 41–7

Grönroos, C (1994) From marketing mix to relationship marketing: Towards a paradigm shift in marketing, *Management Decision Making*, **32** (2), pp 4–20

Grönroos, C (2000a) *Service Management and Marketing: A customer relationship management approach*, 2nd edn, John Wiley & Sons, Chichester

Grönroos, C (2000b) Relationship marketing logic, *Asia-Australia Marketing Journal*, **4** (1)

Grönroos, C (2007) *Service Management and Marketing: A customer relationship management approach*, 3rd edn, John Wiley & Sons, Chichester

Grunig, J E (2009) Paradigms of global public relations in an age of digitalization, *PRism*, **62** (2)

Gummesson, E (1987) Using internal marketing to develop a new culture – The case of Ericsson Quality, *Journal of Business and Industrial Marketing*, **2** (3), pp 23–8

Gummesson, E (1994) Service management: An evaluation and the future, *International Journal of Service Industry Management*, **5** (1), pp 28–36

Hallahan, K (2010) Public relations media, in (ed) R L Heath, *Handbook of Public Relations*, 2nd edn, Sage, Thousand Oaks, CA, pp 623–41

Hoffman, D and Novak, T (1996) Marketing in hyper-media computer-mediated environments: Conceptual foundations, *Journal of Marketing*, **60** (3), pp 50–68

Hollensen, S (2010) *Marketing Management: A relationship approach*, Pearson Education, Harlow

Judd, V C (1987) Differentiation from the 5th P, *Industrial Marketing Management*, **16**, pp 241–7

Kahn, W A (1990) Psychological conditions of personal engagement and disengagement at work, *Academy of Management Journal*, **33**, pp 692–724

Kalla, H K (2005) Integrated internal communications: A multidisciplinary perspective, *Corporate Communication*, **10**, pp 302–14

Kistruck, G M and Beamish, P W (2010) The interplay of form, structure and embeddedness in social intrapreneurship, *Entrepreneurship Theory and Practice*, **2** (1), pp 735–61

Kolhi, A and Jaworski, B (1999) Marketing orientation, in (ed) R Deshpandé, *Developing a Market Orientation*, Sage, Thousand Oaks, CA, pp 7–44

Lachotzki, F and Noteboom, R (2005) *Beyond Control: Managing strategic alignment through corporate dialogue*, John Wiley & Sons, Chichester

Lambert, A (1995) *Company Brochure: People in Business*, London

L'Etang, J L (2005) Critical public relations: Some reflections, *Public Relations Review*, 31, pp 521–6

Levitt, T (1960) Marketing myopia, *Harvard Business Review*, 38, pp 24–47

Littlejohn, S W and Foss, K A (2008) *Theories of human communication*, 9th edn, Thomson Higher Education, Belmont

Macey, W H and Schneider, B (2008) The meaning of employee engagement, *Industrial and Organizational Psychology*, **1**, pp 3–30

MacLeod, D and Clarke, N (2009) *Engaging for Success: Enhancing performance through employee engagement*, Office of Public Sector Information, London

Melcrum (2005) *Employee Engagement: How to build a high-performance workforce: Executive summary*, Melcrum Publishing, London

Piercy, N and Morgan, N (1991) Internal marketing: The missing half of the marketing programme, *Long Range Planning*, **24** (2), pp 82–93

Piercy, N, Harris, L C and Nikola, L (2002) Marketing orientation and retail operatives' expectations, *Journal of Business Research*, **55** (4), pp 261–73

Plowman, K D, Winchell, B and Wakefield, R I (2014) Digital publics: tracking down and reaching out to them, paper presented at Become, International Public Relations Research Symposium, Bled, Slovenia, July 4–5

Porter, M (1985) *The Competitive Advantage: Creating and sustaining superior performance*, Free Press, New York

Rafiq, M and Ahmed, P K (1993) The scope of internal marketing: Defining the boundary between marketing and human resource management, *Journal of Marketing Management*, **9** (3), pp 219–32

Ravald, A and Grönroos, C (1996) The value concept and relationship marketing, *European Journal of Marketing*, **30** (2), pp 19–30

Robinson, D, Perryman, S and Heyday, S (2004) *The Drivers of Employee Engagement*, IES Report 408, Institute of Employment Studies, Brighton

Ruck, K and Welch, M (2012) Valuing internal communication: Management and employee perspectives, *Public Relations Review*, 38, pp 294–302

Quirke, B (2000) *Making the Connections: Using internal communications to turn strategy into action*, Gower, Aldershot

Schein, E H (1990) Organizational culture, *American Psychologist*, **45** (2), pp 109–19

Smidts, A, Puny, A T H and Van Riel, C B M (2001) The impact of employee communication and perceived external prestige on organizational identification, *Academy of Management Journal*, **44** (5), pp 1051–62

Solis, B (2011) *Engage! The complete guide for brands and businesses to build, cultivate and measure success in the new web*, John Wiley & Sons, Chichester

Sowa, B C (2005) Internal communication, in (ed) R L Heath, *Encyclopaedia of Public Relations*, Sage, Thousand Oaks, CA, pp 430–34

Varey, R J and Lewis, B R (1999) A broadened conception of internal marketing, *European Journal of Marketing*, **33** (9/10), pp 926–44

Vargo, S L and Lusch, R F (2004) Evolving to a new dominant logic for marketing, *Journal of Marketing*, **68**, pp 1–17

Verčič, A T, Verčič, D and Sriramesh, K (2012) Internal communications: Definition, parameters and the future, *Public Relations Review*, **38** (2), pp 23–30

Welch, M (2012) Appropriateness and acceptability: Employee perspectives of internal communication, *Public Relations Review*, **38**, pp 246–54

Welch, M and Jackson, P R (2007) Rethinking internal communications: A stakeholder approach, *Corporate Communications: An International Journal* 12 (2), pp 177–98

Wellins, R and Concelman, J (2005) Personal engagement: driving growth at the see-level, in W H Macey and Benjamin Schneider, The meaning of employee engagement, *Industrial and Organizational Psychology*, 1, pp 3–30

White, C, Vanc, A and Stafford, G (2010) Internal communication, information and sense of community: The effect of personal influence, *Journal of Public Relations*, **22** (1), pp 65–84

Wilson, A, Zeithaml, V A, Bitner, M J and Gremler, D D (2008) *Services Marketing: Integrating customer focus across the firm*, 1st European edn, McGraw-Hill, Maidenhead

Windsor-Lewis, S (2002), in (eds) L Smith and P Mounter, *Effective Internal Communication*, 2nd edn, PR in Practice Series, Kogan Page, London

Woodall, K (2006) The future of business communication, in (ed) T L Gillis, *The IABC Handbook of Organizational Communication: A guide to internal communication, public relations, marketing and leadership*, Jossey-Bass/John Wiley, San Francisco, CA

Leadership and trust – how to build a trustworthy company
The importance of communication

06

MARTIN MATHEWS and KATALIN ILLES

OBJECTIVES

The purpose of this chapter is to:

- Investigate current ideas on trust, leadership and communication.
- Provide clear guidelines to help leaders and companies better understand how to build (or rebuild) trust through efficient communication and 'fair' company policies.
- Rethink several 'classic' or 'standard' approaches to leadership.

Introduction

There are many reasons for leaders to strive to create a trusting work environment made up of trusting relationships. These include:

- better cooperation;
- more effective problem solving;

- a positive work climate;
- higher employee engagement;
- higher job satisfaction; and
- lower levels of turnover.

As a concrete example, consider this quote from the CIPD 2013 Employee Outlook report: 'As I work for a small company, trust and respect are everything. We are all honest and open with each other and help each other out where we can. We have great directors who want to do everything they can to see we succeed.'

According to the 2011 Workplace Employment Relations Study (Wanrooy *et al*, 2011) employees who feel committed to their organization carry out more tasks then required of them: 79 per cent of employees who share the values of their organization use their initiative to do more than just their required task; 91 per cent of those who were satisfied with their involvement in decision making felt loyal to their organization; and 87 per cent of those satisfied with their involvement in decision making felt proud to work for their organization. In spite of the strong evidence for the positive impact of employee engagement and empowerment on loyalty and trust, a recent study of first-line managers (Hales, 2005) confirmed that close supervision (a clear sign of mistrust) is widespread and that the devolution of responsibility to teams and individuals (a clear sign of trust) remains rare.

Trust has suffered a serious decline since the 2008 global financial crisis. The 2014 Edelman Trust Barometer shows the largest ever gap between trust in business and government since the study began in 2001. Trust in a CEO is at 43 per cent while it is 67 per cent in an academic and a 'person like yourself' scores 62 per cent. Only one in four general public respondents trust business leaders to correct issues and even fewer – one in five – to tell the truth and make ethical and moral decisions. Government leaders scored even lower across the board.

Trust is a key component of human life. Without trust the workplace is a group of individuals who focus on personal survival rather than creation and contribution. Research in the field of knowledge management and knowledge creation concludes that trust is a prerequisite to creativity in an organizational context (MacLeod and Clarke, 2008). If we are to make the fullest use of the knowledge locked in our minds we need to trust and be trusted. Employees need to feel protected and cared for so that they can focus their energies on creation rather than survival.

To build trust leaders and top management need to rethink their role(s) in 21st-century firms. The old way of leading by command, control and charisma through superior knowledge and personality is still present in many organizations but it does not fit a fast-changing business environment. Increasingly, better educated employees know what is happening sooner than leaders do and they often know what needs to be done. It is no longer a good idea to think that leadership is mainly 'done' by the few to the many. The mainstream leadership model of business and public organizations needs to be renewed to reflect more values-based relationships and transparent behaviour. Leaders must listen to the needs of their stakeholders, and communicate their long-term commitment and responsible intent to re-establish trust.

Rethinking leadership myths

Before looking more closely at the relationship between trust leadership and communication, we start with a short discussion of what leadership may or may not actually be.

As Otto Scharmer (2009) suggests, the primary leadership challenge today is the fact that our economic reality is shaped by globally *interdependent ecosystems*, while organizational leaders, by and large, operate with an *organizational egosystem* awareness. By this he means that business ecosystems are interdependent globalized networks where people must cooperate in order to achieve their individualistic, self-interested egotistical aims. Scharmer proposes that there is an underlying contradiction between the need to cooperate with others (inside a company or between clients and suppliers, for example) and our desire to reap individual rewards (cf Adam Smith). Most leadership issues can be boiled down to this primary contradiction: economic reality works as a global ecosystem, and individuals and institutional leaders are focused according to their institutional egosystem awareness.

We can observe the following leadership myths.

- *The leader is the guy at the top.* The challenges that organizations face today cannot be solved with this obsolete mindset. To find appropriate solutions more people in the organization need to be involved; 'there are other things that people do better. So it's recognizing those sorts of things and making sure we're all contributing' (CIPD, 2014).

- *Leadership is about individuals.* Leadership is a distributed or collective capacity of the system not just something that individuals do. Leadership is about the capacity of the whole system to sense and actualize the future that it wants to emerge.

- *Leadership is about creating and communicating a vision.* The problem with this myth that it focuses primarily on broadcasting a message rather than on something much more important: *listening*. The world is full of grandiose leadership visions that were beautifully communicated before they crashed and burned. Think Enron, Lehman Brothers, GM, AIG and Goldman Sachs. These visions were totally out of touch with reality.

All great leadership starts with listening. That means listening with an open mind, heart and will. It means listening to what is being said as well as what isn't. It means listening to the latent needs and aspirations of all people. Listening is a major component of trust building and strengthening relationships among people; by listening to employees managers show their benevolence and goodwill towards them.

Leadership is a collective process, encompassing both 'leaders' and 'followers'. These are not static labels and leaders can act as followers and followers can act as leaders in certain circumstances (Ladkin, 2010). 'Leadership practice takes shape in the interaction of people and their situation, rather than from the actions of an individual leader' (Spillane, 2004: 3).

When we stop thinking about 'leadership as a position' and embrace its continuously emerging nature then we can create a new, more engaging work environment where the 'right answers' do not have to come from the boss all the time, and creative ideas can be presented by all members. This opens up possibilities and creates more transparent work environments based on trust and shared purpose.

Listening is the first step towards creating trusting relations inside the company. A relational leader has a mindset of continuously creating, building and fostering close relationships which are the pillar of a trusting environment.

What drives trust?

Research (Gillespie and Mann, 2004) has highlighted seven leadership behaviours for building trust:

1 Behavioural consistency increases predictability.

2 Behavioural integrity underlines the coherence between words and actions.

3 Sharing and delegating increase engagement through participatory decision making.

4 Open, honest communication provides information about motivations and decisions.

5 Demonstrating concern and taking others' interest into account.

6 Communicating a shared vision increases cohesiveness.

7 Explaining shared values provides moral leadership and provides guidelines for action.

The drivers of trust

The Institute of Leadership and Management September 2014 report, *The Truth about Trust,* found that employees identified the five drivers of trust shown in Figure 6.1. Openness is the single most important driver. It corresponds to employees' desire to understand leaders' motivations and the reasons for their actions. It also represents an increasing desire for honest relations with senior management. Effective communication is closely related to openness and honesty. It corresponds to employees' need for clarity. Leaders must communicate common values, clear expectations and feedback on performance. They must back up the 'talk' with the 'walk', which is why integrity – joining actions to words – is also highly valued. Openness contributes to employees' understanding of leaders' integrity; that they can be trusted because they 'tell it like it is' (even if it is bad news) and have no hidden agenda.

It is difficult although not impossible to rebuild broken trust over time. For this to happen, leaders must listen to the needs of the employees, take the right actions and communicate the right messages consistently over a long period. Restoring and enhancing trust go beyond simply being a good communicator. They mean rebuilding relationships and creating conditions to support the positive expectations of employees. They require transparency, honesty and commitment from the leaders. These leaders need to communicate their intentions and capabilities clearly and consistently (Kramer and Lewicki, 2010).

FIGURE 6.1   Top five drivers of trust (% respondents)

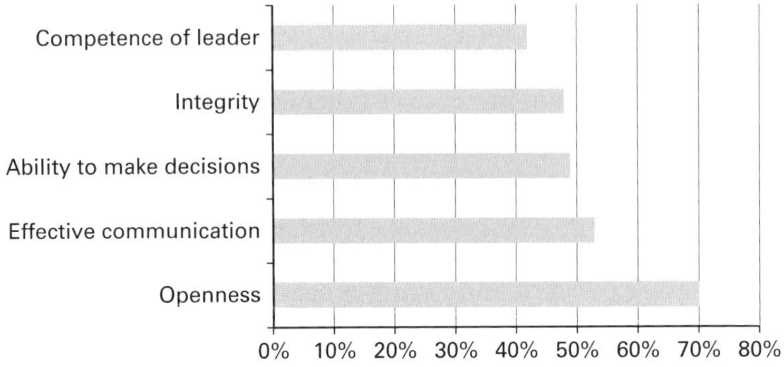

SOURCE: Institute of Leadership and Management (2014)

Internal communications affect the trust that employees feel towards their senior management. One element of communication that leaders must take into account is its 'richness', by which we mean communication that contains high-quality information: generally face-to-face communication as it is considered more reliable than written communication. Face-to-face communication seems to allow employees to evaluate rapidly the openness and honesty of managers and thus allow them to trust.

Employees are less interested in formal 'stuffy' communications (e-mails or memos) than seeking informal opportunities to build relationships with their senior managers. There is a mismatch between the ease of electronic communication, seen by managers to be just one form of communication, and their employees' desire to talk and exchange.

Employees dislike the overuse of electronic communications (Twitter, blogging, etc) and corporate communication departments 'spinning' (Mishra and Mishra, 2005). While these techniques and technologies allow leaders to communicate more frequently and easily, they are interpreted as being less immediate and more remote. Many managers cited by the CIPD study (2014: 12) emphasized the need to 'go and meet' their teams. Employees want to see their leaders in person and in action. This enables them to interact with them personally. To create trust, it is important for leaders to be seen in person and frequently.

The ABIP model

The ABIP model shown in Figure 6.2 was developed by Mayer *et al* (1995) and extended by Dietz and Den Hartog (2006). It has become a widely used tool to help explain why people may trust others. We evaluate the trustworthiness of other people according to four criteria: ability, benevolence, integrity and predictability. Managers need to demonstrate each and every one of these criteria in their daily words and deeds. But because employees' trust in their leader may also be a function of their trust in their company, there must be sound human resource policies in place to make trust grow.

FIGURE 6.2   Ability, benevolence, integrity, predictability

Ability	Benevolence	Integrity	Predictability
(knowledge, skills, professionalism)	(showing interest, recognizing individual needs, being approachable)	(organizational values, ethical behaviour)	(acting consistently, walking the walk)

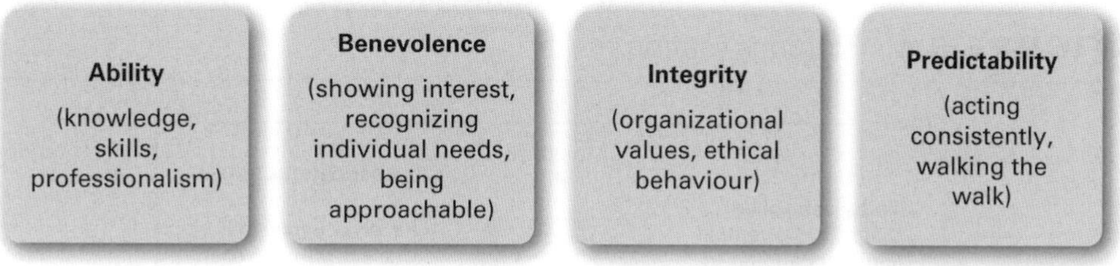

Listening is key to effective management

Through effective communication, leaders lead. Good communication skills enable, foster, and create the understanding and trust necessary to encourage others to follow a leader... Without effective communication, a manager is not an effective leader. (Barrett, 2006: 22)

Some organizations have embraced the concept of 'communicative leadership'. This refers to leaders who 'engage others in communication' and listen as well and share their views in the process. 'Leadership occurs through the process of interaction and communication' (Barge and Hirokawa, 1989).

Communication is a transmission of meaning from one person to another or to many people. It happens either verbally or non-verbally. When it works well it is a simple process. as in Figure 6.3. In reality communication is more likely to resemble Figure 6.4, where the message is lost or distorted in the noise of the organization.

FIGURE 6.3 The communication triangle

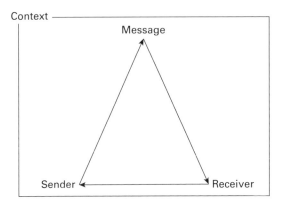

SOURCE: Barret (2006)

FIGURE 6.4 Communication reality

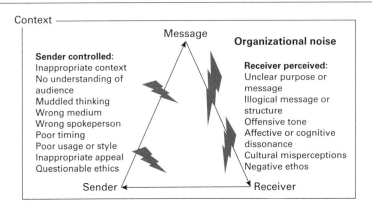

Adapted from Barret (2006)

Sometimes the fault is on the sender's side. Typical mistakes include inappropriate context, not understanding the audience, lack of clarity, choosing the wrong medium of communication, choosing the wrong spokesperson, bad timing, inappropriate style or body language or questionable ethics. Any element that diminishes the receiver's capacity to understand the message will diminish that message's potential to increase trust. If a message is confused then the receiver (the trustor) will have difficulty finding the 'elements of proof' (of integrity, ability, etc) that contribute to their evaluation of the sender's trustworthiness. At worst a garbled message will contribute to distrust because the receiver may interpret such a message as an attempt to lie or deceive. On the receiver's side the problem could be caused by unclear purpose or message; offensive tone; affective or cognitive dissonance; cultural misperception or negative ethos.

According to Barrett (2006), leadership communication happens at core, managerial and corporate levels. Good communication at all levels requires emotional intelligence or interpersonal skills and an understanding of cross-cultural differences. Leaders need to be able to interact effectively with others as individuals or groups. Listening is an essential skill in all situations and it is particularly important for leaders and managers to really hear what others say, not simply what we think we hear them say.

Communication becomes even more complex when we need to consider how to communicate to all internal and external stakeholders. As audiences become larger and more diverse, it is vital to communicate with an open mind, open heart and open will. As mentioned above, the perception of openness contributes to trust because it reinforces the receiver's belief that the sender is honest. Receivers look for clues in order to trust; if the message is perceived as honest, these clues are given more weight in their evaluations of trustworthiness. Leaders are the company's face and voice to the public and they need to work closely with communication specialists to avoid blind spots. It is crucial that they communicate honestly and authentically, showing the human passion behind the leadership role and expressing a positive ethos inside and outside an organization.

Repairing trust

An interesting way to think about creating trust in the work environment is to look at ways that trust is destroyed (a list of don'ts) and then continue the reflection on how to rebuild trust (a list of dos). In this way we can build up a catalogue of ways and means for leaders to create trust in the workplace.

There will be times where leaders must repair trust – after layoffs, poor results or responding to the aftermath of a crisis – or quite simply after periods of poor leadership. Before looking at how to rebuild trust, here's a quick look at how a leader may destroy trust. These are some of the most common causes of trust *destruction* in companies (by leaders):

- Disrespectful behaviours: blaming people, disregarding feelings, ignoring inputs.

- Communication problems: not listening to others, not trying to understand the other's point of view.

- Unmet expectations: broken promises, breaches in the psychological contract.

- Ineffective leadership: poor decisions, favouritism, punishing those who challenge authority.

- Incompetence: making mistakes, not taking responsibility.

- Incongruence: not aligned with core values, not honouring core values, actions not matching words.

In terms of communication, the following elements are possible avenues to trust reparation and creation (CIPD, 2014).

Explanations and accounts

After a trust breach the adequacy of the explanation was found to be central to regaining trust. The characteristics of the explainer and the explanation impacted on whether the deceived was willing to trust again. Explaining, for example, that an error was due to incompetence rather than malfeasance may be easier to accept. Taking responsibility for mistakes contributes to trust reparation.

Apologies

Many would consider that 'talk is cheap' and refrain from apologies, particularly if admission of wrongdoing could lead to legal liability and damages. Apologizing and showing humility are a way of demonstrating concern for the other and taking personal responsibility. Goldman Sach's CEO, Lloyd Blankfein, apologized in 2009 for his bank's involvement in the global financial crisis and set aside $500 million to help small businesses in the recession.

Any apology is better than no apology, and perceptions of sincerity are important for acceptance. Apologizing as soon as possible after the broken promise is important, as is the necessity to accept responsibility rather than trying to blame an outside element. Finally, apologies are more effective when both parties had already built up a trusting relationship.

When rebuilding trust leaders must communicate three essential dimensions: ability, benevolence and integrity (Mayer *et al*, 1995), because employees will evaluate the trustworthiness of their leader(s) according to their perceptions of these three dimensions.

Ability

'People gauge trustworthiness on the basis of that person's leadership actions and practice' (CIPD, 2014). Trust is domain specific. You may trust a friend to save your life if you fell in the canal because he is a good swimmer, but you may not trust him to cut your hair. It follows that leaders should possess the technical skills and knowledge necessary to accomplish their tasks but also the openness and honesty to admit to not knowing everything. Ability in a leader also includes his or her perceived understanding of the environment, business sense and judgement.

Benevolence

'I tend to take an interest in people. I ask them how they're going and what they are doing'; 'I let them talk around their issues, ask them how they feel about that... you know where they could go to get help' (CIPD, 2014). This is the perception of a positive orientation or goodwill towards the trustor (the employee in our case). Employees want to feel that the boss is on 'their side', will not harm them and will harbour positive intentions towards them. This desire is linked to the employees' vulnerability towards the leader. The leader should demonstrate a genuine concern for others. This includes ensuring that company policies are not only fair and equitable (distributive justice) but are also applied fairly (procedural justice).

Integrity and predictability

'If you say you're going to do something, do it. I've worked for plenty of people that have said "Oh yes, we'll do this" and nothing ever happens' (CIPD, 2014). Integrity involves the trustor's perception that the trustee adheres to a set of principles that the trustor finds acceptable. Following (and communicating clearly) a set of principles defines personal integrity. Questions such as the consistency of the leader's past actions, his or her credible communications, and belief that the leader has a strong sense of justice all contribute to the employee perceiving the leader as having integrity. Integrity can be simplified in communication terms as 'doing what you say you do'. Leaders should communicate values that drive them so that others can see consistency rather than randomness.

Building trust

Why line managers are vital to building trust

Employees trust line and middle managers more than other management levels. Yet paradoxically, line managers themselves are among the least trusting members of the firm (9 per cent said they trust few people or absolutely no one according to the Institute of Leadership and Management 2014 survey) (see also Figure 6.5 data from the Edelman Trust Barometer, 2014). It is vital therefore that leaders develop close relationships with their line managers as they assume a key day-to-day role in managing teams and are in close contact with customers.

FIGURE 6.5   Trust in organization by management level

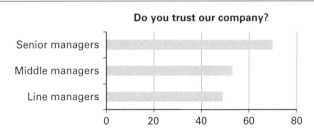

SOURCE: Edelman Trust Barometer (2014)

Line managers or supervisors are more likely to be trusted by employees possibly because the frequent face-to-face contacts allow each party to evaluate the other's trustworthiness. It is also possible that line managers resemble their employees and co-workers (we tend to trust those who are similar to us) and also because there is a smaller power distance between these two hierarchical levels when compared to employees and senior management. Because trust is transitive (if A trusts B and B trusts C, then A will trust C), these close trusting relationships have a positive knock-on effect throughout the organization. It is important then for senior managers to create trusting relationships with these line managers in order to increase trust in the organization.

Part of the challenge in building trust for a leader is the impossibility of meeting all employees every day and interacting on a face-to-face basis, which is frequently the best way to inspire trust. Leaders can create trust ripples through the company. Building on previous remarks, it is important for leaders to demonstrate concern, respect and fairness in their actions and communications. Leaders should communicate openly, honestly and frequently. They must communicate their passion for their job and their firm, but also communicate their expertise, authenticity and integrity.

Building trust in your immediate circle

Trust is a two-way street. We trust those who trust us. As such, leaders can develop trust in their teams (and demonstrate to other managers how to do this). By making themselves vulnerable to others by being honest, sharing ideals, etc, leaders will encourage employees to reciprocate this trust.

Hurley (2006) divides the question of how to develop trust with close collaborators into two factors: personal and situational. Leaders should understand three personal factors of subordinates: 1) their risk tolerance, 2) how well adjusted they are (ie whether they are comfortable with themselves and their position and see the world as a generally benign place), and 3) the relative power differences in the relationship, as high power on the leaders' behalf will lead to increased feelings of insecurity.

Then leaders should appreciate the situational factors, which are security, similarities between leader and follower, alignment of interests, as well as questions of ability, benevolence and integrity. Security is the opposite of risk. Fewer people will trust if the stakes are high. One should attempt to start with small stakes and build up over time. People generally trust other similar people more readily than someone from a different culture, country, university or even profession. This is why it is important for leaders to build teams and a corporate culture based on discussed and agreed values and rules: it binds employees into a cohesive group. When people's interests are aligned, then trust is a natural response. As Hurley says: 'a good leader will turn critical success factors for the company into common interests that are clear and superordinate' (2006: 58).

Creating a trustworthy company

Because a person's trust depends a lot on context, trust in a leader depends partly on the trust the workers have with their middle managers, leaders and the trust they have in the company itself. This 'space of trust' (CIPD, 2014) allows for interpersonal trusting relationships to develop.

Employees trust their company according to its perceived *fairness*. This includes distributive, procedural and interactional justice. A clear sense of norms of behaviour, values and procedures informs employees' sense of control thus reducing their perceptions of vulnerability.

CASE STUDY   John Lewis

The John Lewis Partnership runs over 40 shops in Great Britain. It is a well-respected firm that dates back to 1864. John Lewis has put into place national policies that reflect the firm's benevolence towards its employees, such as creation of a 'registry' where staff can go (outside their line managers) for help in a wide variety of problems, both professional and personal. The registry is like a union or ombudsman run by the company but with a large degree of independence. Some examples of assistance include:

- Help with financial problems.

- Professional problems, when for example a more senior colleague is behaving incorrectly, unprofessionally or illegally.

- Personal problems which may require time off work.

(**SOURCE**: CIPD March 2012 Research Report)

When building trust inside a company, leaders have to manage not only their relations with employees and supervisors but also the relationships employees have with the organization. The following factors are shown to increase employees' trust in their companies:

- There is a clear link between *job security* and trust in the employer. Job security sends a strong message of benevolence and makes people feel less vulnerable and therefore reduces their feelings of risk.

- *Performance management*, where managers work with employees to set expectations, measure and review results and reward performance, increases trust because it communicates to employees what is expected of them and what they can expect in return. An accurate and impartial performance system demonstrates that the senior management is both competent and benevolent. It also conveys messages of integrity if it is perceived as being fair.

- *Training* increases employees' trust as it demonstrates benevolence (concern for the employees' skills and employability) and the competence of managers. It may also be an example of senior management displaying trust (we trust you to stay in the company), and should be communicated as such.

- *Procedural justice*, the perception of fairness in procedures used to make company HR decisions, is closely linked to employees' perceptions of fairness and integrity of the senior management.

- *Distributive justice*, the perceived fairness of outcomes (salaries, bonuses, etc but also questions of leave and training, for example), has a direct link to perceived trustworthiness of supervisors and managers.

Company cultures that foster a sense of collective purpose and mutuality of interest create 'a trust bank' (CIPD, 2014) that leaders can draw on in times of trouble.

Group activity – Discuss in groups the following remarks and questions

1 When you hear the word 'trust' what thoughts, associations and feelings come to you?

2 On a scale of 0 to 10 (0 being 'I never trust anyone at all' and 10 being 'I always trust everybody unconditionally') how trusting is your outlook on life in general?

3 Make a list of the people you trust. Why do you trust these people?

Concluding thoughts

Creating a trusting organization leads to higher performance, more creativity, better working conditions, higher job satisfaction and lower staff turnover. In a trusting environment employees are more ready to 'go the extra mile'.

Trust is not, however, the end goal of leadership; rather it is a measure of the *quality* of the relationships inside a company and in particular the relationships between senior management and their employees. Line managers are particularly important as 'transmitters' because of their direct, constant, day-to-day contacts with front-line staff. Leaders and managers should pay particular attention to them when looking to build trust.

It is impossible to order or to buy trust. Trust builds up slowly over time. 'Trust arrives on foot but leaves on horseback' goes the French saying. Nevertheless, managers should bear in mind how employees evaluate the trustworthiness of other people. A leader or manager wishing to create a trusting environment should assess any actions, announcements, policies, etc in the light of the four criteria that constitute the ABIP trust model developed by Mayer *et al* (1995).

The ABIP trust model

People evaluate the trustworthiness of another person according to:

- The *ability* of leaders (their knowledge, skills, professionalism).

- Their *benevolence* towards us (do leaders show interest, do they recognize individual needs, are they approachable?)

- Their *integrity* (organizational values, ethical behaviour, joining words to actions).

- Their *predictability* (do they act consistently, walk the walk?)

It follows therefore that rebuilding trust is always going to be hard work. When looking to rebuild trust leaders can and must supply plausible explanations for past events, treat their audience with respect and look to apologize if necessary.

Finally, people also trust their organization – or do not. Building a trusting company means putting into place policies that answer to the ABIP model described above. Job security (as far as is possible) demonstrates benevolence. Clear transparent rules, regulations and policies such as performance management allow employees to evaluate their firm's (and their leaders') integrity and predictability.

Revision questions

1 Workers who trust their boss(es) work better. Do you agree?

2 Describe any personal experiences you may have of a trusting or distrusting company.

3 As a consumer, which companies do you trust? Which ones don't you trust?

4 Which parts of the ABIP model are apparent in the following quote: 'As I work for a small company, trust and respect are everything. We are all honest and open with each other and help each other out where we can. We have great directors who want to do everything they can to see we succeed'?

Further study

Ballinger, G A, Schoorman, F D and Lehman, D W (2009) Will you trust your new boss? The role of affective reactions to leadership, *The Leadership Quarterly*, 20 (2), pp 219–32

Dirks, K T and Ferrin, D L (2002) Trust in leadership: meta-analytic findings and implications for research and practice, *Journal of Applied Psychology*, 87 (4), pp 611–28

Kelley, K M and Bisel, R S (2014) Leaders' narrative sense making during LMX role negotiations: Explaining how leaders make sense of who to trust and when, *The Leadership Quarterly*, 25 (3), pp 433–48

Shawn Burke, C, Sims, D E, Lazzara, E H and Salas, E (2007) Trust in leadership: A multi-level review and integration, *The Leadership Quarterly*, 18 (6), pp 606–32

References

Barge, J K and Hirokawa, R Y (1989) Toward a communication competency model of group leadership, *Small Group Behavior*, 20 (2), pp 167–89

Barrett, D J (2006) Strong communication skills a must for today's leaders, *Handbook of Business Strategy*, 7 (1), pp 385–90

CIPD (2012) *Where Has All the Trust Gone?* CIPD Sustainable Organization Performance, Research Report, March, http://www.cipd.co.uk/hr-resources/research/where-trust-gone.aspx

CIPD (2013) *Outlook Report*, http://www.cipd.co.uk/binaries/employee-outlook_2013-autumn.pdf

CIPD (2014) *Experiencing Trustworthy Leaders*, CIPD, University of Bath, http://www.cipd.co.uk/binaries/experiencing-trustworthy-leadership_2014.pdf

Dietz, G and Den Hartog, D (2006) Measuring trust inside organizations, *Personal Review*, 35, pp 557–88

Edelman Trust Barometer (2014) http://www.edelman.com/insights/intellectual-property/2014-edelman-trust-barometer/

Gillespie, N and Mann, L (2004) Transformational leadership and shared values: The building blocks of trust, *Journal of Managerial Psychology*, 19, pp 588–607

Hales C (2005) Rooted in supervision, branching into management: Continuity and change in the role of first line managers, *Journal of Management Studies*, **42** (3), pp 471–507

Hurley, R (2006) The decision to trust, *Harvard Business Review*, September, pp 55–62

Institute of Leadership and Management (2014) *The Truth about Trust*, September, ILM, Lichfield

Kramer, R and Lewicki, R L (2010) Repairing and enhancing trust: Approaches to reducing organizational trust deficits, *The Academy of Management Annals*, 4, pp 245–77

Ladkin, D (2010) *Rethinking Leadership*, Edward Elgar, Oxford

MacLeod, D and Clarke, N (2008) *Engaging for Success: Enhancing performance through employee engagement. A report to the Government*, Department for Business, Innovation and Skills, London

Mayer, R C, Davis, J H and Schoorman, F D (1995) An integrative model of organizational trust, *Academy of Management Review*, 20, pp 709–34

Mishra, A K and Mishra, K E (2005) Trust from near and far: Organizational commitment and turnover in franchise-based organizations, presented at the 65th Annual Meeting of the Academy of Management, Honolulu, Hawaii

Scharmer, O (2009) *Theory U: Leading from the future as it emerges*, Berrett-Koehler, San Francisco, CA

Spillane, J (2004) *Distributed Leadership: What's all the hoopla?* Institute for Policy Research, Northwestern University, Evanston, IL

Wanrooy, B, Helen Bewley, H, Bryson, A, Forth, J, Freeth, S, Stokes, L and Wood, S (2011) *The 2011 Workplace Employment Relations Study*, 6th edn, UK Data Service, London

Effective team-working in contemporary organizations

07

NEIL MOORE

OBJECTIVES

This chapter explores effective team-working in contemporary organizations by:

- Investigating the important role groups and teams play in 21st-century organizations.

- Discussing the difference between groups and teams in the organizational context.

- Considering the role and importance of both formal and informal groups in organizational life.

- Investigating and discussing the key factors that affect team effectiveness.

- Exploring the challenges faced by teams as they engage in important activities such as decision making.

Introduction

Helen Keller, the American author, political activist, lecturer, and the first deaf-blind person to earn a Bachelor of Arts degree, said that 'Alone we can do so little; together we can do so much.' This quote emphasizes the potential benefits that can accrue when individuals work together effectively. Groups and teams form an essential element of any organization. In 2009 the National Statistical Service of Finland estimated that two-thirds of wage and salary earners worked in permanent working groups or teams (Statistics Finland, 2009). In the 21st century those of us working in organizations are increasingly likely to belong to one or more groups or teams. From those operating at the highest levels of an organization down to those working at the lowest, the ability to work effectively as a member of a team has become an essential skill.

This chapter begins by explaining why groups are an important feature of contemporary organizational life and exploring the difference between a group and a team. It then moves on to discuss the role of formal and informal groups in 21st-century organizations and progresses to consider how the key factors of organizational context, task environment, team composition and team development affect team effectiveness and performance. The chapter concludes by exploring the challenges faced by groups as they engage in important activities such as decision making.

Why groups?

People have an innate tendency to gather together in groups. We are social animals with a strong sense of belonging. In order for us to function effectively we need interaction and communication with others. In addition to meeting these basic needs individuals who belong to groups receive a range of other benefits. For instance, group membership can provide status, recognition, prestige and power, and challenges and issues may be more easily overcome through group rather than individual action. For example, when individuals become members of a trade union they are collectively able to exercise power and influence. Similarly, the notion that there is strength in numbers may provide security and protection to individuals who belong to groups. Feelings of vulnerability can dissipate when individuals are involved in group activities. If, for instance, groups engage in collective decision making members are likely to feel less vulnerable if a decision proves to be a bad one – responsibility is shared and individual risk reduced.

Activity – The Bilderberg Group

Each year an elite group of the world's most powerful individuals, The Bilderberg Group, meet up to network, discuss current global affairs and share expertise. The membership is limited to a select but diverse group of politicians, lobbyists, industrialists, academics and royalty. Shrouded in secrecy, the four-day conference attracts criticism from those who suggest that attendees are involved in a 'sinister conspiracy' that reinforces, without accountability, the dominance of a 'transatlantic capitalist cabal'. Regardless of the objectives and motives of the group, for many membership is a sign that someone has 'arrived' as a politician, business leader, administrator or opinion-influencer. Those who are invited are afforded status, recognition and prestige and are perceived to have significant power and influence (Parkinson, 2015).

The Bilderberg Group is an extreme example of how affiliation to a group can provide members with power, status and recognition. Think about groups that you are familiar with, in either a social or work context, and list the benefits that individuals receive from being members of the group.

Groups or teams?

A significant amount of scholarly activity has been undertaken to define the terms 'group' and 'team'. According to Handy (1993) a group is 'any collection of people who perceive themselves to be group'. Similarly, Shaw (1981) argues that a group comprises of two or more individuals that influence each other and are influenced by others outside the group. A more insightful definition is provided by Schein (2010) who emphasizes the psychological dimension of group membership and defines a group as any number of individuals who interact with each other, are psychologically aware of one another and who perceive themselves to be a group. In contrast, many teams are considered to be a type of group that consists of an interdependent collection of people who adopt a shared approach and are united in the pursuit of a common purpose and goals for which they share responsibility (Franz, 2012; Gaffney, 2013; Landy and Conte, 2010). Mullins (2013) compares the different perspectives on groups and teams and provides a helpful insight: 'Whereas all teams are, by definition, groups it does not necessarily follow that all groups are teams' (p 308).

Although the academic debate surrounding the different characteristics of groups and teams is interesting and thought provoking, in practical terms it is acknowledged that it is most common to refer to teams, rather than groups, when considering employees who work together in an organizational context. However, for the purposes of this chapter the terms 'team' and 'group' will be used interchangeably – here the focus is not upon those who work in isolation, but rather those who are interdependent and work with others.

Formal and informal groups

When we observe the chart that shows the various units, departments and groups an organization consists of we see the formal structure of the organization. However, in reality organizations also have an informal structure that is created from the intricate network of relationships that depend upon social processes and interactions.

Formal groups

Martin (2005: 834) suggests that formal groups are 'Designed and imposed by managers on the workforce as a way of achieving organizational objectives through structures, departments and teams'. Such groups are the building blocks of the formal dimension of any organization. The formal organization is characterized by tangible features such as key performance indicators and other measures of efficiency and effectiveness; job descriptions; organization-wide policies and procedures (eg health and safety, absence procedures); managerial spans of control (ie the number of employees that report to a manager); organizational mission statements; and structural charts.

Informal groups

According to Mullins (2013: 312): 'Informal groups are based more on personal relationships and agreement of group members than on defined role relationships.' Such groups are reliant upon social dependency and mutual support and are a key aspect of the informal network of relationships and structures that are a crucial part of organizational life. This informal organization coexists with the formal organization and has a range of important functions; see Table 7.1.

TABLE 7.1   The functions of the informal organization

Function	Description
Motivation	The informal organization can be a means of motivation through social relationships and informal approaches to tasks. For example, members working in informal groups may develop their own ways of working based on the norms and values of the group rather than the formal policies and procedures prescribed by the organization.
Satisfaction	The informal organization can help employees satisfy their belonging and relatedness needs. Because informal groups are dependent on social relationships and friendships, they provide opportunities for members to socialize and form strong cohesive bonds.
Security	The informal organization can have a stabilizing effect on employees. The implicit accepted standards, norms and behaviours that exist outside the formal organization can provide employees with a sense of security and reassurance.
Communication	The informal organization, and the groups that belong to it, can provide supplementary avenues of communication. The informal communication channel known as the 'grapevine' is a crucial network in many organizations. Although this can be a very fast and efficient means of communicating, its informal nature can mean that it becomes a conduit for the dissemination of rumours, gossip and inaccurate information.
Comparison	The informal organization can enable employees to explore the strengths and weaknesses of the formal organization. For instance, by comparing the actual tasks that they undertake on a day-to-day basis with their formal job description, employees can highlight any discrepancies or inefficiencies that may exist.

SOURCE: Mullins (2013: 95)

Helen Lacey has recently moved from one team to another within a public sector organization. The move has occurred because Helen has been promoted to the role of team leader. Helen's team consists of eight administrative staff who have worked together for five years or so. The team is very closely knit and has a reputation for being effective but unconventional. For example, the team consistently meets deadlines but uses informal techniques and approaches that do not conform to departmental policies and procedures.

During her initial meeting with her new line manager Helen has been instructed to ensure that the team begins to conform to the formal operating policies and procedures that are prescribed by the organization.

Develop a clear plan that will enable Helen to ensure that her new team maintains and improves its current effectiveness whilst changing its operating procedures to conform to the standards prescribed by the organization. In particular make sure that your plan takes into consideration the following important areas:

- Justification for why the change is necessary – Helen will need a persuasive argument to convince her team that the change is necessary.

- Identification of the types of resources that Helen will need to support the changes she intends to make.

- Explanation of how Helen can make sure team members do not revert back to their traditional ways of working once the changes have been implemented.

Describe each stage of the process and incorporate clear justifications for the steps you recommend.

Team effectiveness

Although people are predisposed to social interaction and collecting together in groups this is not a guarantee of effective team performance. A major concern for any leader or manager is whether or not individuals can successfully work together to achieve organizational objectives. The factors that influence team effectiveness are varied and complex but can be divided into the categories shown in Figure 7.1.

FIGURE 7.1   The factors affecting team effectiveness

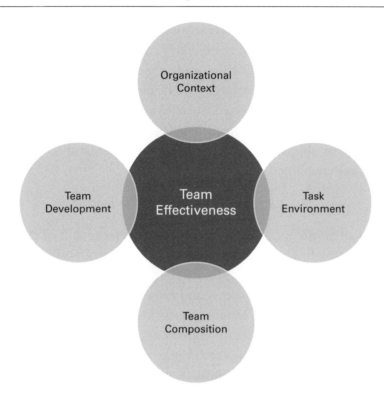

Organizational context

The context in which an organization operates has a range of influencing factors that have the potential to affect group effectiveness and performance.

Staff policies and procedures

Reward systems, training approaches, appraisal mechanisms and opportunities for growth and development are examples of HR policies that can have a direct influence on team effectiveness. For example, according to Landy and Conte (2010), a key factor common in many successful teams is a reward system that focuses on collective results rather than individual behaviours.

Management style

The prevailing management style of an organization will influence how teams perform. For instance, according to McGregor (1960) managers can be categorized as either Theory X or Theory Y. Theory X managers assume that workers are lazy and have to be forced to perform whereas Theory Y managers assume that workers are self-motivated to perform well and enjoy the experience of work. These contrasting views clearly have the potential to influence team effectiveness. Theory X managers are likely to adopt a style of management that closely controls team activities and as a result may be inflexible and rigid. In contrast, Theory Y managers will be more willing to empower teams to be autonomous and self-directed. Such teams have the potential to become more effective in key areas such as problem solving and decision making, because they are able to identify and generate successful solutions to the challenges they encounter.

Growth

The success of an organization is an important determinant of team performance. According to Franz (2012) market growth has a positive correlation with team performance. Individuals have an innate desire to be associated with successful teams. Team success and growth often build confidence and act as catalysts that further enhance performance. In contrast, teams that belong to organizations that are in stagnant or declining markets often struggle to meet their targets and as a result may slip into a downward spiral of underperformance and ineffectiveness.

Externalities

Team effectiveness is frequently affected by external threats. For instance, teams may alter their approaches and patterns of behaviour in response to the appointment of a new leader or the threat of disbandment due to an organizational restructure. Such threats have the potential to motivate team members to become more effective and seek to improve their performance.

Activity – Case study

Andrew Burke is a sales team leader working for Precision Solutions. Andrew's team is responsible for selling IT equipment to schools, colleges and universities. Over the last six months trading conditions have become increasingly difficult because a new competitor has entered the market and has begun to target customers of the company. Andrew has sensed that his team members are becoming increasingly stressed and concerned with the situation.

What steps can Andrew take to maintain and improve the effectiveness of his team?

Task environment

Team effectiveness can be affected by the nature of the task that the team is performing. The characteristics that determine the nature of a task include the following.

Ergonomic factors

These relate to the physical setting that teams operate in. If team members are in close proximity to one another this can enable teams to work effectively. For instance, team members that work together in an open-plan office are likely to have greater feelings of affiliation and belonging than team members who are separated from each other by physical barriers such as walls or partitions. Where workers operate in isolation leaders have to create opportunities for team members to regularly engage with their colleagues. For example, a team may be engaged in a task that requires its members to work in shifts. To maintain effectiveness and performance it is important that when workers end their shift they have opportunities to interact with the team members who are taking over the task – this helps to ensure consistency and alignment.

Levels of communication

For teams to be effective and perform well members need to be able to communicate with each other. As noted above the physical environment in which teams operate has the potential to hinder or improve team interactions. Similarly, the ways in which teams are structured can affect the flow of communication between its members. Figure 7.2 shows the most prevalent communication patterns that are found within teams, based on the work of a number of researchers, including Bavelas, 1948; Leavitt, 1951; Mullins, 2013; Shaw, 1978.

- *Chain configurations* – these tend to be utilized for simple tasks that do not require multiple interactions between team members. Communication flows from one team member to the next without being shared with the wider team. This can be effective if messages are simple and short, for instance if basic instructions are being passed from one team member to the next. However, if messages are complex and detailed they may become distorted as they are transferred.

FIGURE 7.2 Networks of communication

Chain Configurations

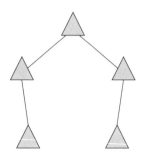

Y Configuration

Circle Configuration

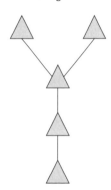

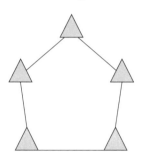

Wheel Configuration

All-Channel
Configuration

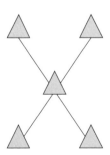

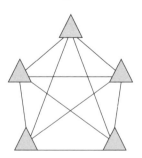

SOURCE: Bavelas (1948), Leavitt (1951), Mullins (2013) and Shaw (1978)

- *Y configuration* – this is a modified version of the chain. Here two team members report to one person who then communicates to the next person in the chain and so on. This type of configuration is often seen in organizations with a hierarchical structure. In this situation members of the board of directors will communicate with the chief executive officer who communicates with a middle manager who in turn communicates with a supervisor. As with the chain configuration there is potential for messages to become distorted as they are passed between individual members without scrutiny from others. In this example, members of the board have to trust that their communications are clearly and effectively passed along the chain down to the supervisory level.

- *Circle configuration* – this configuration has the potential to be the most satisfying for members because it encourages high levels of participation. Because the network does not have an identifiable leader who is central to all communications, members may feel empowered and able to influence team decision making more effectively. This type of configuration is seen in situations where teams are decentralized and self-managed. Such teams tend to be effective at making complex decisions and dealing with change but, because of the absence of a recognized leader, the quality of communication may be variable and inefficient.

- *Wheel configuration* – in contrast to the circle configuration the wheel is a centralized network. Here there is an identifiable link person, most often the team leader, who is at the hub. All communication between team members flows through the link person and consequently there is a high degree of coordination. This is helpful when dealing with relatively simple tasks that have to be completed quickly and efficiently. However, the network can be problematic if the demands on the link person become too great. In busy situations there is a tendency for the link person to become overloaded and as a result communication may become inefficient. Another problem that can emerge is that, in contrast to the leader who is at the centre of communication in the team, team members may feel isolated from one another and consequently may become frustrated.

- *All-channel configuration* – this type of network maximizes the interaction between team members. All members can freely communicate with one another and levels of participation are very high. This configuration is very effective in enabling teams to solve complex problems where a range of perspectives and viewpoints is required. For example a unique challenge, such as the redesign and launch of an existing product into a new overseas market, may require the formulation of a project team that has members drawn from a range of different backgrounds and operational areas. In order to maximize the broad range of insights represented in the team members should be able to communicate freely and effectively with each other.

Technology

Technology has the potential to enhance or inhibit team performance. Indeed the adoption of technology has been cited as producing both positive and negative consequences for team operations and processes. In many instances technology has been shown to improve output and enhance effectiveness. For example, in manufacturing industries the introduction of technology has enhanced the performance of assembly line workers and enabled teams to overcome difficult challenges such as health and safety issues. However, critics argue that technology also has the potential to 'dehumanize' the workplace and act as a barrier to effective team performance. For instance, mechanized assembly lines may require workers to operate at a pace that inhibits interaction with other team members. Low levels of participation and social interaction have the potential to make workers feel isolated which, in turn, can limit team cohesiveness.

One of the most profound effects of technology on team-working has been the way in which it has facilitated the growth and development of teams that are organizationally or geographically dispersed. Accelerating globalization, coupled with advances in information and communication technology, have resulted in the development of virtual teams that consist of members who, despite being separated, are able to work together closely (Mullins, 2013; Shen *et al*, 2014). Townsend *et al* (1998: 18) characterize virtual teams as 'groups of geographically and/or organizationally dispersed co-workers that are assembled using a combination of telecommunications and information technologies to accomplish an organizational task'.

Activity – The virtual intern

According to *Advertising Age* a Chicago-based advertising agency, CBD Marketing, offers virtual internships to those looking to gain experience in the industry. Virtual teams of interns are allocated a project and are supervised remotely by an experienced member of staff. The programme utilizes standard information and communication technologies such as a laptop, videoconferencing and internet access to develop a virtual working relationship with interns who reside in locations outside usual geographical boundaries (SOURCE: Brohan, 2015). Explain the advantages and disadvantages of:

1 Working as an intern in a virtual team.

2 Supervising a virtual team of interns.

Team composition

The performance of a team is also dependent upon its composition. In particular, the size of the team, its permanence and the compatibility of its members play a crucial role.

Size

Large teams often become unmanageable because communication and coordination become problematic. The larger the team the greater potential there is for members to become isolated and feel that their contribution is unnoticed and/or does not significantly add to overall output. Such problems may result in large teams losing cohesion and failing to cooperate effectively. Without cohesion members are less likely to work harmoniously and are unlikely to feel a sense of belonging to the team. Clearly such problems have the potential to negatively impact upon both individual and team effectiveness.

Permanence

The length of time that a team is in existence has a bearing on its effectiveness. Some teams are formed for a particular task and disbanded once it is completed. Such project-focused teams usually consist of members who are aware that the group has a clearly defined lifespan and as a result aim to establish effective working relationships quickly and efficiently. In contrast some teams are focused on a continuous task and consequently are relatively permanent structures within organizations. For instance, once it is established, a customer services team is likely to be a permanent feature of an organization. Members of such teams are likely to have a reasonable length of time to establish relationships with others in the team and develop effective working patterns. The challenge for team leaders in this situation is to maintain performance and effectiveness when new members join the team. Likewise the longer the team is established the more likely it is that it will become too cohesive. When this happens groups can suffer from additional problems that can inhibit their performance – see the section on challenges faced by teams later in this chapter.

Compatibility

This refers to the level of congruence between team members. Where teams have members who have a lot in common it is likely that relationships will be more harmonious and as a result team effectiveness will be higher. For example, if individuals feel united with other team members because they share similar experiences, interests and values the team is less likely to be fragmented and members will experience high levels of belonging and relatedness.

Although homogeneity can be helpful in developing and maintaining unity, differences in some areas can help to improve team performance. For example, team members may have a lot in common in terms of their backgrounds, experiences and values but may be very different in terms of the skills and knowledge they possess. Although such differences have the potential to cause team conflict and dislocation, if they can be reconciled and accommodated they can become a source of strength for the team. For instance, teams that have members with different but complementary skills can deal with complex and challenging problems more effectively than those where there is less variation in the skills sets of team members.

Team development

The effectiveness of a team will be influenced by the extent to which it has matured and developed. The phases of development that teams progress through have been considered by a number of scholars. For instance, Bass and Ryterband (1979) suggest that groups follow a four-stage pattern of development. Phase one focuses on membership establishment and involves the development of mutual trust and acceptance. Phase two involves developing effective communication between team members. As members learn to accept and trust each other communication flows more freely and decision making and problem solving become more effective. Phase three is characterized by increased levels of motivation and productivity. Effectiveness increases as the team progresses beyond the earlier stages and becomes unified in terms of its purpose, goals and objectives. In the final stage, phase four, the team has reached full maturity and the key tasks are to control and maintain performance. The team is cohesive and members have developed effective working relationships that enable them to respond flexibly and creatively to new challenges as they arise.

Another model that focuses on the stages of group development was formulated by Tuckman and Jensen (1977). Their model has five sequential stages:

1 *Forming*. This is the introductory phase, which is characterized by anxiety amongst team members. As the team comes together for the first time, members begin to get to know each other and establish their position within the group. At this stage the team's precise purpose, structure and mode of operation may be unclear and as a result individuals may feel confused and may seek reassurance and clarity.

2 *Storming*. As the structure of the team begins to coalesce and members become more familiar with one another the niceties of the forming stage tend to recede. People begin to feel more confident and may become more forceful and open in their approach. Differences of opinion are likely to emerge and conflicts between team members may be a common occurrence. This is a crucial time for most teams because unless this stage is managed effectively there is a possibility that the team may become stuck or even collapse as disharmony takes hold. However, if progression through this stage is successful teams emerge with stronger relationships and greater clarity of purpose.

3 *Norming*. As conflict and hostility recede the team is then able to begin to establish the ground rules it will use as it begins to perform its allotted tasks. These rules, or norms, serve to identify what is acceptable and unacceptable behaviour in the team and also establish the operational standards that will enable the team to achieve its goals and objectives.

4 *Performing.* Successful progression through the previous three stages of development will enable the team to enter the performing phase. Here the team is able to function effectively because it has established a cohesive structure that provides support and clear direction to its members. The team has reached maturity and is focused on its purpose.

5 *Adjourning.* This stage is an addition to Tuckman's original model (Tuckman, 1965) and recognizes that, as outlined above, many teams may be disbanded after their objective has been met. Dissolution can be a difficult period because team members may feel isolated and vulnerable as they leave the security of the group. Managers can reduce the difficulties associated with this stage by encouraging members to be aware of forthcoming opportunities outside the current team situation.

A key aspect of Tuckman and Jensen's model is that successful progression through the stages of development can only be achieved if the challenges and difficulties encountered at each stage are resolved. For instance, ground rules will be difficult to establish if unresolved conflicts and hostility remain as the team attempts to progress to the norming stage. Similarly, unless clear operating procedures are established and agreed, teams will find it difficult to reach full maturity and perform at their maximum levels of efficiency.

Activity – Case study

Brian Hetherington works in a call centre. He was recently promoted to the role of team leader and is about to take charge of a new project team that will work together for the next six months on a project that aims to develop a new social media strategy for the product development department. Brian's team will consist of eight members who have been drawn from across the organization.

Using Tuckman and Jensen's stages of group development model, formulate a plan that clearly outlines the steps that Brian will need to take to ensure that his team works effectively. Your plan needs to identify the specific actions that Brian should take at each stage of the model to help his team to meet its objective.

In summary, the effectiveness of teams is dependent upon the organizational context in which it operates, the nature of the task that it is required to perform, the composition of the team and the stage of development that the team has reached. These factors have the potential to enhance or inhibit the performance of a team, so managers need to monitor each factor closely as they aim to improve effectiveness.

The challenges of team-working

Although it has been acknowledged that there is a tendency for organizations in the contemporary business environment to rely heavily upon team-working as a way of organizing and managing their staff it is important to recognize that team-working is a not a panacea that will solve all of the problems encountered by an organization. Indeed, as shown in this chapter, teams create a unique set of challenges and issues that need to be addressed if organizational success is to be achieved.

'Risky shift phenomenon'

Potentially one of the most challenging and problematic areas for teams is decision making. Increasingly, both major and lesser organizational decisions are being made by teams and groups rather than individuals. As a result deficiencies in group decision making have attracted a great deal of scholarly attention. For instance, it has long been recognized that decisions made by groups tend to be more risky than those taken by individuals (Bettenhausen, 1991; Forsyth, 2006, Franz, 2012; Stoner, 1961). This is known as the 'risky shift phenomenon' and, according to Martin and Fellenz (2010), is caused by:

- *Reduced responsibility* – group members may feel less individual responsibility for decisions because failure is likely to be attributed to the group as a whole rather than any one individual.

- *Cultural aspects* – if individuals in the group are comfortable with embracing risk because this is a norm of their prevailing culture they are more likely to accept this when they engage in group decision making.

- *Informed decision making* – when making decisions groups can explore more options and consider a broader range of information than individuals. This reduces the potential for impulsive and irrational decision-making behaviour.

- *Majority decision making* – where group decision making is based on the opinions of the majority the views of individuals may be ignored. Those in the minority may feel frustrated and disgruntled as their contributions are not taken into account. By failing to consider a broad range of viewpoints and perspectives group decision making may become riskier and more extreme.

- *Group polarization* – this refers to the situation where group members alter their views so that they are more congruent with what they perceive to be the prevailing values of the group. This shift in position often occurs after group discussions have taken place and results in individuals adopting more extreme perspectives than they would if they were engaged in individual decision making.

FIGURE 7.3   The observable characteristics of groupthink

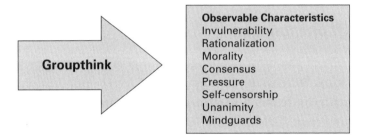

'Groupthink'

Allied to the risky shift phenomenon is the tendency for groups to engage in 'groupthink'. Janis (1982) defined groupthink as 'a deterioration of mental efficiency, reality testing and moral judgement that results from in-group pressures'. Groupthink has a negative impact on team performance because members value consensus and harmony above all; and as a result the comprehensive exploration and evaluation of critical aspects of problems and challenges are compromised. Janis identified a number of observable characteristics that suggest that a team is engaged in groupthink:

- *Invulnerability* – the team suffers from the illusion of invulnerability and becomes overly optimistic.

- *Rationalization* – opposing opinions that challenge the team consensus are discounted and discredited in order to protect prevailing viewpoints.

- *Morality* – the team is convinced that it is 'doing the right thing' and is blinded to the moral and ethical considerations of its proposed actions.

- *Consensus* – the team has an overwhelming desire to maintain harmony and as a consequence any dissenting members or opponents are stereotyped as being dangerous or divisive.

- *Pressure* – the team brings pressure to bear upon members who do not conform to and/or accept the norms, values and dominant opinions of the group.

- *Self-censorship* – each team member is expected to suppress individuality and free expression in order to maintain group cohesion.

- *Unanimity* – because team members comply with the group and dissenting voices are not heard there is a false sense of unanimity.

- *Mindguards* – if dissent begins to emerge within the team mindguards act quickly to apply pressure to restore the status quo by filtering challenging information, protecting the leadership of the team and deflecting opposition.

Measures to prevent groupthink

There are number of actions that can be taken to guard against groupthink. Martin and Fellenz (2010) develop Janis's work and suggest the following preventative measures that teams can implement:

- *Appointment of a devil's advocate* – this is a person whose express purpose in the decision-making process is to explore the opposing point of view. The individual is tasked with challenging key aspects of the decision being made by the team and in so doing forces the group to consider alternative perspectives.

- *Adoption of a scenario-planning approach* – allied to the use of a devil's advocate is the implementation of a scenario-planning approach. This requires team members to construct a range of scenarios that explore the range of possible outcomes that may occur as a result of a decision. By exploring the 'What if?' question teams are required to look outside the team and investigate the wider context in which the decision is situated thereby avoiding the inward-looking approach displayed by teams suffering from groupthink.

- *Use of subgroups* – teams may be split into subgroups that focus upon particular aspects of a decision-making task. This provides an opportunity for members to focus on key aspects without being overwhelmed with the entirety of the task. Also, when subgroups feedback their findings to the wider team this can generate alternative perspectives and discussion that may otherwise have been missed. Subgroups may comprise both internal and external team members. The consideration of outsider viewpoints has the potential to broaden the focus of the team and can guard against the team becoming complacent and blinkered to outside threats and opportunities.

- *Recognition of the influence and power of senior members of the team* – senior team members have formal power which can lead to subordinates suppressing their own views in fear of being punished. To avoid the undue influence of senior members, teams should establish procedures and processes that encourage all members to contribute without fear of retribution. For example, senior members could be encouraged to contribute to discussions after others have expressed their views. This prevents senior members from signalling their views and preferences prior to the input of subordinates. Similarly, teams should aim to foster a culture in which senior members can be criticized constructively. Such openness and honesty are conducive to the development of an atmosphere of trust and will encourage all members to express doubts and fears as they arise.

Activity – Decision making

Think of a time when you have been involved in group decision making. Reflect upon what happened and then consider the following questions:

- To what extent do you think that the decision-making process was open, honest and fair? For instance, were all viewpoints considered equally?

- What measures were taken to ensure that all members were allowed to contribute to the process?

- Given what you have read in this chapter, what could have been done differently and how specifically could it have been improved?

Concluding thoughts

This chapter has explored team-working in contemporary organizations. The key points can be summarized as follows:

- The majority of employees working at all levels in contemporary organizations are required to operate interdependently with others and as a result belong to a range of work groups and/or teams.

- Organizations consist of both formal and informal groups. Formal groups appear on organizational charts and are structured around explicit policies and procedures that are deliberately planned to meet stated objectives. In contrast, informal groups arise from social interactions and are loosely structured.

- Effective team performance is dependent upon the organizational context in which the team operates, the task environment in which it is located, the composition of the team and the stage of development of the team.

- Increasingly in 21st-century organizations team-working is regarded as being a universal panacea to emerging challenges and issues. However, it is essential that it is recognized that teams can create a unique set of challenges and issues. This is clearly evident in the area of decision making where organizational decisions are increasingly being made by teams and groups rather than individuals. As a consequence, an understanding of common team-working problems, such as the risky shift phenomenon and groupthink, is essential.

Revision questions

1 What are the advantages and disadvantages of working in a team?

2 Identify the functions of the informal dimension of an organization and provide an example of each.

3 What are the factors that influence team effectiveness? Using examples, explain how an understanding of these factors can help a manager to improve the effectiveness of his or her team.

4 Risky shift phenomenon is a challenge faced by many teams. Explain the term and outline the measures that managers can take to prevent it from affecting team decision making.

5 Using examples to illustrate your answer, identify the characteristics and behaviours that you would observe if you were a member of a team that was suffering from groupthink.

Further reading

Lepsinger, R and DeRosa, D (2010) *Virtual Team Success: A practical guide for working and leading from a distance*, John Wiley & Sons, Chichester

Salas, E, Tannenbaum, S, Cohen, D and Latham, G (eds) (2013) *Developing and Enhancing Teamwork in Organizations: Evidence-based best practices and guidelines* (Vol 33), John Wiley & Sons, Chichester

West, M A (2015) *Effective Teamwork: Practical lessons from organizational research*, 3rd edn, Blackwell, Oxford

References

Bass, B M and Ryterband, E C (1979) *Organizational Psychology*, 2nd edn, Allyn and Bacon, New York

Bavelas, A (1948) A mathematical model for group structures, *Human Organization*, 7 (3), pp 16–30

Bettenhausen, K L (1991) Five years of group research: What we have learned and what needs to be addressed, *Journal of Management*, **17**, pp 3540–81

Brohan, L (2015) *Virtual Internships: A new solution for hiring millennials seven steps for agencies to develop virtual intern programs*, retrieved on 1 September 2015 from http://adage.com/article/small-agency-diary/virtual-internships-a-solution-hiring-millennials/299289/?utm_source=Small%20Agency%20 Diary&utm_medium=feed&utm_campaign=Feed:+AdvertisingAge/Small%20 Agency%20Diary

Forsyth, D R (2006) *Group Dynamics*, 4th edn, Wadsworth, Belmont, CA

Franz, T M (2012) *Group Dynamics and Team Interventions: Understanding and improving team performance*, John Wiley & Sons, Chichester

Gaffney, S (2013) *Groups, Teams and Groupwork Revisited: A theory, methodology and practice for the 21st century*, CreateSpace Independent Publishing Platform, amazon

Handy, C (1993) *Understanding Organizations*, Penguin, Harmondsworth

Janis, I L (1982) *Groupthink: Psychological studies of policy decisions and fiascos*, 2nd edn, Houghton Mifflin, Boston, MA

Landy, F J and Conte, J M (2010) *Work in the 21st Century: An introduction to industrial and organizational psychology*, John Wiley & Sons, Hoboken, NJ

Leavitt, H J (1951) Some effects of certain communication patterns on group performance, *The Journal of Abnormal and Social Psychology*, **46** (1), p 38

McGregor, D (1960) *The Human Side of Enterprise*, McGraw-Hill, New York

Martin, J (2005) *Organizational Behaviour and Management*, 3rd edn, Thomson Learning, London

Martin, J and Fellenz, M (2010) *Organizational Behaviour and Management*, 4th edn, Cengage Learning Business Press, London

Mullins, L J (2013) *Management and Organisational Behaviour*, 10th edn, FT/Prentice Hall, London

Parkinson, J (2015) *Just who exactly is going to the Bilderberg meeting?* retrieved on 23 July 2015 from http://www.bbc.co.uk/news/magazine-33067655

Schein, E H (2010) *Organizational Culture and Leadership, Vol 2*, John Wiley & Sons, Chichester

Shaw, M E (1978) Communication networks fourteen years later, in (ed) L Berkowitz, *Group Processes*, Academic Press, New York

Shaw, M E (1981) *Group Dynamics: The psychology of small group behaviour*, 3rd edn, McGraw-Hill, London

Shen, Z, Lyytinen, K and Yoo, Y (2014) Time and information technology in teams: A review of empirical research and future research directions, *European Journal of Information Systems*, **24** (5), pp 492–518

Statistics Finland (2009) retrieved on 2 September 2015 from http://www.stat.fi/ajk/tiedotteet/2009/tiedote_009_2009-08-13_en.html

Stoner, J A F (1961) A comparison of individual and group decisions involving risk, in (ed) R Brown, *Social Psychology*, The Free Press, New York

Townsend, A M, DeMarie, S M and Hendrickson, A R (1998) Virtual teams: Technology and the workplace of the future, *Academy of Management Executive*, **12** (3), pp 17–29

Tuckman, B W (1965) Developmental sequence in small groups, *Psychological Bulletin*, **63** (6), p 384

Tuckman, B W and Jensen, M A C (1977) Stages of small-group development revisited, *Group & Organization Management*, **2** (4), pp 419–27

Managing internet user behaviour within organizations
Inter- and intra-generational trends

JESSICA LICHY

OBJECTIVES

This chapter sets out to provide a snapshot of emerging trends in internet user behaviour within organizations today by:

- Tracing key milestones in internet developments, perception and usage across different user groups within organizations.

- Discussing the relevance of using segmentation by 'generation' in the online environment.

- Illustrating how 'generation' (and other factors) can influence internet user behaviour.

- Exploring the impact of the 'generation gap' in the consumption of the internet.

08

Introduction

As information and communication technologies (ICTs) play an increasingly prominent role in our daily lives, both professionally and socially, understanding how the different age groups use the internet is of topical interest to a diverse community of internet users including managers, educational practitioners, parents, researchers and policymakers. This chapter provides a 'brick in the wall' overview of emerging trends in internet user behaviour across the different generations, with specific reference to how individuals consume the internet in the workplace.

The online population of internet users is frequently segmented into distinct 'generations' to illustrate how different age groups of individuals make use of ICT in their everyday activities: to work, learn and build relationships. It is widely acknowledged that each generation has its own behaviour, attitudes, beliefs and lifestyle, quite distinct from the other generations. As ICT is now a fundamental part of many people's day-to-day working lives, issues surrounding how each generation interacts with ICT have surfaced.

The notion of segmenting a group of individuals by generation is not new. It has been used for decades in marketing, for example, to explore how consumers buy (select), pay for and use (consume) various products and services. This notion is now used in the online environment to distinguish one generation of internet users from the other generations. In today's technology-driven society, the way in which each generation consumes the internet has attracted much interest from researchers and practitioners worldwide. ICT, especially social media, has blurred the boundary between work and downtime. Many employees regularly go online in their downtime to continue working; conversely, there are those who use the internet during work time for recreational purposes (to do online shopping, book travel arrangements, use dating and chat sites, pay bills, take part in e-auctions, etc). People of all ages use technology for interpersonal communication, information retrieval and downloading entertainment, but there are differences in the extent to which ICT is central to their lives and the contexts in which they use it (Van Volkom *et al*, 2014). *Managing* the use of the internet is a thorny issue.

As will be discussed in this chapter, various studies available in the public domain point to the broad differences between the generations in their internet user behaviour: preferences for internet access, virtual and mobile devices, privacy concerns, building trust online, and so on. Managers need to be acquainted with the different user trends of each generation in order to avoid potential conflict and misunderstanding. The main problem is that new ICTs are constantly being launched with the result that the way in which people interact with the technology is continually evolving; their expectations and behaviour tend to change when new devices are adopted, for example the growing reliance on instant communication.

New technology also brings new syntax, lexicon and jargon. Certain global brands are now being used as verbs – such as 'Facebook' (Can you Facebook me later?), 'Google' (You should Google it for more facts) and 'Skype' (I Skyped him yesterday). The same pattern is noticeable with nouns; 'inbox' (I will inbox you about that) and 'private message' or simply PM (would you PM me?). The evolution of the English language is a natural process. Modern ICT is merely accelerating the pace of deconstruction and reconstruction. Words that have fallen out of use (like dongle, tether and troll) are now being recycled to refer to new ways of interacting with internet technology; thus 'dongle' is a small device for accessing wireless broadband, 'tethering' refers to using a mobile device to connect to the internet, and 'trolling' means to post a deliberately provocative message online with the intention of causing maximum disruption and argument. Words have also been taken from non-technical domains and applied to the world of ICT such as 'spamming', 'mining' and 'streaming'. New vocabulary has been created though fusing words such as 'crowdsourcing' (using the talents of the online crowd), 'hotspot' (where mobile devices can get wireless broadband access to the internet), 'hot-desking' (the practice of not giving employees their own desk at work; instead the company provides a pool of fully equipped desks). Words have also simply been invented, for example 'emoticon' (a sequence of printable characters intended to represent a human facial expression), 'phishing' (to trick an internet user into giving his or her login name and password) or 'selfie' (self-taken photograph of self). In the workplace, the less techno-literate colleagues and the non-native speakers can find it confusing to be constantly confronted with new words and phrases.

Technological change has always been a feature of modern society but nowadays the cycles of change are shortening and internet user behaviour is evolving quicker than ever before, with the result that it is becoming increasingly difficult for managers to know exactly how technology is being used by employees. It is also becoming very complex to keep pace with the changes taking place; once research is published, the data is quickly out of date.

FIGURE 8.1   The generation divide. Mind the gap!

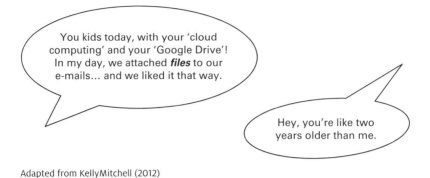

Adapted from KellyMitchell (2012)

For the purpose of this chapter, the term 'technology' is used to refer to web and internet applications such as search engines, social networking applications, online financial platforms, web 2.0 tools, etc. Although 'internet' and 'web' are frequently (but incorrectly) used interchangeably, the internet refers to a large system of interconnected computer networks spanning the globe, whereas the World Wide Web is a subset of computers on the internet. In today's society, the pervasive nature of modern technology is creating a new form of 'digital' gap across the different age groups present online, arising from differing perceptions and uses of internet-based technology.

Younger internet users are accustomed to using technology but there is a difference in the degree to which they collaborate, interact and share knowledge online. Anyone born in the 1970s is likely to have been brought up with access to digital communications technology in the form of personal computers, mobile phones and computer/video games consoles. In contrast, individuals born in the 1980s are likely to have grown up surrounded by smart mobile phones, Wi-Fi, interactive computer games and cloud computing (shared resources, software, data access and storage resources). The net outcome is a difference in the way information is stored and retrieved online; for example, a preference for web 1.0 (e-mail) versus web 2.0 tools (Google Drive).

Talkin' 'bout my generation

The logic of 'generation' stems from the work of Mannheim (1952) in the field of sociology, which produced the revolutionary concept of 'Generational

Theory' (or GT). The core tenets of GT remain relevant today; namely the concepts of generational location, generation as actuality and generation units. Generational location is a passive category based on the chronological span of time for the birth years of a cohort of individuals. This location is thought to affect the potential of the generation. Despite the numerous competing versions acknowledged for theorizing the use of GT (Pendergast, 2010), Mannheim's generational theory is still popular and supported within research into the 'generational effect' in the domain of human science and social science (Donnison, 2007), particularly in the use of modern technology. The sociological approach of Mannheim's GT, as recalled by Namer (2006), emphasizes the link that constructs a generation (born within the same generation) and the generation unit, which is composed of elements that structure this link. Mannheim draws attention to the acceleration of the process related to the emergence of new generations due to the succession of increasingly rapid changes that characterize the contemporary era. Technological developments provide a pertinent example of dynamic change.

Based on year of birth, each generation shares a common 'location' in a social and historical context that limits the members of that generation to a specific range of experiences, thoughts and behaviour. Generational actuality moves from the passive location designation to consider the way a generation responds to 'social changes and how these responses form the persona of the generation' (Donnison, 2007: 4). Thus, for a cohort having the same birth year or 'generational location', its members share a set of similar experiences within the same socio-economic conditions during their formative years. For example, it is possible to distinguish between members of a generation who grew up with the internet from birth and members of a different generation who learnt to use the internet either at school or in the workplace. Each generation will have a different perception and usage of the same technology. For managers, recognizing how employees of different ages use ICT is the first step to developing an awareness of generational internet user behaviour. Without this knowledge, a manager could misinterpret the work methodology of an employee or draw the wrong conclusion regarding the motivation of the employee. For example, a manager who lacks awareness of internet user behaviour may think that an employee is *not* working if the employee is using a social network on a professional platform (such as LinkedIn). Similarly, it is difficult for some managers to comprehend how an employee can work while using a smartphone, watching a YouTube clip, sharing personal information over Instagram and communicating with friends and family via Facebook and Twitter. Young internet users are more proficient at multitasking than older generations.

The main objective of GT is to understand and characterize cohorts or groups of people according to their membership within a generation, which might be objectively identified through the year of birth. The features of a generation are defined according to a dynamic approach derived from a sociocultural theoretical framework encompassing a large and a collective perspective rather than an individual focus. This approach goes beyond individuals as it reveals shifting patterns and cultural tendencies across the whole generational group. The notion of 'generational group' is a multidimensional concept since it is defined by different stakeholders: demographers, media and journalists, popular culture, marketers, consumer researchers and the members of the generation themselves. Furthermore, the living generations (while members are still alive) will continue to evolve and redefine themselves according to changes in the sociocultural context.

In one of the most thorough examinations of generations within multi-disciplinary literature to date, Attias-Donfut (1991) argued that the concept of generation refers to four dimensions within the human science disciplines:

1 A demographical dimension including all individuals within the same age range/group.

2 A genealogical and familial dimension (parents/children).

3 A historical dimension (the average time for a person to get old enough to be autonomous and get involved in the adult society).

4 A sociological dimension, which represents a generational cohort or a group of individuals sharing a set of certain practices and representations as they have approximately the same age and consequently have lived in the same period of time.

Based on the GT framework, Attias-Donfut (1991) defines the concept of generation as an affiliation relationship similar to the generations of parents and their children. In this case, individuals do not have exactly the same age. It can also be a historical period of 20–30 years, which represents the necessary time to renew the organization's top leadership. Furthermore, the concept of generation includes people of similar age who share common experiences that have shaped their lives and their way of thinking. Common experiences would typically include periods in history such as world wars, the 'swinging 60s' or 'Y2K' (the idea that at the end of 1999, ICT systems would stop functioning). It is thought that by sharing similar experiences, individuals belonging to the same generation define themselves according to the characteristics of their time and are aware of what makes them different from previous generations.

Mannheim's GT allows researchers and practitioners to investigate explicit and tacit consumption features as well as to understand the complex behaviours of the consumer society, composed of different generations. While dates may vary from one study to another, it is generally acknowledged that there are six main living generations within today's society, four of which coexist in the workplace today (Baby Boomers, Gen X, Gen Y and Gen Z):

GI Generation (1901–1924)

Silent Generation (1925–1942)

Baby Boomers (1943–1960)

Gen X (1961–1981)

Gen Y (1982–1998)

Gen Z (1999–2019)

The generational framework is burdened by two key limitations and assumptions (Pendergast, 2010). First, the difficulty of using the GT framework is that there is no absolute consensus as to the exact calendar years or a universal definition of each generation. The second challenge is the cultural background of the GT framework, which is originally a US concept and thus more applicable in Western and Anglo cultures. However, the globalization of society, and the dissemination of US culture through the use of ICT, has contributed to the development of the GT concept within non-Anglo cultures. Moreover, it should be noted that within the Western world, many variations can exist within the regions, both geographically and culturally, which means that in reality the list of generations is broadly indicative but somewhat general. There is a similar classification of generations in different countries especially for the three generations from 1943 to 1998, namely Baby Boomers, Gen X and Gen Y. The members of these generations evolve as a collective entity with their unique generational characteristics. They have occupied different phases at different times, passing through the lifecycle stages from childhood to adulthood, and in the process they have acquired a set of values and beliefs that have formed the uniqueness of their generational traits.

Pendergast (2009) draws attention to the 'generational type' of each generation with its unique attributes. It is believed that each generation belongs to one type, and that these types repeat sequentially in a fixed pattern. The characteristics of each generation reflect past and present changes that make its members unique in terms of social behaviour and consumption practices. Broadly speaking, Gen Z have subconsciously integrated ICT into their daily lives. Social networking, online games, video-sharing sites and gadgets such as iPods and smartphones are permanent fixtures of youth culture. Digital media have changed the way young people learn, play, socialize and participate in civic life. There is now a 'digital divide' between in-school and out-of-school use of technology that reflects the widening gap between children's home life and the emphasis of the school curriculum. Older Gen Z who have already entered the workforce are comfortable using both corporate ICT and their own digital devices. However, managers now face the challenge of dealing with employees who choose to use their own devices and software to get a task finished quicker or more accurately than if they had used the corporate system. While the 'BYOD' (bring your own devices) initiative is positive for productivity, it raises serious issues for data privacy and data retrieval from personal devices when the employee leaves the organization.

Gen Y, the *digital natives*, are heavy internet users (both professionally and socially); they were the last age group to know life before the World Wide Web changed the way the internet is used. Gen X, the *digital immigrants*, are moderate-to-heavy internet users (more professionally than socially); they learnt how to use ICT mostly at school but also at home. The Baby Boomers are moderate internet users, having learnt ICT skills at work, ie in a formal, professional context. Baby Boomers tend to use the internet in a functional or practical way rather than for recreation. It is interesting to note that this last group has experienced more changes than normally occur over several generations (Hitt *et al*, 2005). The eldest two age groups (*GI generation* and *silent generation*) are least likely to have integrated ICT into their lives. Many are aware of the technology but do not use it often – or at all.

Age difference in internet use: mind the gap

Numerous technological advances have been introduced since the 1980s. The personal computer, mobile communications and cloud computing have transformed society beyond recognition. The 'digital revolution' has brought about an era of creative destruction. Information and communication technologies are disrupting and shaping future job creation (and job destruction). Modern office technology has drastically reduced the need for secretarial, administrative and support staff, yet created a need for webmasters, programmers and coders. Younger internet users generally have an advantage over older ones; young adults often have the required skills and ability to undertake many of the new web-based jobs that have been created, to such an extent that it sometimes seems that agility and flexibility may outweigh experience and managerial skills.

The internet is an intergenerational piece of technology. Many different types of user behaviour now coexist in the online environment. Younger adults tend to consume internet-enabled devices effortlessly; they have been using the internet longer and more frequently than their older counterparts (Olson *et al*, 2011). By contrast, older adults are less experienced and less comfortable with ICT in general, particularly the use of tactile screens on digital devices such as phones, computers and tablets. When upgrading technology and procedures at work, managers need to bear in mind that some employees may need to be upskilled or reskilled.

As the age composition of the workforce is gradually changing, a clearer understanding of the generations in the workplace is needed. Each generation reacts and interacts with technology in a different way. The 'older' generations face the challenge of training and/or managing the younger tech-savvy employees, many of whom are connected yet 'deficient in communication skills' (Hartman and McCambridge, 2011: 22). The younger generations are driving technological change and the ensuing evolution in internet user behaviour (Livingstone, 2008). Older generations tend to become interested in new ICT when they see the younger generation using it (Bailey and Ngwenyama, 2010; Paz, 2004). In other words, technology diffusion occurs when younger users transmit skills to older users, encouraging participation in ICT despite the generational gap. The younger generations are accustomed to 'actively, instantly and autonomously mastering information digitally' (Haste, 2009: 4), leaving the older generations to catch up. Although it is possible to exist without being connected to the internet, there are many reasons why older generations would benefit from discovering life online, the main argument being to combat loneliness by connecting with like-minded internet users via online communities.

Charlton (2014) points to the emergence of a profound generation gap resulting from different internet user behaviour between children, parents and grandparents. Comparing the Baby Boomers with Gen Y, Loroz (2006) found Gen Y to be more materialistic and more likely to use brands as communication devices, but less religious or spiritual. No significant difference was found between the two generations regarding the ethics of their consumption or concern for the environment. Unsurprisingly, Gen Y were found to be more techno-literate. They see technology as something that is part of their lives, not something they have had to adopt or try to integrate. Technology is inseparable from who they are and what they do (Beckstrom *et al*, 2008). Less is known, however, about the extent to which Gen Z (the children of Gen X) resemble the other generations. Wallop (2014) suggests that Gen Z seem smarter, safer and more mature than Gen Y. However, it is too early to predict the extent to which Gen Z will change as they enter the workforce over the next few years.

As a result of growing up with the internet, it often seems that Gen Z have better online collaborative skills than older generations but weaker face-to-face social skills (Knoll, 2014). Even allowing for technophobic subcultures, it is clear that the connected lifestyle of the younger generations separates them from previous generations. Gen Y and Gen Z grew up 'surrounded by technologies and digital tools that enable a wider range of communication possibilities and greater connectivity than ever before in the developed world' (Barzilai-Nahon and Mason 2010: 396). They are often described as 'savvy computer users' (McMahan *et al*, 2009: 61) who use technology to get information from each other, rather than from traditional institutions or corporations (Li and Bernoff, 2008). For this reason, it is thought that new methods of transmitting knowledge may be needed to communicate with Gen Y and Gen Z (Pelton and True, 2004; Sojka and Fish, 2008) such as virtual user groups, social networks, forums, blogs and wikis (Viot, 2010). While it is impossible to predict how today's schoolchildren will behave in tomorrow's workplace, it is likely that their familiarity with tablet computers for learning collaboratively will lead to a more interactive approach to work.

Gen Z is the first entirely digital generation. This affinity with technology has been linked to the concept of the *digital native* (Prensky, 2001); that is, the belief that the younger generations expect digital technologies to be a component of their life (Moos and Honkomp, 2011). Owing to their technology awareness, they are thought to approach learning and work in fundamentally different ways from other generations (Palfrey and Gasser, 2008).

They are comfortable using blogs, instant messaging (IM) and social networking during their free time and it seems logical that they will want to use the same networking tools at work (Morgan, 2008). The popularity of global networking sites such as Facebook, Twitter and Google+ reveals a need for young people to seek network ties as ends in themselves (Stevens *et al*, 2008). Facebook has even been likened to a nation state by David Post, evoking the definition of Benedict Anderson's *imagined communities* (Fisher, 2010). Given the popularity of social networks, and the focus on integrating lifelong learning into society, there is perhaps an argument for integrating learning materials into social networks, although this would be problematic in areas where internet access is restricted or censored.

Gen Y, and to a lesser extent Gen Z, are powerful agents of change, particularly technological change. They form a new generation of networked individuals who appear to be more socially responsible and wary of global brands, advertising and logo-driven materialism (Williams and Page, 2011). Their different behaviour raises questions about the continuity/rupture of social behaviours in terms of work, consumption, leisure and lifestyle. It is likely that the unique characteristics of these young adults will make them different from previous generations in terms of values, attitudes and beliefs. In the workplace, managers should bear in mind that Gen Y and Gen Z have been educated to use ICT to work collaboratively and interactively. Consequently, it would be productive to engage younger employees in policy and decision making rather than impose outdated work methods.

Stereotypes aside, a distinct divide exists between the older generations (Silent Generation, Baby Boomers, Gen X) and the younger generations

FIGURE 8.2   Generation stereotypes of ICT users

Adapted from Özer (2013)

(Gen Y and Z). The adoption of digital technology by the younger generations has occurred at a rapid pace, leaving research gaps in the field. Many of the younger generations are unfamiliar with a broad range of basic life skills: less likely to know how to do DIY (do-it-yourself home maintenance), sew or cook for themselves. With ubiquitous GPS, many never learn to use physical landmarks to guide them (Howe, 2014). Some young adults have difficulty imagining how people managed looking up information, meeting up with friends in public places and dealing with getting lost without a smartphone or internet-enabled device. It never occurs to them that people visited the library, scheduled meet-ups and learnt to read a road map. Constant access to the internet makes the younger generations believe that everything can be searched for on the smartphone, to the detriment of developing life skills. Young employees need to be (tactfully) reminded that the internet can crash at any moment – with no warning. The ability to work offline is still needed.

One of the problems with keeping abreast of trends and evolution in internet user behaviour across the generations is the reliability of the information. For instance, textbooks often focus on specific aspects of internet usage, but as a book can take two or three years to appear in print the contents can be out of date by the time it is consulted. Academic journals usually provide a more contemporary view than do textbooks; but are written in somewhat convoluted language and can also take up to two years to be published. A quick search on Google will reveal an abundance of online commentary, predominantly from bloggers and journalists who want to put forward an opinion. The problem is that opinions tend to be subjective and can sometimes be based on an oversimplified interpretation of the changes taking place today. Considerable caution therefore needs to be exercised when accessing such data. Ideally, to get a balanced view, it is worth taking time to read academic, professional and government publications on the subject, in addition to comments posted on blogs and social media platforms.

Limitations of the GT approach

Opinions are divided over the legitimacy of simplifying the behaviour of a whole generation. Many sweeping statements have been made about age and digital competence based on the premise that constant exposure to technology since birth will enable young people to be able to use it effectively and effortlessly (Coombes, 2009). Quite often, those who comment about generational technology usage tend to be academics, journalists or techies – three groups who usually understand ICT developments better than the average person.

Vaidhyanathan (2008) and Hargittai (2010) flag up the dangers of presuming that the younger generation have universal internet access. This supposition masks the diversity in skills, knowledge and behaviours among users of digital technologies. It is essential to bear in mind the needs and perspectives of the whole population including those who are not socially/financially privileged and find themselves excluded from internet access. The notion of a tech-savvy youth exaggerates the need for educational reform to cope with the generational evolution. More important, there is a general lack of empirical evidence to substantiate these sweeping assumptions. The collaborative research of the World Internet Project (WIP, 2015) looking at the social, political and economic impact of the internet and other new technologies presents a very different view from 'market research' reports on internet usage in different countries such as *Internet World Stats* (Miniwatts Marketing Group, 2015).

Intergenerational understanding can be fraught by an insistence on identifying all young people as savvy internet users. It may be more accurate to define internet users by how they use the technology rather than by generation. From a management point of view, if the skills of young employees are overestimated there is a risk of underestimating the support that some people may need. All too often, corporate processes and public services are digitized with an emphasis on speed and accessibility rather than on quality and utility.

It is often presumed that young people prefer certain forms of interaction over others, leading to the development of policies, systems and devices that match those presumptions. In doing so, the marketing cliché is reinforced; a heterogeneous group of potential internet users is moulded into a one-size-fits-all system that might not meet their needs. Young people then adopt the new technology, conforming to the marketing ideal. While internet usage is high among the different communities of users (except for the over-65s) it is far from universal; the highly tech-literate behaviour that is often cited as the 'norm' amongst younger users is not so widespread at all. Managers need to be aware of the generational differences as far as ICT usage is concerned, without reading too much into the theoretical assumptions.

How to distinguish the different generations in the workplace

Based on various studies undertaken by the Pew Research Center (2015), Table 8.1 summarizes the influential events that are thought to generate certain broad traits in each age group. Each generation can be illustrated by well-known figures. However, it is crucial to bear in mind that generations worldwide will vary considerably owing to the different contexts including the structure of society, economic development, political system, and so on. Table 8.1 draws predominantly on Western, Anglo-centric cultures.

The table presents an overview of significant events in history that have influenced each generation, together with the characteristics that each generation tends to manifest as a result of their shared experience. To investigate the extent to which affiliation to a particular generation may determine internet user behaviour, participant observation (Kawulich, 2005) was used to gather data about internet user behaviour (namely, how and why people use the internet). Data was gathered over a two-month period from four generations of employees who work in an international training company based within an urban conurbation in England.

The data revealed a number of facets of internet usage across the generations. Similar to earlier telecommunications technologies (telegraph, telephone, radio, television), the internet is used by every generation but not necessarily in the same way. It is highly likely that the different internet user behaviours can be explained by the way in which an individual learnt about ICT (at home, school, work or self-taught). Reisenwitz and Cutler (1998) identify two key factors that encourage ICT adoption: 1) when using the technology is mandatory (at work or school); and 2) when internet skills are learnt in a formal setting. In both cases, internet adoption is faster than if individuals had purchased the equipment for home use and taught themselves the skills. Consequently, each generation of internet users manifests a behaviour that is particular to that generation, as summarized in Table 8.2.

TABLE 8.1   Generations in the workplace: descriptions

	Influential events	Broad traits	Personified by
Silent Generation (1925–1942)	WWII, Great Depression, Cold War, Korean War, suburban expansion, satellite launches, introduction of radio and fax machine. Grew up in an era where unemployment meant hunger, and work was often a job for life. AKA *traditionalists, builders* and *the War Babies*	Sacrifice, loyalty, discipline, respect for authority.	Robert F Kennedy, Elizabeth Taylor, Martin Luther King, Jr, Gloria Steinem
Baby Boomers (1943–1960)	Inception of modern ICT, mass consumption, bull market in 90s followed by financial crisis and real estate downturn (delaying retirement). Many now care for elder family member, introduction of television and personal computing. AKA *digital analogues*	Knowledge is power, 'driven' work ethic (competitive, long working hours), assume diversity, tech-savvy with basic technology, preference for personalized interaction rather than via ICT, envisage working during retirement.	Bill Clinton, Oprah Winfrey, Richard Branson, Susan Sarandon
Gen X (1961–1981)	Have experienced significant changes in society, for example the high divorce rate and shift from traditional to nuclear families, AIDS, terrorism, regional conflicts, deteriorating environment, changes in consumer advertising. Grew up with video games, MTV and television shopping channels. A preoccupation with material possessions and shopping. Introduction of mobile phone, Walkman and home computer. AKA *baby bust, slackers, why me generation,* the *latchkey generation, digital immigrants*	Pragmatic, accept diversity, vigilant about their future, use technology, consider hard work necessary, self-reliant, individualistic, agree to share knowledge.	David Cameron, Stella McCartney, Gordon Ramsay, Victoria Beckham

TABLE 8.1 *cont'd*

Gen Y **(1982–1998)**	Grew up in era of overprotective parenting (nurturing) and blended (re-formed) families. Have seen many civil wars around the world (especially in Africa) and 9/11 terrorist attacks. Death of Princess Diana and Mother Theresa. Introduction of internet, IM (instant messaging), smartphones (text messaging), social media. AKA *millennials, digital natives*	Celebrate diversity, optimistic/realistic, rewrite the rules, disregard of institutions, immediacy, assume technology, cyber-literate, like to be nurtured, sharing knowledge is power. Need of guidance for face-to-face communication.	Malala Yousafzai, Usain Bolt, Kate Middleton, Justin Beiber
Gen Z **(1999–2019)**	Growing up in a world of information overload/information obesity, big data, massive broadband, digital devices since birth. Bombarded day and night by ICT. 'Family' is a loose concept; many school friends come from single (or even same-sex) families. Their parents are often older and comfortably affluent but with heavy financial commitments. AKA *rug rats*	More inquisitive and open-minded about new ICT, digital technology is integrated into family life, little or no inhibition for trial and error of new digital devices, familiarity with tactile screens, techno-literate before being able to read and write, able to locate and use apps for entertainment and information, able to make and post clips on YouTube, creativity and time out are sedentary and virtual (instead of physical), able to download and upload entertainment and music.	Willow Shields, Shiloh Jolie-Pitt, Suri Cruise, Brooklyn Beckham

Adapted from Bassiouni and Hackley (2014), Howe (2014) and Batat (2014)

TABLE 8.2   Comparative internet user behaviour across the generations

Baby Boomer Generation	GEN X
Search for information: Likely to use phone or ask someone	*Search for information*: Either online or phone someone
Social media: Skype and limited use of Facebook	*Social media*: Facebook, LinkedIn, Google+, Skype
Gadgets used: mobile phone for text messaging, desk-top computer, fax	*Gadgets used*: mobile phone/smartphone, laptop, iPad, Apple TV, corporate ICT, TV (especially Sky boxes)
Main ways of communicating: landline, physical visits	*Main ways of communicating*: mobiles (text and calling), Skype, Twitter, e-mail, landline
Apps used: n/a	*Apps used*: Facebook messenger and FaceTime, leisure apps, transport and travel apps, newsfeed, DropBox, Viber and WhatsApp
www usage: Facebook, online shopping for bulky goods, online travel (uses paper tickets), e-mail, sites for leisure pursuits, sometimes Skype (still using Teletext and Ceefax),	*www usage*: information search, online banking, online grocery shopping, online travel (uses paper and e-ticket), paying bills online, online dating, online auctions, online purchase of music and entertainment
ICT skills: learnt at work and/or self-taught	*ICT skills*: learnt to use ICT at school
Connectivity: Doesn't take phone to bed	*Connectivity*: Doesn't take phone to bed

GEN Y	GEN Z
Search for information: online (particularly Google and YouTube)	*Search for information*: online (particularly Google and YouTube)
Gadgets used: mobile phones and smartphones, phone cameras, laptops, tablet computers/iPad, iPods	*Gadgets used*: mobile phones and smartphones, phone cameras, tablet computers/iPad, iPods, game consoles, creative and technological toys (speaking/moving toys)
Social media used: Facebook, Twitter, Instagram, Snapchat etc	*Social media*: Facebook (accounts made at younger ages), Instagram
Main ways of communicating: mobiles (text, occasional call), blogging, Tumblr, Skype, e-mail, Tango, Twitter, Facebook messenger, Snapchat	*Main ways of communicating*: mobiles (text), Facebook, FaceTime, WhatsApp
Apps used: Snapchat, FaceTime, Facebook messenger, for everyday information such as weather forecast, shopping, news...	*Apps used*: Facebook messenger, gaming apps, Snapchat, Viber, Instagram, Vine
www usage: information search, price comparison websites, music streaming and downloading entertainment, interaction with peers, user-generated content and 'citizen journalism', online travel (uses e-tickets), online grocery shopping, online payment, online banking, online car-share	*www usage*: YouTube downloading and uploading, information search (vocal), gaming, YouTube videos of TV programmes
ICT skills: learnt at home/school	*ICT skills*: access to ICT since birth
Connectivity: Takes phone to bed	*Connectivity*: Takes phone to bed (if parents allow)

It is worth bearing in mind that the number of internet users will continue to rise as the ageing analogues adopt ICT in order to avoid social isolation. The needs of these late adopters will be reflected in the increased demand for simplicity – but the wider effects of internet adoption and the impact of internet usage will not be seen until later. This is because information and communication technologies are subject to what is known as the 'rear-view mirror effect' (McLuhan, 1964) – they cannot be identified until they have finished having an effect and are in the past.

Although Baby Boomers make use of ICT, their use of Skype and Facebook is limited to basic functions; for example staying in touch with relatives (especially younger relatives) and with close friends. Older internet users are often self-taught or instructed by a younger family member. Baby Boomers (and to a lesser degree Gen X) are very aware of the danger of divulging large amounts of personal and financial data online. By contrast, Gen Y and Gen Z appear oblivious or unconcerned by the danger of divulging large amounts of personal and financial data online. Gen Y use Facebook for interacting with their social contacts and family members. Gen Z have integrated their use of digital technology into family life, through game consoles, Wi-Fi and smart mobile phones in their bedrooms.

The widespread popularity of social media means that managers may need to rethink corporate policy on technology usage. Employees need guidelines on how they are expected to use ICT at work, for example:

- Length of time authorized for using online networking for both personal and professional use (lunchtime, break time or completely banned in company time).

- General behaviour expected at work regarding the use of the internet, e-mails, smartphones and social media – particularly networking sites, blogs and tweets.

- Importance of maintaining a professional style in online communications and avoiding criticizing or arguing with customers or colleagues or making derogatory comments about individuals related to the company (even in a personal capacity).

- Privacy/confidentiality of company data.

Despite the examples cited throughout the chapter outlining differences in generational internet user behaviour, there is growing evidence to suggest converging internet usage. Key areas of convergence include the reliance on search engines (particularly Google) and the use of communication tools, especially e-mail and internet telephony (such as Skype and FaceTime). People are using online services to make everyday tasks easier, cheaper or faster to complete; in a personal context (cost comparisons, e-tailing, checking bank statements online, planning leisure activities, etc) and in a professional context (faster decision making, better-quality information, customer contact, greater productivity, flexibility of working from home, etc). For most people, the internet seems to be an indispensable tool, both for work and leisure.

Managers must harness the opportunities provided by ICT in such a way that no one feels excluded. Woog (2015) suggests a number of ways in which workers from different generations can learn from each other, listed in the following box.

What older workers can teach younger workers

- *Hard times:* Younger workers did not experience the recession of the 1970s, and there are still people in the workplace who remember the Depression; older workers can pass on wisdom about economic cycles and provide a long-range overview of life.

- *Loyalty:* It may be unusual these days, but sticking with one employer can have its own rewards. Older workers know what it means to commit through thick and thin. It may not be easy to stay the course with one company – especially when a quick job change may bring instant gratification, more pay and better perks – but older workers know that some companies do take care of the employees who stay and take care of the company.

- *Experience:* Whether it concerns corporate policies, company politics or industry knowledge, older workers know the ropes. Most of them are happy to pass on what they know about people, jobs and success.

- *Interpersonal skills:* Older workers are social animals, very skilled at one-to-one relationships. All the technological knowledge of younger workers does not compensate for their lack of interpersonal competence. Older workers can teach younger ones about basic workplace interpersonal skills such as common courtesy and team play.

- *Regrets:* Older workers usually have a good understanding of what they regret in their career choices. People usually regret not what they did, but what they did *not* do. Older workers can use those regrets to pass on ideas about how to steer a career so it can be more fulfilling.

- *Independence:* For years, younger workers have been taken care of by parents and their communities, but now they are on their own. Older workers know how to depend on themselves. They can teach new workers that when they are at work, they cannot count on anyone to take care of them.

What younger workers can teach older workers

- *New technology:* Clearly, younger employees are likely to know how to use modern ICT. If they do not, they are comfortable learning how. And, like most people with a skill, they are usually happy to pass on what they know.

- *Diversity:* Younger workers come from diverse households and backgrounds. Their 'wider perspectives' can help open older workers' eyes to the changing world and workforce.

- *Job hopping:* Older workers have been told that only bad, disloyal or incompetent employees leave. In fact, today only the superstars jump from job to job. While older workers may regard career change as negative, young people understand that it can be fulfilling, energizing – even life-changing.

- *Risk taking:* Younger workers are extremely entrepreneurial. They can think ' out of the box', especially when compared to people who have spent their careers respecting corporate hierarchies and processes, avoiding risk. A new era demands a new way of thinking and problem-solving approach.

- *Balancing work/life issues:* Older workers did not excel at managing the work–life balance. Younger workers are not career driven; they can show older workers different attitudes and values.

- *Fulfilling dreams:* Older workers have had many responsibilities throughout their careers but now that they are without children and mortgages, they can go out and fulfil their dreams – but they may not realize it. If they see how younger workers act and feel, they can follow their lead.

These basic examples outline a number of ways in which different generations can learn from each other and create empathy in the workplace. Learning is undoubtedly a lifelong process. When new skills are learnt through collaborative efforts, meta-activity occurs. Modern technology widens our vision of possibilities; ICT has shaped and will continue to shape how we live, work and study. To ensure the smooth running of the organization, it is constructive to embrace (rather than reject) digital technology and the new culture of the digital workplace.

The digital revolution is impacting every level of society; there are a number of implications that concern policy makers, internet users, business managers (in terms of organizing resources) and researchers (in terms of methodology and further study). Each implication is looked at below.

Implications

For policy makers and internet users

This chapter traces the generation divide, highlighting Mannheim's framework of Generational Theory, then discusses the issue of how different generations use the internet. The discussion calls into question the theoretical framework on the grounds of oversimplification, drawing attention to the danger of assuming a whole generation behaves as a homogeneous segment. Although a good framework – one that fits – is better than no framework at all, it is worth bearing in mind the limitations of theoretical concepts. Theories, by their intrinsic nature, guide people to see what they predict people *will* see... which can lead to overgeneralizing and overreacting to situations based solely on theoretical evidence. What is needed is a flexible framework that focuses on describing internet usage in the context of modern-day consumer behaviour. Existing Anglo-American business models do not seem to take into consideration the complexity of evolving internet user behaviour or the generation divide online. Moreover, it is known that user perceptions play a critical role in the adoption of ICT but very little is known about how perceptions or beliefs may change as users gain experience. More research on a wider scale is needed to produce a post-adoption behavioural framework that explains the perceived usefulness and enjoyment experienced by the different generations of internet users.

A key theme of this chapter is technological divergence (ie the different ways in which people use the internet). Over the past decade developments in technology meant that internet access is no longer restricted to a desk-top computer. Users have the choice between mobile connection and fixed access; and this divergence has accelerated segmentation by providing technology to suit individual user needs. Older internet users seem to access the internet in a functional/practical way (often from a desk-top PC or laptop); younger users are more likely to try new internet-enabled devices that allow mobile and wireless access (particularly via smartphones and tablet computers). The chapter did not set out to explore the impact of technological divergence on internet user behaviour but it would be an interesting area to monitor as the youngest internet users, Gen Z, enter the workforce. Over the next decade, it is likely that Gen Z will express an interest in teleworking (working from outside the traditional place of employment). Modern technology enables internet users to connect from anywhere, via any ware, and at any time; there is no need to be physically present in the workplace for working online. As a result, employer and labour organizations will be compelled to address the issue of 'remote access' and draw up guidelines for teleworking.

A further theme discussed in the chapter concerns the myths that surround the so-called tech-savvy younger internet users. The seemingly widespread adoption of the internet in society often overshadows the fact that there are individuals (not necessarily the older generations) who have missed the opportunity to develop digital skills. This oversight needs addressing because it has an economic impact. The majority of internet users use the internet in a very limited way; less than a tenth of 1 per cent is accessed; people can feel overwhelmed by the volume and complexity of the information available. It would therefore seem constructive to produce a public information campaign that would inform and educate the general public on how to access the internet, how to use online services more effectively and how to download apps. People need to *see* how the internet can improve the way they communicate (being able to talk longer for cheaper) and how it can provide better-quality content (ie access to superior graphic quality or more accurate information). Above all, as technology becomes more sophisticated, marketing efforts need to respond not only to the changing consumption patterns but also to the need for user-friendly ICT.

Long term, failure to participate in the digital society could hinder a person's educational achievement, employment opportunities and access to public and commercial services that are only available online. As access to the internet is akin to a civil rights issue for the 21st century, computer literacy has become an essential skill. For this reason, it is important to encourage the use of ICT across different user groups in society. The problem now is how to communicate with the different generations; a problem not just for policy makers but also for business managers as well.

For business managers

For businesses to compete in today's highly competitive market, managers need to acknowledge the dominant role played by information in industrial and economic business processes. The onus is on managers to keep abreast of technological developments regarding methods of obtaining information and its availability. Managers also need to recognize the significance and value of human capital as a factor of scientific and technological progress. In an ideal world, business managers would communicate to academics the skills that they feel graduates should acquire in order to be employable (ie the relevant professional competences, knowledge and skills to solve applied problems). The generational divide and the divide between digital skills used in-school and out-of-school are part of an ongoing debate about adult authority in educating, socializing and managing youth. Some critics argue that new media empower youth to challenge the social norms and educational agendas of their elders in unique ways.

The management skills acquired in a formal academic context are often out of sync (or out of date) with the skills required in today's global workplace, particularly the skills needed to manage employees who are in different phases and generations of ICT adoption and usage. It may seem daunting (for older or inexperienced employees) to have to learn new ICT skills but it is now a prerequisite, as an increasing number of routine business services are being transferred online (recruitment, procurement, accountancy, etc). It is constructive to offer training to employees throughout the organization to help them become accustomed to using interactive/collaborative tools, for example, to communicate in a forum, to exchange information, to access public services online or to navigate consumer portals. This has implications for future research.

For future research

This chapter discusses the difficulties of studying the internet from a user perspective. Both the technology and internet user behaviour are constantly evolving, and change is taking place at an increasing speed. Much of the data available in the public domain uses questionable methodology to explore internet user behaviour and it can be challenged on many points. Even though ongoing research provides greater insight into internet usage, the evolution of technology and trends means that having a holistic view of internet user behaviour will become increasingly difficult. To understand the evolution of ICT adoption and usage, it would be constructive to explore individual segments of internet user behaviour (by generation) rather than trying to explore the whole population of internet users; for example how different linguistic and cultural communities are converging on certain aspects of internet user behaviour and diverging on others. This perspective ought to reveal the ongoing evolution in patterns of convergence and divergence.

The growth of the internet has been spectacular but it is not simply growing: it is changing rapidly. It was designed to support communication between computer systems in academic and scientific communities; it was not designed to cope with an ever-growing population of networked mobile users and business applications. Nobody owns the internet: there is no centralized governing body; it cannot be turned off. The openness of design has enabled the internet architecture – the assemblage of thousands of individual networks intercommunicating with a common protocol – to grow to a global scale. Today, however, the structural limitations of the internet are becoming apparent and its future is being discussed worldwide. Structural limitations refer to technical or performance restrictions or constraints that cannot be resolved with current paradigms as far as our understanding/ knowledge goes. The most pressing challenge is to provide internet users with access to online services that are efficient, transparent, interoperable, flexible, timely and *above all* secure. There is an urgent need to make the internet more robust, versatile and equipped with suitable governance models. This is a topic in its own right, calling for large-scale investigation and cooperation between internet users, government and businesses worldwide.

In addition to these technical considerations, parallel studies are required to monitor the evolution of various emerging segments of internet user behaviour. Further limitations of the internet include the ongoing inconsistency among internet service providers in terms of quality of connectivity, reliability and cost-effectiveness. More worryingly, perhaps, there is increasing disconnection between the 'real world' use of technology and how it is taught in schools and used in business. It will be an interesting topic to focus on over the next few years: the older generations are eventually going to be out of the picture. The English-speaking world (particularly the United States) is a good starting point to watch for indications of emerging trends in ICT, as they use technology in a different way in businesses and in learning. With respect to the generation gap, a dynamic area to investigate would be the younger internet users (Gen Z), to take a closer look at how these 'digital gurus' use social networks for work, study and recreation in different national contexts – and the extent to which they are driving change.

Concluding thoughts

This chapter presents a contemporary snapshot of internet user behaviour across different generations at a precise moment in time. The internet represents the ultimate expression in free thinking and creativity. Internet users worldwide have access to a colossal volume of data and unbounded communication. The way in which individuals interact with the technology depends on many factors, particularly the generation into which the individual was born. Although internet usage is constantly evolving with advances in technology, it is constructive to have an awareness of the various user behaviour patterns of each generation.

The chapter discusses the broad generational traits and explores disparity in internet usage. Ongoing technological developments and the evolution in internet user behaviour make it increasingly difficult to know exactly what people are doing online; as soon as internet research is finished and published, the analysis is out of date. Thus it is only possible to provide an approximate view of the changes that have been taking place and the likely outcomes of those changes.

Revision questions

1 Explain *why* monitoring the internet user behaviour of young adults is essential in today's global online world.

2 Discuss *how* managers can effectively monitor the internet user behaviour of Gen Y and Gen Z.

3 *How* can this knowledge be used to ameliorate present-day society?

Further study

Doohwang, L, Hyuk Soo, K and Jung Kyu (2011) The impact of online brand community type on consumer's community engagement behaviors: Consumer-created vs marketer-created online brand community in online social-networking websites, *Cyberpsychology, Behavior and Social Networking*, **14** (1/2), pp 59–63

Dreamgrow.com (2012) The power of free stuff: Social media incentives, accessed 25 May 2015 at http://www.dreamgrow.com/the-power-of-free-stuff-social-media-incentives

Duke, C (2011) 5 Tips for amplifying customer engagement', *CRM Magazine*, **15** (11), p WP6, Academic Search Complete, EBSCO*host*, viewed 13 April 2014

Fowler, G (2012) Are you talking to me? *Wall Street Journal*, 18 June, accessed 25 May 2015 at http://online.wsj.com/article/SB10001424052748704116404576263083970961862.html

Nigam, S, Cook, R and Stark, C (2011) Putting the joy back into the airport experience: Can social networking platforms make a genuine contribution to increasing commercial revenues and engaging customers? *Journal of Airport Management*, **6** (1), pp 7–11

Schroeder, J and Salzer-Meorling, M (2005) *Brand Culture*, Routledge, New York

Socialmediatoday.com (2011) The engagement trajectory: How consumers socially engage with brands, *Social Media Today*, accessed 13 April 2015 at http://socialmediatoday.com/jasonsmith/332501/engagement-trajectory-how-consumers-socially-engage-brands

Yan, J (2011) Social media in branding: Fulfilling a need, *The Journal of Brand Management*, **18** (9), pp 688–96

Background materials

13 tips for managing social networks, http://www.placedesreseaux.com/Dossiers/
reseaux-sociaux/developper-votre-audience-web-1.html#.UXfcN2thNdQ.e-mail

Negative effects of facebook, http://www.youtube.com/watch?v=-X38N8lS78g&
feature=related

Social media in plain english, http://www.youtube.com/watch?v=MpIOClX1jPE (TED)

The effects of social media on society and marketing, http://www.youtube.com/
watch?v=Vqb8nKbOo-c&feature=related

What is social media? (Eric Qualman), http://www.youtube.com/watch?v=
5mid8p4A6Eg&feature=related

References

Attias-Donfut, C (1991) Générations et âges de la vie, *PUF Coll Que sais-je?*,
no 2570, Paris

Bailey, A and Ngwenyama, O (2010) Bridging the generation gap in ICT use:
Interrogating identity, technology and interactions in community telecenters,
Information Technology for Development, **16** (1), pp 62–82

Barzilai-Nahon, K and Mason, R (2010) How executives perceive the net generation,
Information, Communication & Society, April, **13** (3), p 396

Bassiouni, D and Hackley, C (2014) Generation Z children's adaptation to digital
consumer culture: A critical literature review, *Journal of Customer Behaviour*,
13 (2), pp 113–33

Batat, W (2014) Comment les adolescents définissent-ils leurs propres compétences
de consommation? Une approche par les portraits, *Recherche et Applications
en Marketing*, **29** (1), pp 27–60

Beckstrom, M, Manuel, J and Nightingale, J (2008) The wired utility meets
the wired generation. Electric light and power, accessed 13 April 2015 at
http://www.elp.com/index/display/articledisplay/342495/articles/electric-light-power/
volume-86/issue-5/news-analysis/the-wiredutility-meets-the-wired-generation.html

Charlton, R (2014) Generation Z, accessed 8 August 2015 at
http://spaceliferob.blogspot.fr/2014/08/generation-z.html

Coombes, B (2009) Gen Y: Are they really digital natives or more like digital
refugees? *Synergy*, 7 (1), pp 31–40

Donnison, S (2007) Unpacking the millennials: A cautionary tale for teacher
education, *Australian Journal of Teacher Education*, **32** (3), pp 1–13

Fisher, M (2010) Should Facebook declare itself a sovereign state? accessed 12 May
2015 at http://www.theatlanticwire.com/features/view/feature/Should-Facebook-
Declare-Itself-a-Sovereign-State-1657

Hargittai, E (2010) Digital na(t)ives? Variation in internet skills and uses among members of the 'net generation', *Sociological Inquiry*, **80** (1), pp 92–113

Hartman, J L and McCambridge, J (2011) Optimizing millennials' communication styles, *Business Communication Quarterly*, **74** (1), pp 22–44

Haste, H (2009) *Identity, Communities and Citizenship*, commissioned as part of the UK Department for Children, Schools and Families' Beyond Current Horizons project, led by Futurelab, Bristol, p 4

Hitt, M, Ireland, R and Hoskisson, R (2005) *Strategic Management: Competitiveness and Globalization*, 6th edn, South-Western College Publishing, Thomson, OH, pp 108–9

Howe, N (2014) Are you born to be better off than your parents? accessed 25 May 2015 at http://www.forbes.com/sites/neilhowe/2014/07/16/part-1-generations-in-pursuit-of-the-american-dream

Kawulich, B B (2005) Participant observation as a data collection method. Forum Qualitative Sozialforschung (online) Berlin, accessed 28 May 2015 at http://nbn-resolving.de/urn:nbn:de:0114-fqs0502430

KellyMitchell (2012) Generation X vs Y, accessed 28 May 2015 at http://www.kellymitchell.com/2012/03/generation/

Knoll, Inc (2014) *What Comes After Y?* (pdf) accessed 9 August 2015 at https://www.knoll.com/media/938/1006/What-Comes-After-Y.pdf

Li, C and Bernoff, J (2008) *Groundswell: Winning in a world transformed by social technologies*, Harvard Business Press, Boston, MA, p 9

Livingstone, S (2008) Internet literacy: Young people's negotiation of new online opportunities, in (eds) T McPherson, J D and C T MacArthur, *Digital Youth, Innovation and the Unexpected*, The Foundation Series on Digital Media and Learning, MIT Press, Cambridge, MA, pp 101–22

Loroz, P (2006) The generation gap: A Baby Boomer vs Gen Y comparison of religiosity, consumer values, and advertising appeal effectiveness, *Advances in Consumer Research*, 33, 308–9

McLuhan, M (1964) *Understanding Media: The extensions of man*, Routledge, New York

McMahan, C, Hovland, R and McMillan, S (2009) Online marketing communications: Exploring online consumer behavior by examining gender differences and interactivity within internet advertising, *Journal of Interactive Advertising*, **10** (1), p 61

Mannheim, K (1952) The problem of generations, in (ed) P Kecskemeti, *Essays on the Sociology of Knowledge*, Routledge & Kegan Paul, London, pp 276–322

Miniwatts Marketing Group (2015) Internet World Stats: Usage and population statistics, accessed 9 August 2015 at http://www.internetworldstats.com

Moos, D and Honkomp, B (2011) Adventure learning: Motivating students in a Minnesota middle school, *Journal of Research on Technology in Education*, **43** (3), pp 231–52

Morgan, J (2008) Blogs, wikis increase fund firms' collaboration, *Money Management Executive*, November 17, **16** (44), pp 1–8

Namer, G (2006) *Karl Mannheim, sociologue de la connaissance : La synthèse humaniste ou le chaos de l'absolu*, L'Harmattan, Paris

Olson, K E, O'Brien, M A; Rogers, W A and Charness, N (2011) Diffusion of technology: Frequency of use for younger and older adults, *Ageing International*, 36, pp 123–45

Özer, T (2013) Generations (X, Y, Z, Alpha, Baby Boomers), accessed 25 May 2015 at http://www.birhabersin.com/2013/12/generations-xyzalphababy-boomers.html

Palfrey, J and Gasser, U (2008) *Born Digital: Understanding the first generation of digital natives*, Basic Books, New York, p 6

Paz, J (2004) Navigators and castaways in cyberspace, in (eds) M Bonilla and G Cliché, *Internet and Society in Latin America and the Caribbean*, Southbound & IDRC Books, Ottawa, ON, pp 147–92

Pelton, L E and True, S L (2004) Teaching business ethics: Why Gen Y? *Marketing Education Review*, **14** (3), pp 63–70

Pendergast, D (2009) Generational theory and home economics: Future proofing the profession, *Family and Consumer Sciences Research Journal*, **37** (4), pp 504–22

Pendergast, D (2010) Getting to know the Y generation, in (ed) P Benckendorff *et al*, *Tourism and Generation Y*, CABI Publisher, Australia, pp 1–16

Pew Research Center (2015) Generations and age experts, accessed 10 August 2015 at http://www.pewresearch.org/areas-of-expertise/generations-and-age/

Prensky, M (2001) *Digital Natives, Digital Immigrants*, NCB University Press, **9** (5), pp 1–6

Reisenwitz, T and Cutler, B (1998) Dogmatism and internet usage by university students: Are dogmatics late adopters? *Journal of Marketing Theory and Practice*, Summer, pp 43–9

Sojka, J and Fish, M (2008) *Marketing Education Review*, **18** (1), p 25

Stevens, M, Armstrong, E and Arum, R (2008) Sieve, incubator, temple, hub: Empirical and theoretical advances in the sociology of higher education, *Annual Review of Sociology*, 34, p 133

Vaidhyanathan, S (2008) Generational myth, accessed 25 May 2015 at http://chronicle.com/article/Generational-Myth/32491

Van Volkom, M, Stapley, J C and Amaturo, V (2014) Revisiting the digital divide: Generational differences in technology use in everyday life, *North American Journal of Psychology*, **16** (3), pp 557–74

Viot, C (2010) Toi aussi, deviens mon ami, *Décisions Marketing*, 58, p 77

Wallop, H (2014) Gen Z, Gen Y, Baby Boomers – A guide to the generations, accessed 8 August 2015 at http://www.telegraph.co.uk/news/features/11002767/Gen-Z-Gen-Y-baby-boomers-a-guide-to-the-generations.html

Williams, K C and Page, R A (2011) Marketing to the generations, *Journal of Behavioral Studies in Business*, **5** (1), pp 1–17

WIP (2015) World Internet Project, accessed 10 August 2015 at
http://www.worldinternetproject.net/#about

Woog, D (2015) What older workers and younger workers can learn from each
other, accessed 25 May 2015 at http://career-advice.monster.com/in-the-office/
workplace-issues/generational-teachback/article.aspx

Arts pedagogy in management development

09

ANNE PÄSSILÄ and ALLAN OWENS

OBJECTIVES

This chapter aims to introduce the distinctive forms of practice and discourse that arts pedagogy can offer when applied in management development and education by:

- Questioning some fundamental assumptions about knowledge production and management in an innovation context.

- Explaining the development of and reasoning behind the use of arts-based methods to foster criticality and question assumptions informing daily practices.

- Considering the potential in shifting from monological to dialogical approaches when management and management education are conceived of as a relational process.

- Providing examples of the use of arts pedagogy and discourses about it in action.

Introduction

In this chapter we focus on the ways in which managers deal with problems that resist simple solutions. One way is to use rational, logic-oriented, conventional tools as a knowledge manager to identify a solution to the problem and then solve it. Another, to which we give most attention here, is for the manager to act as a knowledge facilitator, placing emphasis on the formulation of questions that need to be asked, rather than proposing ready solutions to complex problems and phenomena. For example, how and why a successful manager (in this chapter we give her the name Mary) spends her time with a multi-professional learning community creating space for a new type of knowledge creation and understanding by questioning her own assumptions and ways of acting – through arts pedagogy. We ask why it is fundamental for Mary to provide space for herself to find out how she could support her employees to act in an innovative manner in their organization.

Arts pedagogy refers to the act of 'people coming together to learn, to make, to express and to think creatively and, therefore, de facto, to think differently' through a range of art forms (Adams and Owens, 2015). In the context of management and management education we are particularly concerned with the way in which the arts can be used to organize critical reflection and as a means of co-creating knowledge to deepen understanding of issues at hand (Pässilä, 2012); for example in enabling Mary to reflect on how she influences others and to identify tensions between different units in her organization, the consequences of which would otherwise be felt, but the causes remain invisible.

We have taken an ethnodramatic approach, weaving theory and research into this dramatic ethnography chapter. Following Saldaña's definition of ethnodrama (2005: 1–2) as one application of theatrical methodology, this is a written research script that consists of 'dramatized, significant selections of narratives collected through interviews, participative observations, field notes, journal entries, and/or print and media artefacts such as diaries, television broadcasts, newspaper articles, and court proceedings'. Our ethnodramatic chapter entails the creation of 'real-life' vignettes that emerged from data, pre-text-based drama performances and dialogues around them, and scenes containing elements of dramatic tension. As authors of this chapter our aim is to communicate research findings in a way that remains ardently faithful to the primary research subjects and the veracity of the data. We also want to bring this sort of discourse to management development and education.

The organization of the chapter

We begin with some fundamental assumptions and questions about knowledge production and management that inform Mary's actions. Next, we present an introduction to the use of arts in organizations with the questions that are asked about this by one of her more sceptical colleagues, Tom. Part of Mary's response to Tom involves sharing the growing body of literature of arts-based approaches and practical examples. Another is an invitation to Simon, a specialist in practice-based innovation in regional development, to make sense of arts-based approaches through an explanation of the theory and practice of Mode 2b knowledge production. This is generated through multi-voiced discussions between organizational actors (employers and employees) and between these actors and their customers and stakeholders. It is triggered by problem setting in practical, localized contexts and can be characterized as social and cross-disciplinary; the underpinning assumption being that we, as people, are continuously constructing meanings of our worlds and ourselves rather than the assumption that there is a reality from which we can separate.

Mary is inspired, but does not know how to 'do it': to make the shift from knowledge manager to knowledge facilitator. This provides the excuse to join in a 'Manager learning community' just being launched by Alexis, an 'arts pedagogue', the name given to professionals skilled in bringing people together to learn, to make, to express and to think creatively and differently (Adams and Owens, 2015). She shares her experience of arts-based methods, explaining unfamiliar key concepts such as 'critical creativity' and 'aesthetic distancing'. While taking part in the Manager learning community, Mary reflects on her own management practice through one form of arts-based initiative: a pre-text-based drama called 'King Lear'.

After participating in the Manager learning community, Mary is able to articulate the need of space for her own practical reflexivity, suggesting that this involves dialogue and critical reflection; that it is not about toolboxes but about learning, about turning to learning.

The cast list is:

Mary – CEO in an industrial company.

Tom – executive board member of Mary's company.

Simon – a specialist in practice-based innovation in regional development.

Alexis – arts pedagogue specializing in the use of arts in organizations.

Venla – Human Resource Manager in a large public institution.

Riisto, Tiina, Niina, Juha, Lena – Manager learning community participants.

Some fundamental assumptions

Mary, like many members of our organizations, whether we are CEO-level managers, operation line managers or employees, has fundamental assumptions and questions about knowledge production and management that inform her actions. One of these is that we seldom raise difficult or sensitive issues as topics in formal conversation, believing this to be a waste of time. Similarly, we tend to avoid even starting to reflect on the power tensions between us during weekly meetings or sharing our fears or dreams in project meetings. We behave in this manner because of assumptions. For example, we assume that emotions are not part of our knowledge production, regardless of the fact that emotions are symptoms of the resistance that emerges when things change, as they do when innovation is being processed. In other words, change causes emotional responses and power tensions which, along with other social and cultural encounters, are not always acknowledged in the knowledge production process. This is normally conceived as being linear and unproblematic based on the assumption that there are those who produce knowledge and store it for others to use as needed.

After talking in the Manager learning community with a specialist in practice-based innovation in regional development (Simon), Mary made the connection with Mode 2b knowledge production and problem-based learning in which culture-based method and problem-based learning process are harnessed to make sense of the realities of the workplace and to manage challenges. Simon introduced Mary to Alexis, an arts pedagogue who specializes in the use of arts in organizations. Simon's Mode 2b knowledge production assumptions resonated strongly with Mary's, as did his use of the concept 'tacit and embodied knowing' (Polayani, 1958). She came to understand this as being the sort of knowledge that cannot be shared with others simply by talking about it or writing it down, as often those who have it do not know that they know more than they can tell (Polayani, 1958). She was intrigued by the idea of organizing reflection in organizations via arts and

FIGURE 9.1   Connections

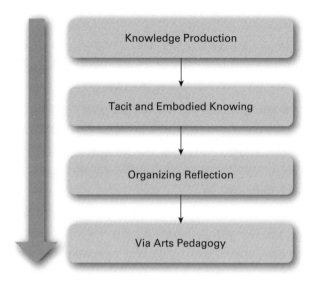

arts pedagogy in ways that built trust, which was a prerequisite of this valuable knowledge being shared. We return to consider Mode 2b knowledge production in more detail later in the chapter, but present the connections Mary noted here (Figure 9.1).

Introduction to arts in organizations

Mary's colleague Tom connected with the concept of Mode 2b knowledge production and ideas of tacit and embodied knowing, but was sceptical about the whole notion of reflection in organizations via arts and arts pedagogy (Meisiek and Barry, 2010, 2014; Boje *et al*, 2003; Clark, 2008; Hotham and Owens, 2011; Meisiek, 2002, 2004; Meisiek and Barry, 2007; Pässilä, 2012; Scheyogg and Hopfl, 2004; Taylor and Ladkin, 2009), as this conversation reveals:

> *Tom:* So what are the identifiable outcomes of the use of arts in organizations?
>
> *Mary:* The approach is more about 'what comes out' rather than predetermined outcomes.

Tom: There's no sense spending time on the kind of things that can't be measured in an organization.

Mary: This obsession with measurement is locking us deeper and deeper in our intra-organization silos. The measurement system does not include, for example, how often we cooperate with colleagues from other units when we cross boundaries and take risks.

Tom: Surely because those are outcomes that can't be planned for? Let's think of our positions in this company, we could really be wasting our time – encouraging our people to work with others outside their unit when they should be achieving the targets they are going to be measured by.

Mary: The same-minded people from the same professional background stick together to work with the same-minded people, R&D in one box, sales unit in their box, operations in theirs. I can understand your concerns, Tom, but we are supposed to be innovative. I've just been talking with Simon and he gave me a really concrete example of a large packaging business he was invited to work with because of the animosity between sales managers and operators on the factory floor which the CEO picked up to be causing increasing concern for some of his major customers. Rather than asking who was not following procedures, in other words whose fault this was, they used a form of research-based theatre to find out what was motivating and what angering people in sales and production. It turned out that production felt sales were spending too much time with customers in hospitality, skiing and eating, and sales felt production always wanted specification far too early. Through research-based theatre the salespeople shared their tacit understanding that there needed to be trust between them and customers so that when things went wrong, which they invariably do from time to time, the customers would not walk away because they knew it would be sorted out quickly. Through arts pedagogy the production and sales teams formulated questions over the silos, enabling them to ask what was important in each other's work that they each should see rather than blaming each with the possible consequence of losing customers.

Tom: Ok, I am beginning to see what you are getting at.

Mary: We are caught in a paradoxical situation – we need to be innovative, think and act outside the box in multi-professional creative ways in order to realize innovation, while simultaneously being required to be increasingly efficient and ever more productive.

Tom: I see what you mean – this is a different sort of 'being creative' than the usual – doing more with less.

Mary: Yes, it can be. The use of arts in organizations operates from within the tension of this paradox, providing ways for organizational actors to define the right questions rather than rushing in to give solutions. We both know like other top managers that we spend 95 per cent of our time trying to formulate the right questions. Many of the problems we face today are perplexing – there are no one-size-fits-all solutions.

Tom: So the use of arts in organizations might be a solution.

Mary: Not necessarily a solution but another approach, rather than always reaching for the conventional rational, logic-oriented tools. If we always use a hammer then the problem is always a nail.

Tom: Rather than a set of tools, you are talking about an approach that allows us to articulate questions that make problems visible that we are perhaps not yet aware of?

Mary: Yes!

Activity – Discussion questions/thinking assignment

- Mary and Tom operate from very different sets of assumptions about knowledge production. How would you characterize these?

- Basic assumptions run very deep in our being in the world and in our practices. We take it for granted that business and economics are about this and that, socialized as we are into these as we work with same-minded people who strengthen these beliefs even further. But how come Mary acknowledges Tom's assumptions and constructs very quickly, but Tom has more difficulty in acknowledging Mary's?

- Is it possible to ever fully articulate our own assumptions or identify our blind spots?

Tom e-mailed Mary later that week:

> I have just done a quick literature search and there are quite a few case studies out there.
>
> I wonder if this could be linked to human capital theory. What I would be interested in is evaluative reports – in an empirical sense – from the perspective of the user. These could really be helpful in identifying the tangible benefits of engagement with the arts.
>
> Regards
>
> Tom

Mary saw that Tom was trying to make connections through the literature with what he was saying and replied very fully:

> It's tricky to reduce this approach to the series of bullet points you seem to be after, Tom. The arts have been used to attempt to sharpen skills needed in the organization – creativity, diversity, imagination, and improvisation -- or have aimed at practical outcomes, for example generating greater numbers of ideas, awareness or impacts on strategy, or at organizing communication and interaction training. These arts applications have been viewed as encounters between different domains, as the artist or arts practitioner enters into the workplace to work with organizational actors and/or arts are brought into the world of the organization (Heinsius and Lehikoinen, 2013). For example, arts-based methods and approaches are applied to idea generation, strategy building, learning and training, branding and problem solving. Arts have also been used as a way of framing how members of a community can explore and reflect on meaningful questions and problems together (Pässilä *et al*, 2013; Pässilä and Vince, 2015).
>
> For example I've just been reading a case study in which a large primary and special care organization was grappling with increasingly vocal public criticism about poor provision. They used arts pedagogical approaches to sensitively surface the emotional relational issue of families trying to secure the best care for their child. Rather than the simple and easy access

they believed they had procedurally ensured they found through making the clients' point of view visible that there were 55 different officers that a family needed to engage with within their own organization!

There are many more studies. Over 10 years ago in a special edition of *Organizational Studies* called 'Theatre in organizations' it was suggested that theatre had 'moved from a metaphor to describe organizations towards a technique to change them' (Scheyogg and Hopfl, 2004), resonating with other publications in communication studies (Boje *et al*, 2003) and management studies (Clark and Mangham 2004a, 2004b; Meisiek, 2002, 2004). While some of the earliest 'theatre in organizations' companies started up in the early 1990s, many have gone on to establish themselves comfortably in the conventional flow of the business and public organizations sectors; other individuals have continued to develop critical and research-driven theoretical lenses and forms of practice such as Barry (2006), Barry and Meisiek (2010, 2014), Clark (2008) and Meisiek and Barry (2007).

Parallel developments at that time were also taking place in the use of other art forms including music, art and dance, and have continued to do so (Schiuma, 2011). Managers and artists have explored the potential of operating as partners to develop new ways of working to realize organizational change and innovation (Taylor and Ladkin, 2009). Pässilä (2012) suggests that we need reflexivity in relation to innovation; she also mentioned to me that 'One of the most distinctive new dimensions of development in management thinking and education since the year 2000 has been the growth of the "Art of management".' Research, academic inquiry and practice have taken place in the educational context of university business schools (Holtham and Owens, 2011; Meisiek and Barry, 2014), and into the ways in which practitioners from across the arts work in private, public and third-sector organizations locally, regionally and nationally through academic inquiry in university arts schools (Heinsius and Lehikoinen, 2013; Korhonen and Airaksinen, 2014).

Schiuma (2011) documents and analyses the evolution of the field in arts and business in which he is concerned with the form of 'organizational value creation capacity' generated by integrating technical and emotive knowledge through the arts as a knowing process. His main focus is on what is going on inside organizations when the arts are employed as products and process by management: 'the deployment of artistic products and processes [is used] to activate and induce the static dynamics that affect the emotive knowledge characterizing employees and organizational infrastructure' (p 11). Schiuma argues that 'the private sector plays a crucial role as a co-creator of society' as it builds the 'ecosystem in which it operates'; an approach predicated on recognizing 'the human-based nature of the organization', a form of business with humanity (p 11).

Other scholars in the field such as Taylor (2008, 2009) and Adler (2010) operate from a liberal arts tradition in the valuing of self and how one relates to the world whilst taking a critical stance in the sense of seeing business and organizations as arenas for social change.

You can see from the above, Tom, that while this is still an emerging field it is a vibrant one.

Best

Mary

A theory and practice of Mode 2b knowledge production

Mary returned to the connection that Simon and Alexis had helped her make between knowledge production, tacit and embodied knowing and organizing reflection via the arts and arts pedagogy. She invited them both to speak to other managers and invited business colleagues.

Simon: I have been studying and following artists' and arts pedagogues' work in practice-based innovation when they use what I call 'cultural methods', and I think this is the most typical innovation method in Mode 2b innovation, which is when the nature of the innovation processes is interpretive and knowledge production is based on the social capital of the people involved. The logic in this is to develop innovation capability to break silos and prevent bottlenecks. The most typical outcomes of this type of knowledge production are organizational innovations, social innovations and service innovations. Innovation is differentiated into science technology innovation (STI) knowledge production – this mode which is based on the production and use of codified scientific and technical knowledge. The other mode of knowledge production is doing-using-interacting (DUI). This is based on informal processes of learning and embodied, experienced-based know-how and I suggest that this mode has two dimensions, namely 2a and 2b: 2b is the thing we are interested in.

Simon referred to Melkas and Harmaakorpi's book (2012), in which they joined the knowledge production discussion by suggesting new subcategories for mode 2 knowledge production. He used Table 9.1 to illustrate Harmaakorpi and Melkas's (2012: 447–8) proposal for new subcategories of Mode 2 knowledge production. (This table is adapted from the original.)

TABLE 9.1 Melkas and Harmaakorpi's (2012) extended model of 2a and 2b knowledge production and innovation policy

Innovation policy types			
Point of view	Science-based innovation (STI, Mode 1)	Practice-based innovation (DUI, Mode 2a)	Practice-based innovation (DUI, Mode 2b)
Most typical innovation types	Radical technological innovations and related concepts	Radical concept innovations – technological system innovations	Organizational innovations – social innovations – service innovations
Most typical fuels of innovation	Proximity	Distance	'Near distance'
Most typical logics	Agglomeration – clusters – economies of scale	Related variety – innovation platforms	Developing innovation capability – breaking silos and preventing bottlenecks
Most typical capital	Intellectual capital – financial capital	Social capital – institutional capital	Social capital – structural capital
Most typical innovation processes	Analytical	Interpretative	Interpretative
Most typical innovation methods	Scientific methods	Methods of intellectual cross-fertilization (including virtual)	Problem-based learning (eg culture-based methods)
Most typical origins of innovations	Science and related expertise	Networks – serendipity – customers	'Ordinary' staff – customers

Alexis simplified the sub-definitions. Subcategory Mode 2a refers to intellectual cross-fertilization, where members from very different organizations and professions come together (managers, researchers, artists), for example in innovation sessions, in which scientific and practical expertise are combined with the help of various ideation and creative methods. Subcategory Mode 2b refers to heterogeneous development of organizations, the effectiveness of which becomes visible more slowly. By 'heterogeneous' we mean cross-disciplinary teams working together, moving outside their own units, their own silos; for example, in primary care and special public health provision bringing client family members together with organizational actors ranging from medical specialist through administrators to receptionists. Such developments may be conducted with arts and arts pedagogy methods and learning by doing, in which the most typical type of knowledge creation process is tacit, and the most typical knowledge base is symbolic.

Alexis extended the invitation to others present to join a new learning community of which Mary was already a part, where together they could define further what this actually meant in practice. Manager learning community participants would include managers from industrial and service companies as well as public sector, experts in drama and arts-based practices, and experts in innovation and organizational development from both consultancy and academy. This learning community would be guided in a way that required all participants to undertake a learning journey that would use the arts, arts pedagogy and in particular pre-text-based drama, to engage in a Mode 2b type knowledge production process.

Example 1: Manager learning community

An example of critically reflective and creative approach to management development and learning

Mary joined 22 other experts forming together a cross-fertilization knowledge production and learning community. She was pleased to be joined by Venla, a manager from a different business field whom she always enjoyed talking to and who she had invited along to hear Simon and Alexis speak. Each of the three three-day blocks was run in a residential Finnish lakeside setting and comprised four zones:

1 Drama with an emphasis on pre-text-based process drama.

2 Knowledge inputs on practice-based innovation.

3 Reflection on personal experiences.

4 Retreat-type of relaxation.

When talking to colleagues after experiencing the first three-day, two-night intensive block of days in the Manager learning community, Mary said:

> It's a messy, difficult and complex learning process, but, applying it properly uncovers contradictions, tests variations, and tries out events from several points of view... I came to the right place to the right people at the right time... The process drama often starts with listening to the start of a deceptively simple story told by Alexis, and then he offers enjoyable ways to actively step into this imagined metaphorical story world. The co-construction process began there, it was a dialogic process, consisting of 'doing', 'watching' and 'interpreting'. It was in the continuous movement between the closely observed reality of the drama and the largely unobserved reality of everyday personal and professional life that possibilities for change and innovation surfaced.

Three key concepts arose: critical creativity, aesthetic distancing and organizing reflection and were much discussed.

Critical creativity

A recurrent term Mary noticed Alexis using was 'critical creativity'. The first thing she grasped was that it was an idea derived from the notion of competing voices in a diverse cultural context – the culture being the organizational culture. Being 'critical' appeared to be central to this and it resonated with critical management approaches such as that framed by Stokes and Oiry (2012) as notions of 'lived experience' in which they emphasize the value of critical perspectives in seeking new competences. Alexis said:

> The type of creation that we have been calling 'art' since the modern age depends to a large degree on the possibility of taking a critical stance in one's own society and culture. Only when creative individuals can rise above their own world for a while... can they

actually make a difference in their culture. As Pascal Gielen says in his book, *Creativity and Other Fundamentalisms*, it starts with self-reflection and self-criticism rising above one's own ego and seeing oneself from some distance.

Imagination and action seemed to be the fundamental constituents in this model of creativity in which engagement and momentum are key rather than quickly reaching for resolution. What this appeared to mean in effect is that ideas, concepts and daily practices are opened up and laid bare, subjected to critical appraisal – not an occasional or superficial questioning of a process, rather it is the regular, daily and perpetual re-evaluating and contesting of the practices.

Criticality in this context of creativity is a vital constituent enabling the imaginative, innovative impulse to be located socially in such a way that it offers a reflection of the social processes that gave rise to the concept in the first instance. The practice is an irritant to the otherwise unquestioned working practices and assumptions.

Aesthetic distancing and organizing reflection

Mary, Venla and Simon talked about how to reflect on their own practice and Alexis shared his idea about how reflection and aesthetic distance are related to tacit and embodied knowing of managing. Alexis talked about aesthetic distance in terms of the way arts can be used to make the familiar strange so that we see it 'afresh' or 'anew', just as for example a photograph of something we see every day but taken from a different angle makes us stop and perhaps reconsider it in the light of the new perspective offered. He pointed out that one of the key challenges in organizing reflection is to move away from seeing reflection as looking back at how something was done or could have been done differently and to move towards creating distance from which to connect with what is still being felt.

Venla: Aren't we connected to a wide range of past emotions in the present – even if we are not fully conscious of them?

Alexis: Yes, I understand aesthetic distancing as a process that encourages an important contradiction: remaining connected to the emotions generated within organizations and, at the same time, being able to sufficiently distance oneself from their effects. Aesthetic distance encourages reflection on the emotions at work and, as a consequence, invites reinterpretation of practice.

Simon: Wasn't this concept of aesthetic distancing originally invented by the German playwright Bertolt Brecht in the context of drama and theatre?

Alexis: Yes, ontologically, Brecht highlighted critical reflection achieved by artistic experience. He argued that fiction and truth are different domains and need not be mixed. He maintained distance between the role and the actor as well as between the play and the world. Instead of creating an illusion – the idea behind Aristotelian drama or tragedy – Brecht created epic drama that shattered the illusion of the stage. Brecht used different types of alienating effects – aesthetic distancing – to provoke reflective thinking in the audience.

Mary: So aesthetic distancing facilitates knowledge production, deepens understanding of power relations, and offers space for reflection?

Alexis: Yes, for example difficult or sensitive issues can be approached through metaphors, images, stories, performances and role-play. For example, a social enterprise I was working with was running a public consultation process about the potential public use of a deserted railway building in the middle of a market town. Feelings were running high as members of the community had a very wide range of strongly held views, ranging from lack of parking, to loss of business, to the desperate need of a community and local business hub. A series of nine public focus groups were held but instead of coming only to state a personal view, arts-based methods were used to create time for participants to not only speak but to listen to each other. One local businesswoman who had entered the room and immediately stated it needed knocking down in order to make a car park as her customers had nowhere to park said at the end, 'Well, we need a car park, but maybe not there.' What had allowed her to pause and think through or think afresh about her opinions and assumptions were the 100 photographs of various non-realistic still images of two to three people in staged poses which had been carefully used to allow for dialogue. Aesthetic distancing is used in Mode 2b knowledge production because it offers the potential and space for multiple worldviews (polyphony) to emerge and be interpreted and reflected. Aesthetic distancing allows us to explore the invisible and link our sensible sensitivity to difficult 'taboos' – like matters in knowledge production.

Venla: So, the first push for change comes from the understanding of experiences of ourselves; we create an expansive interpretation from our own and others' experiences?

Mary: Self-defined needs and possibilities are the cornerstones of the change.

Organizing reflection

Venla: What do you mean by organizing reflection?

Alexis: Organizing reflection is part of an approach to critical reflection that seeks to question taken-for-granted power relationships. When we bring the arts and arts pedagogy along, I use the concept of aesthetic distance in order to address a paradox in organizational experience which is: how can we remain connected to the emotions we feel in organizations at the same time as being capable of sufficiently distancing ourselves from their effects in order to reflect on our emotions at work?

Venla: So reflection through sensory experience is 'beyond the head', it is related to my embodied way of making sense of personal and social emotions.

Alexis: Yes, the movement between reflection and imagination is an important component. It encourages connection with emerging emotions, which shape our thoughts and reactions when engaging with the unknown. Imagination invites playfulness to be a continuous aspect of critical reflection.

Vince and Reynolds (2009) summarize the characteristics of critical reflection that distinguish it from other approaches to reflection:

The task of critical reflection is to identify and question taken-for-granted beliefs and values, particularly those that have become unquestioned or 'majority' positions.

Critical reflection pays particular attention to the analysis of power relations and relations between power and knowledge. Regardless of the particular perspective a critical approach is based on, it will emphasize the value of questioning and challenging existing structures and practices.

Critical reflection implies a shift of focus from an individual perspective on knowledge (skill or competence) towards a collective, situated process that assists inquiry into actual and current projects and their organizational consequences.

Critical reflection identifies social and collective dynamics within and constructed by our own practice. Reflection on socially constructed, collective experience is important in order to highlight the political, emotional, and ethical components of organizing, as well as its conceptual or technical aspects.

Example 2: Pre-text-based drama

King Lear

One of the drama zones in the Manager learning community focused on 'King Lear'. Alexis was enthused about putting in to practice Cunliffe and Easterby-Smith's (2004) ideas about 'unsettling conventional practice'. His intuition was that the pre-text storyline of 'King Lear' could help them all reflect on what is taken for granted in knowledge management when trying to create space for innovation. This resonated with another study he had recently read: an article by Elena Antonacopoulou (2010). He was inspired by her argument that it is vital to acknowledge that, instead of giving answers to people or advising them how to be innovative, learning should raise questions and dialogue about what is meaningful for people in their work and how they understand the relation between their work, innovation and their role in renewing practices. He chose the King Lear pre-text-based drama to challenge the assumption that the innovations are 'out there', that they can be captured and converted to business profit in the form of controlled R&D projects.

> *Alexis:* the word 'pretext' in English means 'excuse' for action. Pre-text-based drama refers to the source of the drama activity, which begins simply but which can rapidly develop towards more complex problems. Instead of talking about a given dilemma chosen as an entry point in the consideration of a given subject or phenomena, participants step in and out of it, not to lose themselves in an illusion, but in order to see familiar things in a different way.

He shared some of his hunches about the connections that might be made through the pre-text and some of the issues that would arise by speaking his thoughts out loud in the form of questions rather than stating what the outcomes would be:

> *Alexis:* I wonder if it is a commonly held assumption that truth is always valued and is about trust. In 'King Lear' the king is in power but the situation is perplexing. Is it inevitably hard to notice these assumptions when we have power? I wonder if we tend to love the better version or image of ourselves. Maybe this pre-text-based drama line will allow us to explore our assumptions in a critical way; well, let's see what might emerge.

Vignettes taken from the action in the pre-text-based drama King Lear

In this pre-text-based drama using the story line taken from Shakespeare's play, Alexis creates a simple safe frame for participants to step into the carefully observed world of the drama. We join the action 15 minutes into the pre-text, just after participants have heard a thumbnail description of the key characters, and based on this have chosen which they would like primarily to work with.

> *Alexis:* Now you have chosen the roles let me tell you the outline of the opening of the play and then we will do some work on it – stepping into the scenes that interest us. The play takes place in a kingdom where the old king – King Lear – had ruled for many years and kept the peace. (Group look at the map drawn prior to the session by a group of participants tasked with drawing a kingdom.) The king decided that it was time to rest, that the responsibilities had weighed heavy for too long; he would divide the kingdom up into three giving his youngest and favourite daughter the most

opulent part. (The map has been marked into three sections, with the richest part clearly identified.) He called his daughters together and asked each to step forward. The eldest, Goneril, flattered him incredibly, saying that she owed him everything and that the very sun shone from his eyes, along with many more compliments.

Next, Regan flattered him even more to the point where she said life had no meaning without him. The youngest, and one who loved him most, Cordelia, stepped forward and said nothing. She could not bear what she had heard and was not going to play the flattering game just to please him. She knew she had always loved and cared for him and that her sisters did not care at all for anyone but themselves. She could not 'heave her heart into her mouth' as she says, and so says nothing. The king's disbelief turns to anger. He warns her to think again and asks how someone so young can be so cruel. She replies that she is so young but so true, and that he cannot see true worth even in his own family. When the youngest had refused to flatter a second time (despite the warning that 'nothing shall become of nothing') he banishes her.

To start we are going to re-enact the scene as discussed. Can we agree on where Lear enters from, where the daughters stand/sit when giving their 'testimonies'? Should the rest of us watch in role as members of the court or simply watch as audience? While you are watching or participating in the scene I would like you to be thinking about what scene should follow this one. I will tell you what Shakespeare focused on, but this is our pre-text so we can decide.

After the re-enactment, the group generates ideas about the options as to what the next scene might be, then chooses which to re-enact, heightening the language and interweaving play text as appropriate. Alexis clarifies the frame, ie roles, situation, focus and perspective, and Mary noticed that, after the shared experience of the re-enactment and encouragement to imagine the 'what if', came the point where the group's agenda began to be identified and points that resonated with their experience began to surface and be shared.

From the suggested scenes, the group chose to devise a scene in which Lear met a week later with his two daughters, so all three were in the court. The tensions of power newly acquired and relinquished were strong. It was at this point that Alexis made the shift between the carefully observed reality of the drama and the largely unobserved reality of everyday organizational life.

Alexis: How does this kind of situation resonate with your work?

Riisto: This is a really a true situation in a family business I know. The father loved his daughter more than his son. The son became CEO and the daughter became marketing manager. Suddenly the organization had two sub-companies which both had two different managers as well as the third one – the father – who was still very much around when retired trying to control things. The employees were so confused, the situation collapsed and the companies' business started to go down. The father was in between with no proper role – he could not give up managing.

Tiina: This could so easily be about project organization where there is competition about applying for funding. Inside one organization there are several groups that have good ideas; they start to compete. The funding system requires only one application, but the people cannot combine their strengths so the organization needs to decide which project is best and will get the funding and go further. People are lobbying the top manager; different managers are gatekeepers who have power; much depends on who knows whom.

Nina: I am thinking of a member of the organization who is rapidly promoted. She starts to make decisions based not on the advice of experienced colleagues who respond to her request for ideas, but on her own ideas and one other favoured colleague. She thinks she is listening, but is hearing nothing that others are saying and not noticing the resentment building and building as people look for other jobs.

Juha: Then there is the issue of cooperation in which the main partner acts in an unfair way; no one dares say anything except one person who speaks the truth. The intra-political reasons keep everyone else silent. No one helps except one person.

Lena: What about the manager who encourages innovativeness towards new things and change teams and ways of meeting? One member of the team is an outsider who does not want to participate in this new value-innovating process and makes it very difficult for everyone else, but then this very same person takes all the glory and honour of the idea when the manager comes onto the stage.

Participants presented these scenes dramatically and chose Nina's to work on further. Using a range of other pre-text-based drama techniques they explored the different ways in which the manager was not able 'to see' what was happening. They named it 'The Blind Manager'. As they were working in the drama form they began to ask what qualities they would need as a manager to be able to better notice issues that are linked to agency building, transformation matters and details that have an emancipatory nature and potential. Reflecting on the discussions about 'King Lear' they identified different orientations of organizing reflection, one being problem-based, one interpretive, another being critical view.

Concluding thoughts

Despite theories and formal discussions about the importance of managing knowledge production as a fuel for innovation, welfare and growth, another reality seems to exist on the practical grass-roots level of Mary's company where the executives, operational managers and employees are not fully familiar with the learning orientation related to knowledge production. In the course of the Manager learning community, Mary, Simon and Alexis wanted to question the basic assumption that analytical decision-making interactions about structural problems are sufficient. They also point out that Mode 2b knowledge production is likely to be the mainstream when finding solutions for wicked problems, but the tools to support Mode 2b knowledge production are not yet very well developed. For example, in the context of management development and learning, the members of Mary's work community could explore real-life work situations – and their perplexingness – and try to find solutions to problems as well as create new answers and approaches. But Mary acknowledges that this type of knowledge production is tacit and embodied and therefore needs to be facilitated in a different way. Further discussion about this with Simon, Alexis and Venla led to them naming the quality that a manager needs to have to facilitate knowledge production in this different way as 'Sensible sensitivity'. The main reasoning behind the concept was that it is foolish for any manager not to notice small things that are symptomatic of large issues – it is sensible to be sensitive.

Table 9.2 explains for Mary as well as other managers, artists and arts pedagogues why it is fundamental to provide space for ourselves to find out how we can support employees and colleagues to act in an innovative manner – to understand our own sensible sensitivity potential. After the Manager learning community intensive period came to a close Alexis, Mary and Venla decided to meet up regularly with the intent of deepening their understanding of using the arts and arts pedagogy in management contexts. During one of these encounters, they made sense of Table 9.2.

Venla: I sense that there is shift happening; a managerial and leadership shift from knowledge management to knowledge facilitation.

Mary: I recall that Simon said that the most typical innovation processes in Subcategory Mode 2b are interpretative and that the interpretative dimension of innovation refers to a fragmented, ongoing, open-ended and multi-voiced dialogue-based process that emphasizes interaction and communication.

Alexis: Yes, that this involves facing incompleteness and distance, and being willing to live amongst multiple viewpoints and a lack of universal truths – as there may be no single 'answer', but rather multiple suggestions and proposals.

Mary: The ability to create space for social commitment, shared language and trust is fundamental to innovation, and once that space has been created, knowing can be generated together by the members of various professional groups within the organization and between external actors and customers.

Venla: The aesthetic distancing that took place during our shared Manager learning community learning process, where we tried to develop our management practices, revealed relational processes of facilitating knowledge production.

Alexis: Yes, the attempt is to be sensibly sensitive.

Together they started to sketch a model that would show the fundamental elements of the process of understanding the potential of sensible sensitivity. Figure 9.2 shows the process of sensible sensitivity in the knowledge production model in action.

TABLE 9.2   Manager learning community frame of Mode 2b knowledge production via pre-text-based drama

Problem-based orientation of organizing reflection	Interpretative orientation of organizing reflection	Critical view of organizing reflection
Agency building: • Mary exploring how to improve competence linked to productivity and work satisfaction • Mary focuses on problem solving and identifying development needs and technical orientation to improve processes, practices and roles	Transformational: • Mary exploring how to generate alternative interpretations • Mary making sense through a multi-voiced approach, sensing understanding of hidden potential symbolic actions and descriptions to deepen understanding related to one's own role in renewing processes, practices and roles	Emancipatory: • Mary unsettling established ways of working • Mary focusing on allowing reflexivity to emerge to collectively break down assumptions and discussion of existing situations through raised awareness
Knowledge production on: developing one's own work and learning activities that change work practices and personal and professional engagement	Knowledge production on: becoming collectively aware of diversity and transforming one's own behaviour	Knowledge production on: identifying and questioning taken-for-granted beliefs and values as well as by taking account of emotional, social and political processes in the workplace
Pre-text-based drama aiming at gaining deeper understanding of the perplexingness of the problem at hand	Pre-text-based drama aiming at interpreting the existing situation	Pre-text-based drama aiming at exploring the dynamics between various groups of professionals and between them and customers

FIGURE 9.2 Sensible sensitivity in the knowledge production model

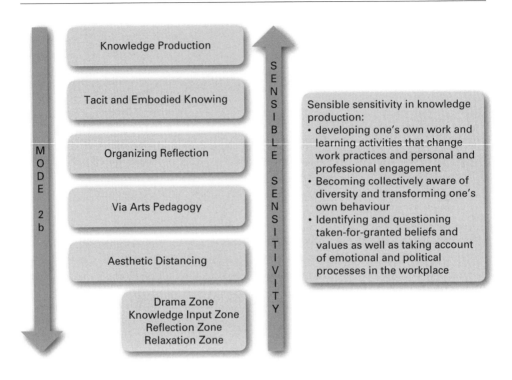

The model is aligned with Mode 2b knowledge production as a specific knowledge transformation 'mechanism'. In this transformation, Mary with the other organizational actors – innovation managers and employees from different professional groups as a community of practice-based innovators – and artists shared their understanding of values, ethics, roles, and interests when applying arts and arts pedagogy in organizational use, agreed as follows:

Mary: The first step is to create a multi-voiced space for organizing reflection via arts and arts pedagogy and inviting diversity into this type of knowledge production and management development. It is about spending our valuable time on new forms of knowledge facilitation. It is about understanding through questioning our own assumptions and ways of acting. Arts and arts pedagogy approaches differ from conventional organization activities, for example daily meetings, because the intent is to collectively learn from the synergies resulting from the utilization of sensing and imagination in reflection; they form a path to further knowledge facilitation. This is not about management toolboxes, but about learning, about turning to learning.

References and further study

There is a growing number of articles that can assist in understanding the topics and issues discussed in this chapter. The titles listed below are indicative for the purposes of assisted development of your thinking: Some of these have been cited but not detailed fully in the chapter text.

Barry, D (2006) The art of..., in (eds) D Barry and H Hansen, *The Sage Handbook of New Approaches in Management and Organization*, Sage, London, pp 31–41

Barry, D and Meisiek, S (2010) Seeing more and seeing differently: Sensemaking, mindfulness, and the workarts, *Organization Studies*, **31** (11), pp 1505–30

Boje, D M, Luhman, J T and Cunliffe, A L (2003) A dialectic perspective on the organization theatre metaphor, *American Communication Journal*, **6** (2)

Clark, T (2008) Performing the organization, in (eds) D Barry and H Hansen, *New Approaches in Management and Organization*, Sage, London pp 401–11

Clark, T and Mangham, I (2004a) From dramaturgy to theatre as technology: The case of corporate theatre, *Journal of Management Studies*, **41** (1), pp 37–59

Clark, T and Mangham, I (2004b) Stripping to the undercoat: A review and reflections on a piece of organization theatre, *Organization Studies*, **25** (5), pp 841–51

Gielen, P (2013) *Creativity and other Fundamentalisms*, Japan Books, Heijningen

Heinsius, J and Lehikoinen, K (2013) (eds) *Training Artists for Innovation: Competencies for new contexts*, Kokos Publications 2, Helsinki: Theatre Academy, University of the Arts Helsinki, https://helda.helsinki.fi/handle/10138/38879

Holtham, C and Owens, A (2011) Using the urban to span the boundaries between diverse disciplines: Drama education and business management, *Practice and Evidence of Scholarship of Teaching and Learning in Higher Education*, ECE Conference Special Issue, **6** (3), pp 292–305

Korhonen, P and Airaksinen, R (2014) (eds) *Hyva Hankaus 2.0*, Draamatayo, Helsinki

Meisiek, S (2002) Situation drama in change management: Types and effects of a new managerial tool, *International Journal of Arts Management*, **4**, pp 48–55

Meisiek, S (2004) Which catharsis do they mean? Aristotle, Moreno, Boal and organizational theatre, *Organization Studies*, **25** (5), pp 797–816

Meisiek, S and Barry, D (2007) Through the looking glass of organizational theatre: Analogically mediated inquiry in organizations, *Organization Studies*, **28**, pp 1805–27

Meisiek, S and Barry, D (2014) Theorizing the field of arts and management, *Scandinavian Journal of Management*, **30** (1), pp 83–5

Pässilä, A, Oikarinen, T and Harmaakorpi, V (2013) Collective voicing as reflexive practice, *Management Learning*, **44** (5)

Scheyögg, G and Höpfl, H (2004) Theatre and organization, editorial introduction, *Organization Studies*, **25** (5), pp 691–704

Stokes, P and Oiry, E (2012) Competency frameworks: What place for lived experience? *Euromed Journal of Business*, **7** (10), pp 4–23

Taylor, S (2008) Theatrical performance as unfreezing: Ties that bind at the academy of management, *Journal of Management Inquiry*, **17**, pp 398–406

Taylor, S and Ladkin, D (2009) Understanding arts-based methods: Managerial development, *Academy of Management Learning and Education*, **8** (1), pp 55–69

Literature about ethnodramatic and critical approaches

Cotter R J, Pässilä, A and Vince, R (2015) New directions for researching critical reflection in organizations, in (eds) T Beyes, M Parker and C Steyaert, *The Routledge Companion to the Humanities and Social Sciences in Management Education*, Routledge, London

Fook, J (2010) Developing critical reflection as a research method, in (eds) J Higgs, A Titchen, D Horsfall and D Bridges, *Creative Spaces for Qualitative Researching: Living research*, Sense Publishers, Rotterdam, pp 44–64

Mienczakowski, J and Morgan, S (2006) Ethnodrama: Constructing participatory, experiential and compelling action research through performance, in (eds) P Reason and H Bradbury (eds) *Handbook of Action Research*, Sage, London, pp 176–84

Mienczakowski, J and Moore, T (2008) Performing data with notions of responsibility, in (eds) J G Knowles and A L Cole, *Handbook of the Arts in Qualitative Research*, Sage, London, pp 451–8

Saldaña, J (2005) *Ethnodrama: An anthology of reality theatre* (Crossroads in Qualitative Inquiry Series, Vol 5) Alta Mira Press, Walnut Creek, CA

Saldaña, J (2008) Ethnodrama and ethnotheatre, in (eds) N K Denzin and Y S Lincoln, *The Sage Handbook of Qualitative Research*, Sage, Thousand Oaks, CA, pp 195–208

A selection of texts on the use of arts in organizations taken from Mary's e-mail

Adler, N (2010) Arts reflection and leadership, retrieved 16 January 2015 from http://www.rh2010.com/bilan2010/pdf/14a17_Adler_v13n4-en.pdf

Berthoin Antal, A (2009) R*esearch Report: Research framework for evaluating the effects of artistic interventions in organizations*, TILLT Europe, Gothenburg

Meisiek, S and Barry, D (2014) Theorizing the field of arts and management, *Scandinavian Journal of Management*, **30** (1), pp 83–5

Pässilä, A, Oikarinen, T and Harmmkorpi, V (2013) Collective voicing as a reflexive practice, *Management Learning*, **44** (4), pp 42–52

Pässilä, A, Oikarinen, T and Kallio, A (2013) Creating dialogue by storytelling, *Journal of Workplace Learning*, **25** (3), pp 159–77

Schiuma, G (2011) *The Value of Arts for Business*, Cambridge University Press, Cambridge

Literature related to practice-based innovation and Mode 2 knowledge production

Gibbons, M, Limoges, C, Nowotny, H, Schwarzman, S, Scott, P and Trow, M (1994) *The New Production of Knowledge*, Sage, London

Hessels, L K and van Lente, H (2010) The mixed blessing of Mode 2 knowledge production, *Science, Technology and Innovation Studies*, **6** (1), pp 65–9

Jensen, M, Johnson B, Lorenz, E and Lundvall, B A (2007) Forms of knowledge and modes of innovation, *Research Policy*, **36**, pp 680–93

Lester, R K and Piore, M J (2004) *Innovation – The missing dimension*, Harvard University Press, Cambridge, MA

Melkas, H and Harmaakorpi, V (eds) (2012) *Practice-based Innovation: Insights, applications and policy implications*, Springer, Heidelberg

Nowotony, H, Scott, P and Gibbons, M (2001) *Re-thinking Science Knowledge and the Public in an Age of Uncertainty*, Sage, London

Relevant literature about organizing reflection via arts and arts pedagogy

Cotter, R J, Pässilä, A and Vince, R (forthcoming 2015) New directions for researching critical reflection in organizations, in (eds) T Beyes, M Parker and C Steyaert, *The Routledge Companion to the Humanities and Social Sciences in Management Education*, Routledge, London

Pässilä, A and Vince, R (forthcoming 2015) Critical reflection in management and organization studies, in (eds) T Beyes, M Parker and C Steyaert, *The Routledge Companion to the Humanities and Social Sciences in Management Education*, Routledge, London

Pässilä, A, Oikarinen, T and Harmaakorpi, V (2013) Collective voicing as reflexive practice, *Management Learning*, **44** (5) http://mlq.sagepub.com/content/early/2013/06/26/1350507613488310.full.pdf+html

Pässilä, A, Owens, A and Pulkki, M (2015) Learning Jam – The back story of creating polyphonic understanding in work-based practice, Conference paper, International Forum on Knowledge Asset Dynamics, Bari, Italy, 10–12 June

Reynolds, M (2011) Reflective practice: Origins and interpretations, *Action Learning: Research and Practice*, **8** (1), pp 5–13

Reynolds, M and Vince, R (2004) Critical management education and action-based learning: Synergies and contradictions, *Academy of Management Learning and Education*, **3** (4), pp 442–56

Vince, R (2002) Organizing reflection, *Management Learning*, **33**, pp 63–78

Vince, R and Reynolds, M (2009) Reflection, reflective practice and organizing reflection, in (eds) S J Armstrong and C V Fukami, *The Sage Handbook of Management Learning, Education and Development*, Sage, London

Literature on the use of pre-text-based drama and other forms of theatre in organizations

Adams, J and Owens, A (2015) *Creativity and Democracy in Education: The practices and politics of learning through the arts*, Routledge, London

Antonacopoulou, E (2010) Making the business school more 'critical': Reflexive critique based on phronesis as a foundation for impact, *British Journal of Management*, **21**

Cunliffe, A and Easterby-Smith, M (2004) From reflection to practical reflexivity: Experiential learning as lived experience, in (eds) M Reynolds and R Vince, *Organizing Reflection*, Ashgate, Aldershot, pp 30–46

Kettula, K (2012) Towards professional growth: Essays on learning and teaching forest economics and marketing through drama, role-play and reflective journals, *Dissertationes Forestales 152*, Department of Forest Sciences Faculty of Agriculture and Forestry University of Helsinki

Meisiek, S (2002) Situation drama in change management: Types and effects of a new managerial tool, *International Journal of Arts Management*, **4**, pp 48–55

Neelands, J (2009) Acting together: Ensemble as a democratic process in art and life, *Research in Drama Education: The Journal of Applied Theatre and Performance*, **14** (2), pp 173–89

Pässilä, A (2012) Reflexive model of research-based theatre – Processing innovation at the crossroads of theatre, reflection and practice-based innovation activities, *Acta Universitatis Lappeenrantaensis 492*, Lappeenranta University Press, Lappeenranta, Finland

Viewing leadership from a systemic perspective

10

WILLIAM TATE

OBJECTIVES

- To present a whole-systems approach to leadership and its improvement that addresses the question: 'How can the organization best consider its own leadership needs, and ensure that appropriate leadership is applied, so that the organization is better led as a whole?' (*Note:* This is very different from asking typical individual-based questions such as 'What qualities do leaders need?' and 'How can we develop better leaders?')

- To shift the focus towards developing the organization's leadership process, and intervening to ensure appropriate leadership is applied in practice, recognizing the collective leadership culture.

- To clarify assumptions, models and theories that underpin the use of organization development (OD)-based leadership interventions that are aligned with challenges, once we can see and understand the contexts as complex systems.

Introduction

Organizations have to respond to changing moods, new ideas, discoveries and emerging disciplines. Things happening in their environment matter to leaders, including – but not limited to – those that directly comment on the leadership process. But what is ephemeral fad and what is here to stay? Language is not immune from fashion. New words can help managers think afresh, exchange ideas, even see their roles differently. The buzzwords *systems*, *whole systems*, *systemic* and *holistic* have entered the organization lexicon. Take leadership in the UK's National Health Service (NHS) and Sir Robert Francis's Public Inquiry into the Mid Staffordshire NHS Foundation Trust failure. His report resounded with 'system' words, using them like stents to free up the flow of meaning in a sclerotic body (*HSJ*, 2015).

Systems jargon is not simply new language in ideas that were first bottled long ago. The 'new' sciences of systems thinking and complexity are reaching parts of bureaucratic bodies previously occluded by comfortingly familiar, but out-of-date, assumptions about what makes organizations effective. Coming under the microscope is the long-dominant, individual-centric view of management. The alternative systems lens through which to magnify the world – including the world of leadership – is now coming into sharper view. Extending the NHS theme, the contrasted quotes below illustrate the change:

> *Yesterday:* If Florence Nightingale were carrying her lamp through the corridors of the NHS today she would almost certainly be searching for the people in charge. (Griffiths Report on NHS: DHS, 1983)

> *Today:* If Florence Nightingale were walking NHS wards today, she would be looking beyond them: out into general practice; into community services; into the private and voluntary sectors; and into social care. She would be looking for the other leaders who would help her make her wards work better. For it has been clear for many years that the NHS cannot provide the best outcomes and experience for patients – and indeed cannot solve its own problems – alone... Among those to whom Florence Nightingale would also be looking are patients. (The Future of NHS Leadership Report: *HSJ*, 2015)

Among shifts hinted at here are from one leader to many, from elites to shared leadership, from personalization of the leader to the activity of leadership, from autocratic styles to more democratic ones, from simple structures to complex relationships and partnerships, and from one-sided delivery to co-creating solutions. Over time, leaders and leadership adapt because their surroundings are continually changing – including the workplace, society, economics and technology.

In Florence Nightingale's era, if we wanted to find out about leadership we would expect to find the answer in the leader. In that conception, leadership is a property of the individual leader (usually senior managers when taking a lead). We are slowly becoming aware that most of the clues to leadership – what it is, why it is seen as failing in a given instance, what is needed, and what breathes life into it – are to be found in the organization context, in the system that surrounds 'leaders'. Seen like this, leadership is a property of the organization. It has its own collective leadership culture, to which managers belong and conform.

From this perspective the leadership activity being played out in the organization can be mapped, studied, managed and improved as a system, not simply applied *to* a system by an individual leader who sees the system as 'out there'. And what is true of leadership per se is equally true of leadership development activities and programmes. Much leadership development activity is still trapped in the old way of thinking rather than being inherently linked with its environment.

The metaphor of the fish tank and the fish

Most employment policies and development practices target individual managers. Such individuals are assumed to be in control of their job – the system doesn't receive much consideration. Yet a better analogy is that managers are all at sea, subject to powerful system waves over which they have little control.

So what do we see if we liken the organization and its people to a fish tank? The matter of how clean, clear, safe and nutritious the system is affects whether the occupants shine in front of interested parties. The fish exist in a complex ecosystem. Bigger and hungrier fish have a say too. But there are other things going on.

When we become more observant we notice how good swimmers some are, who are the star fish, the personal favourites, and who are the less glamorous supporting cast. We observe pecking orders (to mix the metaphors) and detritus. We see species whose job is to clear up the mess at the bottom, and those who service the hygiene needs of those 'higher up' and keep their image clean. We notice fish that compete for attention and favours. We may also sense fear, wariness and caution as the fish keep looking over their shoulder (in a manner of speaking), seeking hiding places from the sharks. There are some fish we rarely see.

Translating the metaphor into organization language

How individual fish swim is akin to competency. Show-offs are good at managing their image. Personal favourites remind us of the dangers of the halo effect: those who look good get more than their fair share of credit and their weaknesses are overlooked. The food chain represents the hierarchical power structure and struggles for ascendancy. As we look up at the less attractive side of those who are climbing the career ladder we are reminded that much of the mess and toxins is emitted by the bigger 'fish'.

Shoals tell us that some people find safety in numbers, combining their strength with others if they are to survive and get their fair share. The range of species reminds us of silos, turf/territory disputes, no-go areas, and in- and out-groups. Some 'fish' are more prepared than others to raise their head above the parapet (mixing metaphors again), while others lie low and try not to be noticed, or they pretend to be busy when they have little to do. Some prefer to be big fish in a small pond, and others prefer the reverse. Some appear to glide effortlessly while paddling furiously out of sight – like the serene swan.

There is food for good behaviour. There are predators, bullies and gangs. There are big fish and small fry. There are acolytes and mischief makers. Rules, protocol, bureaucracy and injunctions try to create order out of chaos but achieve little. A murkiness hangs over the place, making it difficult to see ahead and navigate the system. There's an official and an unofficial feel to the place, things that are rational and other things that are dark and in the shadow. There are some things that are 'undiscussables'. Political undercurrents lie just below the calm surface.

We notice these things if we have developed the ability to see the organization as a whole system. Yet rarely do managers focus on the quality of the fish tank and what surrounds the fish: they mostly notice individual fish and become fixated on them. But if the water is toxic, the fish suffer. If there is no movement in the water, it will be deprived of life-giving oxygen, will stagnate and develop a cloudy bloom, making it difficult for fish to see ahead. Wise owners do not blame the fish for their poor performance. They do not take the fish out from time to time to give them a spot of training, tell them to smarten up and look more lively, and then plop them back in the same dirty water. Instead they clean the tank.

Cleaning the tank is the real work

Toxins arise from natural, accidental or deliberate causes, and from various internal and external sources. The law of entropy captures the natural progression of decay, degeneration and growing disorder that besets any organism. Renewal activity can attempt to recreate order and clean conditions (Tate, 2009a: 187–202). It may also help with unnatural causes, accidental or deliberate. However, as Bettridge and Whiteley (2013) point out, the more pervasive toxins emanate from less tangible external influences, including economic theory and assumptions about what makes for operational efficiency. These too are part of the enveloping system in which people swim. What to some are desirable features may, to others, produce too comfortable a working climate. To some bosses, a fearful work environment is toxic, while to others it is necessary if people are to work hard. Amazon, for example, has been criticized for electronically tagging employees (*New York Times*, 2015). The most powerful toxins can infect a whole organization culture and damage a business's reputation. Differing values – often more McGregor's Theory X than Theory Y concerning employees' assumed motivators – find their echo within the management hierarchy.

The metaphor draws attention to the relationship between the fish and their manager, with colleagues, the culture and all else that surrounds them. It raises questions about the organization's design, operation and management that go deeper than the climate and nourishing the fish. The 'fish tank' that is the organization needs to be understood as a system, one that offers scope for improvement if the 'fish' are to be able to see their way around, handle the political currents, enjoy themselves, feel safe and secure, and deliver what owners want. Questions prompted include:

1 What risks are people taking when they exercise personal leadership?
2 How can leadership be more widely distributed?
3 How can the hierarchy work more effectively?
4 What does no one dare talk about?
5 Where can feedback channels be improved?

(*Note:* The above section is an edited extract taken from Tate, 2013b.)

> ### Suggested action: Responsibility for the fish tank
>
> - Learn to notice the water, to analyse, value and manage the water as much as the fish; don't look through/past it.
>
> - Appreciate that it is healthy water that gives fish life.
>
> - Stop blaming the fish when their performance fails to delight.
>
> - Don't take the fish out for a spot of training to smarten them up, then drop them back in the same dirty water.
>
> - Recognize that fixing the fish doesn't fix a fish tank that's become smelly (unless it's the biggest fish that get fixed).

Seeing challenges as system contexts for interventions

Reflect on the myriad ill-health problems facing large organizations. Think about their challenges and manifestations, not just in the NHS, but in all public services, institutions, companies like banks and supermarkets, governments, global business, even the planet itself. Once you see things in terms of systems, you begin to see them everywhere. You question how you were previously thinking and what you were previously seeing. This is brought out in an extract of a conversation between Matthew Taylor (Chief Executive of the Royal Society of Arts) and Steve Hilton (former Director of Strategy for Prime Minister David Cameron) (RSA, 2015):

> *Taylor:* I have no difficulty with an argument that says that what matters is not human nature so much as the structures in which we find ourselves. This isn't about good guys and bad guys; it is about the way that the systems affect us.

> *Hilton:* Generally, I think people want to be kind and treat others in a decent way. When you end up in a system that gets too big and bureaucratic and removed from that, people are unable to behave in a 'human' way. The systems do not allow them to do that.

The systems mindset illuminates a complaints call centre, an overflowing jail, a shortage of affordable homes, a fractious company board, a backlog of court cases, a money-laundering bank, a lavish reward policy, a G7 summit, Fifa's football governance, child obesity, a polluted ocean. If people are involved in its evolving and complex form, then it's a living ecosystem with multiple interdependencies, much like nature, responding to its environment. This is hardly new; the origins of systems thinking go back over 100 years:

> There used to be 'lack of system', now we have 'the system', that is, every little detail has to go up and down five or six levels of the hierarchy, a mountain of paper is generated... I am now extremely weak and am gradually conking out to the greater glory of 'the system'. (Georgy Chicherin, a workaholic foreign minister in the first Bolshevik government, writing to Leon Trotsky in the hope that he would share such discontent with Vladimir Lenin, the architect of the Russian Revolution, one of the most remarkable, surprising and audacious change management projects in history. (CIPD, 2015: 39–43)

As this Soviet example shows – albeit on a world scale – some systems have or are problems, some have failed or are failing, and some can simply be better understood, managed and led towards improvement. The challenge before us is to see that what we experience in our own organizations, and in aspects of everyday life, become clearer when we understand them as systems. Systems offer an explanation and a way forward. In the same manner, social workers in child-protection work are trained to understand that the family system is the route to understanding a dysfunctional child's behaviour. Leadership is akin to a child of its parent system; that is, leadership behaviour can be traced back to its organization context.

Stuck systems

Systems become stuck and require action to unstick them. This is also true of their subsystems. In the above example the subsystem of leadership was stuck. The process of unsticking began in 1985 with Mikhail Gorbachev's bold reform programme of *perestroika* (restructuring) and *glasnost* (openness).

CASE STUDY   Michael Brown's legacy

Michael Brown, an unarmed black teenager, was shot and killed on 9 August 2014 by Darren Wilson, a white police officer, in Ferguson, Missouri, prompting protests and riots. On 24 November, the St Louis County prosecutor announced that a grand jury decided not to indict Mr Wilson. The announcement set off another wave of protests. In March 2015 the US Justice Department called on Ferguson to overhaul its criminal justice system, declaring that the city had engaged in constitutional violations.

Following an investigation, a scathing report laid bare 'the systemic bias' and abuse that pervades Ferguson's police department and municipal court system. This included Ferguson's justice system acting as a 'collection agency': 'Ferguson has allowed its focus on revenue generation to fundamentally compromise the role of Ferguson's municipal court,' the report said. The court primarily uses its judicial authority as the means to compel the payment of fines and fees that advance the city's financial interests.

Minor municipal code violations turned into multiple arrests, jail time, and payments that exceeded the cost of the original ticket many times over. A new judge, Donald McCullin, appointed in June 2015, ordered that all arrest warrants issued in the city before 31 December be withdrawn. People who have had driver's licences suspended will be able to obtain them and start driving again.

'Ferguson unrest: Judge withdraws pre-2015 arrest warrants', BBC News online, 26 August 2015)

If leadership is the problem, is it also the solution? If so, by whom and of what kind? As long as anyone can remember there has been the lack of a consensus over a leadership approach that responds to complex challenges. Conventional leadership development programmes don't provide the answer. The complexity is more apparent now and better understood than ever it was, requiring us to rethink the contribution of leadership and addressing such questions as:

- How can we balance the individual and the system?
- How do systems relate to leadership development?
- How can systems stop the scandalous waste of leadership capability?

- How do systems affect managers' competency and use of frameworks?

- How does a systems approach improve governance?

(For deeper study and help with such questions, readers may access the Institute for Systemic Leadership website (**www.systemicleadershipinstitute.org**) for books, articles and papers listed under this chapter's references.)

Suggested action: Seeing the system challenges

- Identify system challenges that you face that are stuck.

- Reflect on where leadership is the problem and where it is the solution.

- Build a consensus for a systemic leadership approach.

System blindness and system sight

Almost 100 years ago the prescient Mary Parker Follett realized that organization performance needs to factor in the way relationships affect collective performance: 'We should notice, too, what is sometimes forgotten, that in the social situation two processes always go on together: the adjustment of man and man, and the adjustment of man and the situation' (Parker Follett, 1924: 122).

Echoing Follett in 1936, Kurt Lewin, the founding father of social psychology, propounded his view in the heuristic B = f(P, E). An individual's *Behaviour* is a *function* of that *Person*'s personality, competence, training, etc and his or her *Environment*. Given today's talk of 'skills' shortages, it is salutary to be reminded of Lewin's largely forgotten dictum on how performance is delivered (Tate, 2013b). With a nod to the nascent discipline of systems thinking, Lewin pleaded: 'It is necessary to find methods of representing person and environment in common terms as parts of one situation' (Lewin, 1936: 12).

We now accept that the system is a substantial determinant of organization performance when compared with individuals' contributions. W Edwards Deming, a quality and productivity systems specialist who came to embrace the systems perspective, recognized this:

> Placing blame on workforces who are only responsible for 15 per cent of mistakes where the system designed by management is responsible for 85 per cent of the unintended consequences... A manager needs to understand that the performance of anyone is governed largely by the system that he works in... it is the structure of the organization rather than the employees, alone, which holds the key to improving the quality of output. (Deming, 1986: 23–4)

The social psychology phenomenon known as the 'fundamental attribution error' explains the above and is running unrecognized in the background of most performance and behaviour issues.

The fundamental attribution error

Social psychologists speak of the 'fundamental attribution error' – the tendency for people to overemphasize personality-based explanations for behaviour, while underemphasizing the role and power of situational influences. The consequence is that people assume that what a person does is based more on what kind of person he or she is, rather than the social and environmental forces at work on that person. (Tate, 2009a: 31)

In looking for explanations, reviewers of performance attribute successes or shortfalls to the reviewee's disposition and don't sufficiently consider situational factors (put very crudely: 'all fish, no fish tank'). To address perceived deficits, reviewers seek remedies in the individual more than in the situation. Compounding this effect, consideration of situational factors is made even less likely because of the distorting effect of actor-observer bias; that is, reviewees take situational factors more into account than does the reviewer, and more than would the reviewer as an explanation for his or her own behaviour in similar circumstances. The presence of hierarchy in the relationship further distorts any gap in viewpoints. While the reviewer is given the power to judge others, his or her own behaviour is a direct factor in the relevant performance.

Discomfort with systems thinking

Some people have an aversion to systems and the language of systems. Is the system really real, they question? There are system deniers, those who claim that systems exist only in the imagination – systems cannot be seen or touched. It seems odd to them that systems are talked about as though they have personality and exhibit human-like behaviour, can take decisions and act. For them, systems lack independent agency; all that exists is conversations. It is true that systems are indeed a mental construct, a way people have found of talking about an intangible concept. But systems are in good company; they are as real as, say, hierarchical power, which is another construct. The truth is that we really do experience and feel the power of 'the system'. Ergo, it exists.

The word 'system' is used in several ways: sometimes on a grand scale (eg the NHS system), and sometimes to refer to more local and tangible work arrangements and processes: systems may be macro and micro. The word is also commonly used for IT, and systems are related to culture. But culture says more about values, while system says more about how work gets done, how parts relate to each other and to the whole. The system transcends company boundaries, whereas culture usually refers to a particular organization, profession or other subset. The system seems the more tangible concept of the two: easier to diagnose what changes one could make to the system to bring about improvements, whereas knowing where to begin to attempt to change the culture seems more daunting. People also find it easier to blame the system than the culture.

Systematic is not systemic. These words are frequently confused. A common mistake is claiming that a deep-seated problem is systematic, when systemic is the correct word; see Table 10.1. Given these definitions, it is easy to see why organization failings are systemic rather than systematic. In muddling these words – as many do – thinking becomes confused too. The mistake is easily

TABLE 10.1 Systemic and systematic

Systemic	Located in the system or having an explanation that relates to how a system works
Systematic	Anticipated, well-planned, having clear steps, rational, organized and measured

explained: everyone grows up knowing what 'systematic' means, but for many the word 'systemic' is less familiar, barely understood. Yet the words have almost opposite meanings. When Sir Ian Blair (then the Metropolitan Police Force's Commissioner) tried to explain the fatal shooting of Jean Charles de Menezes at Stockwell underground station in 2005, he described the killing as 'systematic' (Tate, 2009a: 237, 254). In the United States in 2015, shootings of black youngsters by white policemen were examined from a 'systemic' perspective, as we saw in the Ferguson case. Similarly, the frantic scenes at the French port of Calais in 2015 of migrants from north Africa seeking a better life in Europe can be viewed and understood through a systems lens.

There are also various categories of system that need to be seen and understood separately. At one level are 'designed abstract systems', designed to serve some explanatory purpose (Checkland, 1999: 111). Quite different are 'human activity systems', observable in the world and more or less consciously ordered in wholes as a result of some underlying purpose or mission. A key distinction is between 'hard systems', which assume that the world is a set of systems that can be engineered; and 'soft systems', which assume that the world is problematic, but that the process of enquiry into these situations can be organized as a system.

The myth of predictability and control

Managers' training and education place a high value on things being conducted rationally, logically and analytically. There is an implication that managers can predict and control things and deliver planned results accordingly. Managers are taught to value and liken the organization to a smooth-running machine. So they come to believe that what they do in their job should be systematic, and that it is their job to create order and impose solutions, as in the example below:

CASE STUDY   Banking on truthfulness and compliance

Barclays Bank's multimillion-pound academy to train over 2,000 staff in truthfulness and compliance is well-intentioned but may be misguided ('Barclays school to teach staff to avoid scandals', 4 July 2014). The individuals being singled out for retraining are neither naturally wicked nor ignorant of the truth and company rhetoric; they are responding to the way hidden forces in the system in which they work operate. These forces encourage particular behaviour, often contrary to espoused company values and policies. Instead of training, Barclays would do better to understand the way the system works its wicked way on individuals. Without such an understanding at the system level, the bank will drop retrained 'fish' back in the toxic 'fish tank' water and find they swim in the same old way. It is the water that needs refreshing more than the fish.

The rise of 'wicked' problems

Politicians' piecemeal attempts to manage such situations sometimes fail because they confuse complex situations with complicated ones. And they lack a systemic understanding of a complex situation, especially the more acute 'wicked' variety (Grint, 2008). They behave as though the issues are systematic. They think the problems are linear, linking cause and effect, but complex social situations are non-linear. Outcomes from managers' action are often unpredictable. Unintended consequences are common.

In system terms things are said to be 'complex' where the interaction between the parts produces emergent effects that cannot be predicted from those parts. This is especially true of social systems because people's views, experience, values, prejudices, thoughts and ideas, etc and their likely effect on others when interacting are not predictable. By contrast, things are said to be 'complicated' when they consist of many parts, but that with enough expertise or computer processing power, they are amenable to being solved and the right answer found. Grint explains that wicked problems:

- are complex, not complicated;
- have interdependencies that mean they cannot be solved in isolation;
- sit outside a single hierarchy;
- lack a clear definition of what success looks like;
- have no clear stopping point;
- may be intransigent: we may need to learn to live with them;
- contain symptoms of deep division;
- have better or worse development rather than right or wrong solutions;

- require political collaboration rather than scientific processes;
- call for leadership rather than management.

Wicked problems are contrasted with 'tame problems', which may be complicated but not complex. Tame problems lend themselves to known and uncontested solutions; they can be solved by tried and tested good practice, and sometimes by best-practice solutions if the problem is simple and one mind is sufficient. Wicked problems on the other hand require leadership; they necessarily involve many stakeholders and their viewpoints, competing interests and expertise in tackling them. The intractability increases when the solution further fuels the problem, as for example in Germany's generous solution to the problem of large numbers of Syrian asylum seekers in 2015. This solution may lead to more refugees turning up on Germany's doorstep as word spreads, so the problem may recur.

As today's Florence Nightingale hinted earlier, trends in society, economies and modern structures are shaken up by complexity-inducing forces such as globalization, multiculturalism, outsourcing, and cross-boundary partnerships. These push an increasing number of today's organizational leadership challenges in the direction of wicked problems. They call for a multi-experience and multi-perspective response where the task is to ask appropriate questions and engage in collaboration (Tate, 2013b).

Suggested action: Developing system sight

- Embrace the new vocabulary.

- Remember that a manager's performance is a function of personality and environment.

- Recognize the 85/15 per cent split between the system/individual that accounts for mistakes.

- Allow the system to enter the room and to be considered in managers' performance discussions.

Challenging the traditional, individual-centric model

Most people instinctively associate leadership with leaders, especially when bemoaning the lack of it. These leaders are individuals – usually managers but not always – who somehow 'do' leadership. Most of the leadership literature vests leadership in the person of the individual leader, and this is equally true of so-called 'leadership development' (actually usually *leader* development). This focus leads to a preoccupation with the ideal leader's qualities and behaviours, devoid of organization context and relationships. It leads to singular models of leadership for a given organization ('the way we do leadership in XYZ'). The task in this chapter is to break with that tradition and open readers' eyes to something more that is going on in organizations when we think and talk systemically about 'leadership' activity. This amounts to a paradigm shift:

> The familiar approach overlooks key aspects of reality about the application of leadership in an organization. Crucial among these is that a manager's leadership activity is not pursued by individuals acting alone, confidently, trusted, and free of restraint or political interference. Leadership is foremost a social activity, an empathic as much as a cognitive pursuit, one conducted through relationships. Moreover, leadership wholly depends on interacting not just with colleagues and other people, but also with other organizational things. These various interconnecting pieces are part of a complex leadership puzzle located in the manager's immediate environment, in what goes on around and between managers. (Tate, 2013b)

If we accept that leadership is a property of the organization as well as of the individual, then responsibility and agency have a dependent, symbiotic relationship. Individuals' leadership impacts upon the organization. But that system also impacts upon leadership activity. In particular, the system limits how much disturbance it will accept, thereby acting as a constraint on leadership's power.

According to Hernez-Broome and Hughes (2004): 'There is a distinct shifting of emphasis in the academic literature away from seeing leadership as the characteristic of certain individuals... towards a view of leadership that exists only in relationships between individuals.' That recognition of relationship is key. It leads to the question: 'What form of leadership will replace the "heroic" models at the beginning of the 21st century?' (CIPD, 2006). According to Zheltoukhova (2014), 'While the capability of individuals is growing through training and experience, their ability to lead is not always realized, where an organization's context is not set up to meet the need for leadership.'

The heroic leader stands in the way

The heroic model of leadership has had a long life. It continued to hold traction in the 1980s–1990s, despite 'great man' theories having been debunked in the 1950s (Gronn, 1995: 14–27). A consequence is that among older generations a familiar siren call remained: a strong leader was needed 'to sort them out'. But the 'death of deference' makes Generation Y less in thrall to the 'strong leader'. There will always be leaders whom we consider to be wise and experienced, and whose judgement and decisions we value and respond to. But that aside, the trend away from powerful, know-it-all leaders who tell us what to do ushers in more democratic, self-management, peer-based models, as well as systems-based approaches to distributed leadership.

The hero model is not simply outdated: a powerful leader sucks attention and energy upwards and away from what is happening in the system. But that system exists come what may. Whereas the hero is a choice, the system is not. It is whether you pay attention to it that is the choice. And the hero presents a block to managers focusing on what is needed to improve the way the system works, and their involvement and responsibility in that. As we saw with the fish tank, individuals can be a distraction, taking our eye to the nodes rather than what is going on around and between the nodes.

Post-millennial research and new models of leadership are extending what are meant by 'relationship' and 'interconnectedness', and where they are located. We are not simply talking better teamwork here. A systems view takes the discussion much deeper. Systems-based leadership ways of thinking and acting are becoming an essential part of the response to the CIPD's question. 'Whole systems' interventions are gaining popularity. The leadership question becomes: 'How can an organization best understand, expand, release, promote, improve, combine and apply leadership capability suited to its needs?' (Tate, 2013b).

This presents a challenge for the HR profession, one as yet hardly recognized: does its people-focused brief stand in the way of accepting the system's role in organization behaviour? Even more uncomfortable: are people-oriented professionals especially vulnerable to system blindness? Do some see systems where others see only people (Baron-Cohen, 2003), and regard people as the source of organization problems and of the solutions too? Hence the predominance of training as the assumed answer – and its marginal effect.

Suggested action: Challenging the traditional, individual-centric model

- Come to see leadership as a property of the organization/system.

- Recognize that leadership is manifested in and through relationships.

- Understand why the heroic model of leadership is necessarily under pressure.

- Reflect on how the HR profession is challenged by post-millennial research.

Challenging the status quo

A frequent issue is a company's treatment of whistle-blowers, so often a case of 'playing the man and not the ball', to use the football analogy of foul play.

Dr Kim Holt was forced from her job as the designated doctor for children in care at St Ann's Hospital in Haringey, North London, in 2007. She and three other doctors had written to management warning that staff shortages and poor record keeping would lead to a tragedy. Shortly afterwards that fear was realized with the widely reported death of Baby Peter Connelly ('Baby P'), where scapegoating featured strongly, especially at the hands of politicians and others trying to protect their own reputations:

> People attacked me, but actually they would have attacked anyone who challenged that culture, who challenged the system... What is wrong is the cover-up. It is the cover-up that needs to be held to account.
>
> It was only very late on that I realized that what I was doing was showing leadership. You can be a manager and not be a leader. And you can be both. And leaders have particular qualities – very strong values, and having a very clear vision of where things should be, where we should be trying to go.
>
> (Dr Kim Holt, in Timmins, 2015: 49–53)

Dr Holt's experience in raising concerns, speaking up and campaigning for a 'just culture' led to her being given clinical leadership awards. That is another pattern frequently experienced in the life of whistle-blowers. Once the system has failed to crush them, and once cleared of guilt, they are often lauded.

Overcoming homeostasis

There is a further dynamic when it comes to challenging the status quo. Those who have most authority to agree to change are usually those who are most vested in the extant model, values and beliefs. They have the most to lose. In any case, even wise managers who can overcome personal hesitation, or who are under orders, have no choice but to work with the system to change the system. This process of homeostasis applies a natural brake to the business of attempting change.

Where the purpose of an intervention is simply to change the way managers think, this may have an infectious effect on colleagues. The argument here is that the tendency to revert to past habits and wilt under pressure to maintain the status quo does not apply to thinking to the same extent that it does to behaviour and organization change. Thinking may appear less threatening. Moreover, once you have learnt to see all living things as systems, and the scales have fallen from your eyes, there is mentally no going back.

Suggested action: Challenging the status quo

- Keep checking whether you are defaulting to an individual-centric position, and not seeing the system.

- Help your managers change the way they think.

- Strengthen your connections before going out on a limb.

Understanding where failure has systemic roots

Leadership failures receive wide media coverage. In the UK, who has not heard of such scandals as the BBC over Jimmy Savile, or South Yorkshire police at Hillsborough?

Group behaviour is not simply the sum of the behaviour of individuals. It has its own institutional life and responds to other impulses... all the groups we belong to – from family to nation – are subject to compulsions that may well lead to more unrestrained selfishness, more covering up of inconvenient truths, than we would ever display in our personal relationships. (Canon Dr Alan Billings, 'Thought for the Day' on the subject of the Hillsborough Enquiry, BBC Radio 4, 24 September 2012)

Systemic failures do not just reflect the failure of individual leaders in those organizations: they are also major failures of leadership policy and process. In the Hillsborough disaster it comes as no surprise that even the subsequent investigation of the leadership failure was itself an example of systemic failure when police collusion and falsification of evidence went undiscovered and led to a miscarriage of justice, leading to a fresh public inquiry.

In cases like these, the public most want to know *who* failed. They want to see accountability. They want someone in the dock. Yet the legal system itself fails us here, because systems cannot be found guilty; only individuals can. Corporate manslaughter is the closest it gets, and attempts to prosecute are rarely successful. Of the 141 cases opened since the law changed in 2009, only three have resulted in convictions. And even then it is the company and not the system that is in the dock. It is difficult to cross-examine a system.

Following the capsizing of Costa Concordia in 2012, it was the character of Captain Francesco Schettino that was under the spotlight before he was found guilty of manslaughter. Little attention was given to the cruise company's policy of encouraging its ships to go close inshore to give a public 'salute' to past captains (Tate, 2013a). The captain had a relationship going on there, a relationship with the company's head office and its public relations policy.

CASE STUDY   Drowning in bureaucracy

Systems constrain individuals when attempting to take on a leadership role. In a well-reported case, police officers were prevented by regulations from rescuing a drowning child in shallow water; they could only stand by while they waited for fully trained and equipped fire and rescue service officers to arrive. Several factors explain what is going on here:

1 An organization that is risk-averse.

2 Close radio contact between the uniformed police and the control room about the situation they find themselves in.

3 A bank of controllers whose advice to officers is governed by a manual of standard operating procedures.

4 A perceived risk of a police officer (or spouse) losing compensation rights if injured or killed in an incident while acting in breach of standard operating procedures.

5 A quasi-military structure where the first commandment is that the hierarchy must be preserved.

Combined, these factors may stop the police from entering the water.

In strongly hierarchical organizations – as Lawrence Peter (of 'The Peter Principle' fame) put it – 'super-competence in an employee is more likely to result in dismissal than promotion, a feature of poor organizations, which cannot handle the disruption. A super-competent employee violates the first commandment' (Peter and Hull, 1969: 47). The deadly combination of factors in the policing system makes it difficult for an otherwise courageous officer to use personal discretion to waive the rules and use initiative. In the public mind this looks like a lack of leadership, but it is the system that is faulty. (Tate, 2013a)

Widening the system relationships

While leadership is a relationship, an analysis of failures shows that the relationship is not just between people (leaders and their followers), but between leaders and *things*, such as policies, structure, protocols and culture. Other relationships in an organization exist between, say, governance and operations, as in Stafford Beer's Viable Systems Model (Hoverstadt, 2008). The relationship may cross multiple system boundaries, as the Baby P case showed (Tate, 2009b). So, more than skill, and more than leaders, it is usually the *system* of leadership that is found wanting and in need of understanding, examination and improvement.

Too often, the individual thinking pattern is limited to finding and fixing broken parts ('reductionism'), and then reassuring the public and shareholders. Earmarking individuals for retraining is especially popular, but may miss the (systemic) point. The knee-jerk mantra 'lessons will be learnt' will be heard – generally stronger in rhetoric than substance. What is usually missing is a deep understanding of how the organization – and indeed how leadership itself – works as a system.

Complexity and risk avoidance

All organizations are social systems. Complexity has always been present, but not recognized as such. Only recently have we had the benefit of complexity science to help us understand and respond to it. The risk is that leaders (and HR) ignore this complexity and try to manage people as though they are more known, more alike and more predictable than they really are. Some managers ignore the fact that people talk among themselves and have views about work that have impulses that form elsewhere. Managers know nothing of what is going on in people's minds. Yet, in the traditional model, organizations pretend that these forces can be controlled through bureaucratic mechanisms such as behavioural frameworks designed to ensure that people comply with someone else's assumed best-practice model. Unwisely, this restricts variety (as well as initiative and innovation) among managers.

Requisite variety

Expressed in layman's terms, Ashby's Law of Requisite Variety (Tate, 2009a: 129–30) says that, to survive and thrive, the management resources of a system need to contain as much variety as that which it confronts in the challenges it faces from its environment, otherwise it will be overwhelmed by its environment. As early systems pioneers put it, 'only variety can absorb variety' (Hoverstadt, 2008: 47). Many HR policies and practices fly in the face of that law.

Andy Haldane, chief economist at the Bank of England, recalls leadership practices in which messengers of the impending crisis were systematically disciplined or dismissed, probably throughout the entire banking industry (Saunders, 2015). A powerful leader may intentionally suppress variety if it poses an uncomfortable threat to his own confidently held worldview and his personal authority. HBOS chief executive James Crosby's 2004 dismissal of Paul Moore, his percipient group head of regulatory risk turned whistle-blower, was a tragic case in point in the run-up to the 2008 banking crisis.

Besides the risk aspect of neglecting the messy realities of complexity, there is an opportunity here that often goes begging: that is, the emergent possibilities that open up in the interconnections between people. Taking leadership as an example, leadership is an emergent property of a relationship. The risk is that organizations believe that leadership can be adequately specified, studied and worked on via the individual alone. It cannot.

Emergence

This refers to organization behaviour (good or bad) that arises as a property of interaction in the system; behaviour that is not present, observable or obtainable in any of the parts alone. To take a simple example, speed is an emergent property of a car, but speed cannot be found in any of the parts of the car if it is taken apart (Hoverstadt, 2008: 303).

On a similar basis, since leadership is relational, it follows that action, decisions, ideas, energy, etc that arise when two people engage (or any two or more elements engage) is described as being 'emergent'. So we cannot take people away and train them to be leaders and know what will happen if and when they apply their new-found skills since the outcome (and what the organization is looking for from them) depends on the nature of their interaction with other people and with other elements in the system.

CASE STUDY   'Why am I surrounded by idiots?'

A FTSE 100 chief executive once said to his HR Director, 'Why am I surrounded by idiots? Will someone take them away and train them to be leaders?'

When people look out at what surrounds them, they tend to see things that are 'out there', beyond them and beyond their own responsibility and culpability. They are correspondingly blind to issues that are 'in here', either within themselves or happening in the space between them and others. In this case, the chief executive was blind to those alternative perspectives. The CEO placed all the fault in the other party: '*they* are not leaders'. He was overlooking his own role in appointing them, agreeing their goals, appraising their performance, and awarding their bonuses. More important, he was 50 per cent of the relationship he had with each of them.

Leadership is conducted in and through relationships. The leadership manifested is a function of both parties, not just the person being complained about. It is not the responsibility of one party or the other. It is a product of both acting together; it springs from the nature and quality of the connection that they experience in their relationship.

The leadership behaviour is both unpredictable and different from that of either of them acting independently. And the boss's behaviour will be different with each director, and the director's behaviour would be different with a different chief executive. And their behaviour with their chief executive will be different when all directors are together as a management board than when they are alone with the boss. In other words, the behaviour is contextual. Being sent away to be trained to be a leader misses the point. This becomes obvious once you see these relationships as a system, each a different system.

(This real-life situation with the above-quoted CEO has been developed into an imagined conversation to show how its resolution might play out under three possible scenarios, each based on where the particular HR adviser is coming from: a) a training and development mindset, b) an HR mindset, and c) a systems mindset; see **http://www.systemicleadershipinstitute.org/ resources/case-studies/**)

Suggested action: Complex problems and systemic failures

- When something or someone fails, first assume that it is a system issue rather than an individual to be found and blamed.

- When the challenges are complex, bring a range of diverse experiences and perspectives to bear.

- Shun the temptation to believe that a powerful individual will solve problems that no one else has managed to do.

- Don't design arrangements that are more complex than they need to be.

- Embrace and apply systems thinking principles.

Levels of systemic leadership thinking and practice

A spectrum covers systems, management and leadership, and how ideas are developed, taken up and applied. The strands of thought cover two related fields of interest. They address the latest understanding, structure and nature of organizations and work. Running alongside this is interest in the future of management and leadership, preferably linked to the first preoccupation. Common ground comes in the 'new' sciences, especially systems, complexity and chaos theory.

As part of this, and sometimes as a counterweight to the individual-leader perspective, more organization-focused leadership models have been appearing in the last 20 years. These are sometimes used as the basis for leadership development programmes. Some models recognize complex adaptive systems and complex responsive systems, with a leadership reply offered by system(s) leadership, whole-system(s) leadership, systemic leadership, and so on.

Individuals are of course agents, and thankfully many stand out and make their mark as leaders; but in the systems view it is ultimately a well-running integrated system that delivers outcomes and results for customers. Organizations succeed or fail as systems, and a key leadership responsibility is to optimize and continually try to improve that system. The territory falls into four broad levels in the challenge to traditional thinking.

Level 1

At the first level, some protagonists are content simply to highlight the importance of considering the impact that the individual leader has on the organization; ie more than leading people: also leading and changing the organization. This barely qualifies as systemic, though it uses the language and is offered as such by some consultancies.

Level 2

This viewpoint can be found in much of the public-sector literature on system(s) leadership and whole system(s) leadership. It implicitly accepts that an organization's services are delivered by systems more than by individuals acting independently. And systems need managing and leading by 'leaders', who it is said need to understand these things. So, these models include what individual managers (often in senior 'leadership' positions in the hierarchy) need to know and do if they are to succeed in leading and managing their organization as a system (for examples, see Timmins, 2015). Senge *et al* (2015) capture the need: 'The deep changes necessary to accelerate progress against society's most intractable problems require a unique type of leader – the system leader, a person who catalyses collective leadership.'

Such models remain at heart individual-centric, and the leadership talked about sounds heroic. Furthermore, research casts doubt on the assumed ability of a single leader to think outwardly in a systems way and also to display emotional intelligence in relationships (Goleman, 2013). Note too that the approach assumes that leadership is inherent in what these leaders do by virtue of their positional authority, as opposed to acts of personal leadership open to all.

Level 3

At a third level the ideas and theories are more advanced. The shift is towards understanding leadership as a property of the system, and itself a system. Besides helping leaders run big projects, we are interested in how whole organizations can live a different kind of leadership.

'While we all had our heads under the bonnet of the car trying to work out why we lost the election, these people jumped into the car and drove it off' (Andrew Rawnsley, the *Observer*, 6 September 2015, commenting on the campaign to elect a new leader of the UK Labour Party). This illustrates the easy temptation of reductionism compared with more imaginative holism. And it responds to the instinct to analyse rather than synthesize – breaking things down to find the broken parts or elements rather than bringing things together into new wholes. But note that action on developing elements remains a valid and necessary synthesizing activity, as Rawnsley pointed out: 'The MP for Islington North [Jeremy Corbyn] was alone among the candidates in putting on his campaign website a link to the £3 sign-up. The teams of all three of his rivals made a terrible mistake in not spotting how this would radically influence the race.'

Approaches at this level examine how the new sciences of systems thinking, allied with complexity and chaos theory, have the potential to fundamentally alter the purpose, role, shape, nature, possibilities and preoccupations of leaders and leadership, as well as of how organizations work and are viewed. Wheatley (1999) claims that the beginning of the 20th century heralded the end of the hegemony of Newtonian (ie reductionist) thinking: 'In the quantum world, relationships are not just interesting; to many physicists they are all there is to reality... The quantum world has demolished the concept of the unconnected individual' (pp 32–4). She points out that with relationships:

> we give up predictability and open up to potentials. None of us exists independent of our relationships with others. Different settings and people evoke some qualities from us and leave others dormant. In each of these relationships, we are different, new in some way.

According to Senge (1994: 25):

> In the realm of management and leadership, many people are conditioned to see our organizations as things rather than as patterns of interaction. We look for solutions that will 'fix problems' as if they are external and can be fixed without 'fixing' that which is within us that led to their creation.

Level 4

These ways of thinking tell us that human organizations have more in common with nature than has previously been understood and accepted. Nature's life path draws on natural processes for its own self-organization and management.

The Dutch company Buurtzorg (translating as 'neighbourhood care'), established in 2006 by Jos de Blok, is causing some commentators to take notice of the self-management movement. The company employs 9,000 community nurses, largely ex-state employees, who wanted greater freedom in how they manage patients, free of bureaucratic controls. The company now operates internationally (Laloux, 2013).

Suggested action: Levels of systemic leadership

- Learn more about systems thinking and complexity science and relate them to your own experience and daily practice.

- Consider where a problem requires both system and people skill sets (maybe in more than one person).

- Challenge your organization's present state of systems thinking development.

- Check out how systemically embedded providers' approaches really are.

Concluding thoughts

Once we reframe leadership in terms of the organization, and not just the individual leader, that role and relationship need managing on behalf of the employer, otherwise it won't happen. Leadership is a key organization resource, and resources need to be managed. In that sense – paradoxical as it may sound – the practice of systemic leadership needs managing (Tate, 2014), as this chapter has shown. Here are some meta questions:

- How does a systemic perspective change leadership's purpose?
- How does the language of systemic leadership change conversations?
- How can managers change the way they think about leadership and their own role in it?
- How can they keep this in the forefront of their minds, rather than react to things that come their way?
- How can governance become systemically driven?
- How can the process of accountability be robustly managed?
- What should systemic leaders focus their time and energy on?
- Where are the weakest links that are letting down the whole system?
- How can the organization get better at learning from its mistakes?
- How clear is it where responsibility lies for the healthy functioning of the system?

We are aiming for a model for managers to use, based on the principle that 'every good regulator of a system must be a model of that system'. In cybernetics this is known as the Conant–Ashby Theorem. It means that managers should have in mind an understanding of a relevant and effective model of the system they are attempting to manage. 'The manager's ability to manage any system or situation depends on how good their own model is. Without a relevant model a manager cannot manage' (Hoverstadt, 2008: 302–3).

Very few managers have a mental model of the system for which they hold responsibility. If they had, they would be better able to gauge the likely effect of their actions on the system. Instead, managers guess what affects what, announce forecasts and set targets, producing unintended consequences that someone then has to deal with. Without a systems appreciation, and lacking a view of (or indeed responsibility for) the whole system, pressurized managers may push stuff elsewhere with little thought about the consequences.

This echoes Gregory Bateson's admonition that 'We all cling fast to the illusion that we are capable of direct perception, uncoded and not mediated by epistemology' (Brockman, 1977). In other words, we need to know how we know. At the same time, managers need to be aware that they are themselves inside the system. Again quoting Bateson: 'We are not outside the ecology for which we plan – we are always and inevitably a part of it' (Bateson, 1973: 512).

Systems are nested. The manager has responsibility as a regulator of that part of the organization as a system for which he or she has responsibility. There is also the leadership (sub)system and its improvement. The points of advice below, coupled with the diagram of the leadership system (see Figure 10.1), constitute a partial model for the manager to have in mind as a 'regulator' of those systems:

- Concentrate on the whole and the interconnections between the parts.
- Focus on the system's purpose ahead of its processes and procedures.
- 'Look out' for things (synthesis) more than 'look into' things (analysis).
- See what is actually happening ahead of what needs to happen.
- Check what is going on in the organization by personal examination.
- Strengthen feedback loops.
- Understand, facilitate and value emergence.
- Be pulled by what the customer wants; hear the customer voice.
- Understand demand and respond to it (avoid provider-supply dominance).
- Make continual improvement of the system a prime goal of leadership.
- Consider all the players and actors, of which the organization is one.
- Become aware of natural oscillations and progress along a natural lifecycle.
- Stimulate and seek organizational learning.
- Consider practically how 'lessons will be learnt'.
- Embrace the edge of chaos as a necessary concomitant of improvement.
- Value and make the most of uncertainty, rather than espousing certainty.
- Understand the forces leading to entropy – the amount of disorder in any system.

FIGURE 10.1   Systemic leadership: a concept map

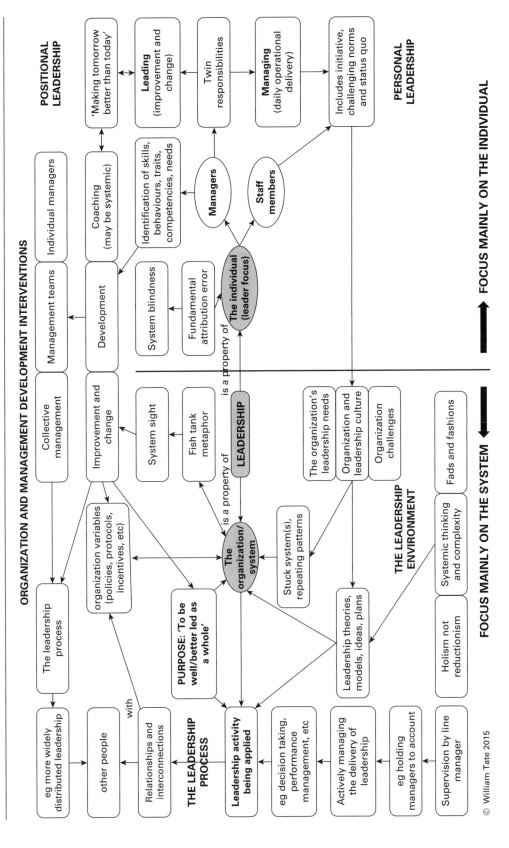

© William Tate 2015

References

Baron-Cohen, S (2003) They just can't help it, *The Guardian*, 17 April

Bateson, G (1973) *Steps to an Ecology of Mind*, The University of Chicago Press, Chicago, IL

Bettridge, N and Whiteley, P (2013) *New Normal, Radical Shift: Changing business and politics for a sustainable future*, Gower, Aldershot

Brockman, J (1977) *About Bateson: Essays on Gregory Bateson*, Penguin, Harmondsworth

Checkland, P (1999) *Systems Thinking, Systems Practice*, Wiley, Chichester

CIPD (2006) *Engaging Leadership* (report), Chartered Institute of Personnel and Development, London

CIPD (2015) Power struggle, *Work*, Chartered Institute of Personnel and Development, Summer, London

Deming, W E (1986) *Out of the Crisis*, MIT Press, Cambridge, MA

DHS (1983) *Griffiths Report on NHS*, Department of Health and Social Security, London

Francis, R (2010–13) *Francis Inquiry: Report of the Mid Staffordshire NHS Foundation Trust Public Inquiry, Volumes 1, 2 and 3*, The Stationery Office, Norwich

Goleman, D (2013) The focused leader, *Harvard Business Review*, December

Grint, K (2008) Wicked problems and clumsy solutions: The role of leadership, *Clinical Leader*, **1** (2), December

Gronn, P (1995) Greatness revisited: The current obsession with transformational leadership, *Leading and Managing*, **1** (1)

Hernez-Broome, G and Hughes, R L (2004) Leadership development: Past, present and future, *Human Resource Planning*, **27** (1), pp 24–32

Hoverstadt, P (2008) *The Fractal Organization*, Wiley, Chichester

HSJ (2015) Future of NHS leadership, *Health Service Journal*, Alastair McLellan, online issue dated 15 June 2015, accessed 3 November 2015 at: www.hsj.co.uk/leadership/future-of-nhs-leadership-inquiry

Laloux, F (2013) *Reinventing Organizations: A guide to creating organizations inspired by the next stage of human consciousness*, Nelson Parker, Brussels

Lewin, K (1936) *Principles of Topological Psychology*, McGraw-Hill, New York

New York Times (2015) Inside Amazon: Wrestling big ideas in a bruising workplace, 15 August

Parker Follett, M (1924) *Creative Experience*, Martino Fine Books, Eastford, CT

Peter, P and Hull, R (1969) *The Peter Principle: Why things always go wrong*, W Morrow, New York

RSA (2015) Being human, *Journal of the Royal Society of Arts, Manufactures and Commerce*, **2**

Saunders, T (2015) The power intoxicant, *OP Matters*, No 26, June, The British Psychological Society, London

Senge P (1994) *The Fifth Discipline Fieldbook*, Nicholas Brealey, London

Senge, P, Hamilton, H and Kania, J (2015) The dawn of system leadership, *Stanford Social Innovation Review*, Winter

Tate, W (1996) *Developing Corporate Competence: A high-performance agenda for managing organizations*, Gower, Aldershot

Tate, W (2009a) *The Search for Leadership: An organisational perspective*, Triarchy Press, Axminster

Tate, W (2009b) *The Systemic Leadership Toolkit*, Triarchy Press, Axminster

Tate, W (2013a) *Leadership – A case of systemic failure*, Croner-i

Tate, W (2013b) Managing leadership from a systemic perspective, (White Paper), Centre for Progressive Leadership, London Metropolitan University Business School

Tate, W (2014) Forward to basics – a new primer: Bringing a fresh look to the building blocks, Parliamentary Commission on the Future of Management and Leadership, evidence submitted by The Institute for Systemic Leadership to the All-Party Parliamentary Group on Management

Timmins, N (2015) *The Practice of System Leadership* (report), The King's Fund, London

Wheatley, M (1999) *Leadership and the New Science: Discovering order in a chaotic world*, Berrett-Koehler, San Francisco, CA

Zheltoukhova, K (2014) *Leadership: Easier said than done* (research report), Chartered Institute of Personnel and Development, London

Leading and managing people through change and resistance to change

11

NEIL MOORE

OBJECTIVES

This chapter aims to explore the leadership and management of people through change by:

- Investigating the internal and external drivers of change that exist in the contemporary business environment.

- Explaining the individual and organizational barriers to change that can impede change initiatives and create resistance to change.

- Outlining the different types of change that may be encountered in 21st-century organizations.

- Considering the key challenges and issues faced by those leading and managing people and organizations as they attempt to deal with change.

Introduction

Benjamin Franklin (1706–1790) famously said that there are only two certainties in life – death and taxes. However, in the 21st century we can add a third: the inescapable truth that we will have to deal with change. Indeed one of the biggest challenges facing us all is the nature and pace of change that we encounter in our daily lives. Change is everywhere and its impact is unavoidable. Increasingly business success, regardless of sector or context, is dependent upon the ability of leaders, managers and other employees to deal with change and its consequences.

This chapter begins by exploring the drivers of change and considers resistance to change. It then moves on to outline strategies for dealing with different types of organizational change and concludes by exploring the challenges faced by leaders and managers as they aim to deal with change situations.

Activity – The changing world of work

According to Frey (2011) many children who are currently in high school will undertake jobs and careers that have not been created yet. He suggests that 60 per cent of jobs that will be undertaken by 2030 do not currently exist. When we consider the past we see this trend beginning to emerge – for instance 20 years ago the role of Web Designer did not exist, likewise 40 years ago the role of Database Manager was meaningless.

Question: Identify a job role that currently does not exist but you think will be of significant importance in the future. What will the role involve? What specific challenges will face those who undertake the role? What specific challenges will face managers who have to work with those undertaking the role?

Drivers of change

To survive and grow, organizations need to be able to respond to the emerging external and internal challenges and issues they encounter. These factors create pressure for change and are often referred to as forces or drivers of change.

External drivers of change

An effective way to explore an organization's external environment and develop an understanding of the drivers for change that prevail within it is to apply the PESTLE framework. Each of the elements of the framework has the potential to affect organizations in a variety of ways. Table 11.1 demonstrates how the framework can be used to explore the many and varied external drivers of change that impact upon organizations.

TABLE 11.1   Drivers of change

Change driver	Description
Political	Changes to political processes and structures regionally, nationally and internationally can force organizations to adapt the ways in which they deal with key stakeholders such as consumers. Increasingly pressure groups are scrutinizing organizational activity and exposing inequalities (eg differences in working conditions and rates of pay); such activities can force organizations to change their modes of operation. For example, in 2014 Greenpeace claimed Lego terminated its 50-year relationship with Shell after coming under sustained pressure from the environmental campaign group because it had a marketing deal with the company to allow its toys to be distributed from petrol stations in 26 countries.
Environmental	Organizations are increasingly expected to act sustainably. This means that there is pressure for them to use their resources in ways that minimize waste and maximize efficiency. Since 2008 Sainsbury's Taste the Difference range of fresh chilled juice drinks have been packed in 100% recycled bottles – this has saved 375 tonnes of new plastic per year.
Sociocultural	Fundamental changes in aspects such as demographics, life expectancy and lifestyle create pressure for change. In addition, increasing global expectations relating to higher living standards, greater purchasing power and augmented consumer choice create pressure and opportunities for organizations to adapt and change. For instance, the record-breaking sales performance of Bentley Motors in 2014, up 23% in the first half of the year, was attributed to unprecedented demand from emerging markets such as China.

TABLE 11.1 *cont'd*

Change driver	Description
Technology	The rapid pace of technological change poses many challenges. For instance, technological change generates new market opportunities via e-commerce and social media and can lead to increases in the range and number of consumers and competitors that an organization faces. For example, cable TV providers face ongoing competitive challenges from satellite TV providers such as Sky.
Legal	Organizations are required to respond to legal and regulatory changes. Increasing bureaucracy related to international trade and consumer legislation can pose significant challenges for organizations and necessitate the implementation of new systems and processes. For example, the Chinese government requires all imported goods to possess compulsory permits and certificates. Imported agricultural goods and foodstuffs have to have a Quarantine Inspection Permit. Compliance procedures can involve the inspection of a company's manufacturing processes and investigation of the safety of products – goods without the appropriate permits and certification will be prevented from entering the country and confiscated.
Economic	The emergence of the global economy has required many organizations to change the ways in which they operate. Globalization has created pressure for organizations of all types to integrate and compete in the world economy. For many, the establishment of strong globally identifiable brands and the relocation of production to low-cost regions are necessities. For instance, in 2003 Dyson, the UK-based vacuum cleaner manufacturer, decided to relocate its manufacturing operations to Malaysia because it estimated production costs would be 30% lower.

Internal drivers of change

In addition to external drivers there are also internal factors that require organizations to adapt and transform their activities. A fundamental internal driving force is the need to replace outdated and ageing resources such as equipment and buildings. Similarly, as staff leave organizations, for example because of retirement, suitable replacements may be required. Most often such changes can be anticipated and therefore can be managed effectively. However, other internal drivers of change are less predictable and as a result can pose more significant challenges. Such drivers include the following.

Performance improvement

As markets become more competitive, organizations are required to become more efficient in their operations and activities. Increasingly there is a tension between maintaining and improving quality and reducing costs. Leaner forms of organizational structure, often utilizing outsourcing and zero-hours contracts, can drive internal change that results in new operating procedures and processes. Clearly, the effects of modernism can be seen as shaping many of these aspects (see Chapter 2).

Technology

As shown in Table 11.1, technology is a key external driving force of change. However, it can also be an important factor in driving internal change. For example, new technologies require workforce changes in terms of new skills and knowledge, new ways of operating and new conditions of employment.

Changing employee expectations

Increasingly employees are seeking to establish sustainable work–life balance. As a result many organizations are under increasing pressure to change the ways in which they organize their activities and operations. Flexible work patterns, job sharing and home working are now regarded by many workers as mainstream practices that should be freely available. Other changes to the psychological contract between employers and employees are also altering employment practices. For instance, for most employees, the notion of a 'job for life' which gives continuous employment with one organization is no longer a realistic expectation. The transient nature of employment in many organizations and industries poses significant challenges and issues for employer–employee relationships and has acted as a catalyst for change in areas such as industrial relations and performance management.

Fashions and trends

Often organizations engage in change because it is expected that they will be at the leading edge of innovation – this can result in 'change for change's sake'. For instance, a move to implement a new production process may be driven by the personal aspirations of the operations manager because he or she wants to demonstrate that they are at the leading edge of innovation. Such motivations may on occasion be driven by an agenda that prioritizes self-interest and values personal control and power ahead of the aims and objectives of the organization.

Activity – Planning for change in SMEs

The issue described in this case study is common to many SMEs. Very often the owner/founder of the business takes full day-to-day control of the enterprise and its operations. This approach is suitable while activities are small scale; however as an organization becomes established and begins to grow this 'hands on' approach becomes increasingly difficult to sustain. This challenge is further compounded when the owner/founder leaves the business – employees often find the transition difficult to deal with.

Flexi-joint is an SME that manufactures industrial products used in a wide variety of industrial applications. It has 76 employees and a turnover of £15.2 million. The business was established 23 years ago by John Gregory and, despite approaching retirement, he plays a full and active role in the day-to-day activities of the company. Recently John has had a few minor ailments that have caused him to spend a few days away from the business and he has become increasingly aware of the dependence his staff have on him. John has begun to think about what will happen when he retires from the business and he is concerned that the company does not have any plans to appoint a successor who will be able to lead the business in the future. His retirement will be a profound change for the business.

Question: How can Flexi-joint deal with this change? Identify the options available and explain the advantages and disadvantages associated with each.

Resistance to change

Although change is frequently a very positive experience that can bring a range of benefits it is often resisted both individually and organizationally. This section considers the individual and organizational barriers that can impede change.

Individual barriers to change

Uncertainty

When people are challenged by the unknown aspects of change or they face uncertainty they may become insecure, fearful and anxious and as a result they may resist change. Uncertainty may result from issues such as misinterpretation, poor communication and lack of knowledge and information (Cullen *et al*, 2014). If workers misinterpret why changes are being introduced, are not communicated with effectively and/or are ill-informed, proposed changes may be perceived as a threat and consequently resistance may follow. It could be, for example, that new rules and regulations relating to working hours are introduced and as a result employees are only offered restricted overtime. Unless the underlying reason is clearly explained and workers are made aware that the change results from new legislation the withdrawal of overtime may be regarded as a management-led cost-saving exercise.

Perceptual filters

Individuals' experience and understanding of the world are constructed by their perceptions of what is happening around them. As discussed in Chapter 2, we all selectively pay attention to, retain and filter the stimuli we encounter and as a result we generate an individualized picture of the 'real' world. This is when we only pay attention to the information that best fits our view of reality; this can prevent us from accepting change. Such bias can act as a significant barrier and impede progress. For example, a recently promoted employee may propose a change to a long-established process. In this situation colleagues may ignore the fact that the newly promoted person has significant and valuable experience and consequently decide to challenge and resist the proposal. By selectively filtering out important information about the person's past a valuable opportunity may be lost.

Patterns of behaviour

Habits play an important role in helping us deal with all manner of experiences and situations. Often we respond in routine ways in which we feel comfortable, secure and familiar. Requests to change long-established habitual patterns of behaviour may require us to move outside our comfort zones and develop new routines and approaches. Such challenges to the status quo may generate resistance and act as a barrier to change because people may be fearful of the risks associated with moving on from the past and generating and adopting new patterns of behaviour. For instance, asking experienced employees to alter the way they perform even the smallest of tasks may be resisted because they may be concerned that they will appear inept and lose face.

Threat to status

Often change may result in individuals losing status within the organizations in which they work. For example, a restructure may cause some employees to adopt new job titles – if the new title no longer includes the term 'manager' and is replaced with the term 'coordinator' or 'supervisor' this may be regarded as a loss of status. When changes result in an erosion of status and symbolic meaning individuals may strongly resist them in order to preserve both intrinsic and extrinsic benefits.

Organizational barriers to change

Organizational structure

Organizations with rigid and complex structures may find it difficult to respond to changes in their operating environments. For instance, in dynamic fast-moving markets organizations with inflexible mechanistic structures are likely, to be unable to respond to the challenges posed by competitors with leaner, more flexible configurations that can be changed and adapted easily to changing environments. In such situations an organization's structure may create inertia that impedes necessary and effective change (Sydow, 2015).

Borders the bookseller is an example of an organization that failed to adapt to change because of structural inertia. The company adopted a strategy of expanding its chain of retail outlets by entering into long-term leases for prestigious high street locations. Because of these commitments, as the competitive environment changed with the advent of online retailing, the company was not able to restructure and reconfigure its operations to meet the challenges posed by emerging competitors such as Amazon, and was liquidated in 2011.

Organizational culture

A fundamental component of the way that an organization operates is its culture. An organization's prevailing culture will help to determine its processes, procedures and 'ways of doing things'. For example, an organization that is dominated by a culture that values tradition will have policies and systems that support and protect well-established customs and practices – if change becomes necessary the organization may struggle to introduce it.

Organizational commitment

In situations where organizations have committed significant resources it may prove difficult for them to contemplate change. Substantial asset investment may mean that an organization is tied to undertaking a particular strategy even if more effective alternatives emerge. For instance, a manufacturer may undertake a large capital investment programme to implement new production equipment only to find that within a short time a more technically efficient system becomes available; in such circumstances a transition to the alternative is likely to be unfeasible. Likewise where organizations commit to long-term agreements with key stakeholders, such as customers and suppliers, contractual terms and obligations may prevent changes to operations and product/service offerings.

Organizational power and influence

Particular groups within organizations may have significant power and influence that they may wish to exert if change is proposed. Such vested interests can act as a barrier to change and may cause resentment and unrest within an organization. For example, a trade union may propose alterations to working practices but senior managers may resist this in order to maintain low costs and secure operational efficiency.

Activity – Change and resistance

Ross Marks is a sales manager who leads a team of financial consultants. He was promoted to the role of manager from the team he now leads after the previous manager retired. He has been in post for three months and he is finding his role very challenging. The team of financial consultants that he leads is long-established and has resisted any changes that he has attempted to implement. Ross is coming under continuing pressure from the regional manager to improve the sales performance of his team and he has been told that he is able to employ an additional consultant to help improve the situation. The job advert has been circulated internally and has attracted two applicants from other regions. Their profiles are as follows.

Consultant 1 is a 48-year-old who has worked with the same team for 15 years and has a successful track record of generating new sales. He is an experienced member of staff who has been considered for promotion on two previous occasions but deemed not to be suitable for a management position.

Consultant 2 is a 23-year-old who has worked in the same team for three years and, although he is relatively inexperienced, has a good set of recent sales figures. His recent performance appraisal indicated that despite showing some promise he is unconventional and will require guidance and support.

Question: Which consultant should Ross select? Provide a clear justification for your decision.

Types of change

So far in this chapter we have explored the internal and external drivers of change and the individual and organizational barriers that may exist when change occurs. This section explores types of change and the impact that each can have. Martin (2005) presents a change matrix that shows how the extent to which change is planned, and the scale of its impact, can create a range of responses – an adapted version of Martin's matrix is shown in Figure 11.1. Each of the elements of the matrix is discussed below.

FIGURE 11.1   Categories of change

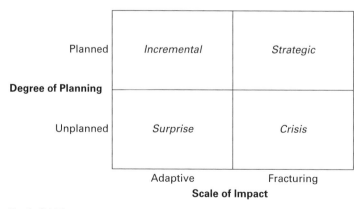

Adapted from Martin (2005)

Degree of planning

The vertical axis of the matrix represents the degree of planning that an organization can undertake in relation to change.

Unplanned – unanticipated and unexpected events can impact on organizations of all types. For example, crises such as natural disasters may take an organization by surprise because their precise nature cannot be predicted. Although we may know that an organization is located within a flood zone, and as a result can prepare for the possibility of disruption, it is unlikely that we will be able to know precisely when and to what extent our operations will be affected. Contingency plans can be made but their implementation may remain uncertain and unpredictable.

Planned – some changes can be anticipated and therefore can be managed through careful planning. In such cases organizations are able to develop well-thought-out strategies and can implement them at a time and pace of their choosing. For instance, managers may identify that service improvements are necessary and may plan a training and development programme to help employees change the way in which they perform particular tasks.

Scale of impact

The horizontal axis of the matrix considers the scale of impact of a change that an organization may experience.

Adaptive – in contrast to the extreme changes that have the potential to fracture an organization, those categorized as adaptive are relatively minor and small scale. These can be seen as the daily modifications and adaptions that are required to ensure that operations are maintained. For example, an employee may be suspended from work while a disciplinary matter is investigated and consequently other staff may be required to provide cover in addition to their existing workload. An important aspect of this is that although in organizational terms sourcing cover for an absent employee may not represent a significant challenge, for those who are required to absorb the additional workload the impact may be significant (working late, taking work home, etc).

Fracturing – this category incorporates profound and significant changes that have the potential to break or even destroy an organization. For instance, a technological advance may cause a long-established product to become obsolete and as a result may be a catastrophic event from which an organization may struggle to recover. An example of this is the move towards downloadable and streamed media content. Many high street movie rental outlets have closed because films and other media can be accessed instantaneously via a broad range of media devices.

Blockbuster (UK)

Blockbuster (UK) went into administration in January 2013 with the closure of 528 branches and the loss of 4,190 jobs. An underlying factor was the inability of senior managers to grasp the extent to which they needed to alter the strategy of the business to respond to changes in their competitive environment and the habits and preferences of customers. As new challenges emerged the executive management team opted to make small changes to the business model, such as allowing customers to trade second-hand items, rather than introducing innovative offerings such as streaming services. (Source: http://www.bbc.co.uk/news/business-21047652)

The synthesis of the vertical and horizontal axes of the matrix generates a typology of change that is composed of the following four elements:

1 *Incremental* – this type of change is expected and is most often on a small scale. It could, for example, result from the analysis of one of a series of processes that are utilized by an organization. The analysis may indicate that a minor modification would enhance other activities – as a result a small-scale planned alteration may be introduced.

2 *Strategic* – this category involves planned change that has implications of major significance for an organization. For instance, an organization may decide to expand its operations overseas. Such a strategic move will require planning and preparation and will carry inherent risks that have the potential to negatively impact on the future direction and success of the organization.

3 *Surprise* – change of this type is relatively minor and unplanned. For example, sudden unanticipated increases in the cost of diesel may force a road haulage company with a large fleet of vehicles to adjust its fuel budget and in turn recalculate its costs. In such a situation a decision will be required as to whether the increase in cost is absorbed by the company or passed on to its customers in the form of higher prices.

4 *Crisis* – this can be regarded as the 'worst case scenario' for an organization. Change is severe and takes the organization by surprise. For instance, the founder and owner of an organization may die in an accident – the unexpected devastating loss of a key employee, whose involvement is crucial to the functioning and success of an enterprise, has the potential to jeopardize its future and may even cause it to cease trading.

Episodic and continuous change

Martin's work on organizational change provides a useful and comprehensive framework that enables us to explore the different types of change that an organization may encounter. However, there are many approaches to categorizing change; a simpler typology was developed by Weick and Quinn (1999). They suggest that organizations will experience either episodic or continuous change.

Episodic change

This is intentional revolutionary change that is infrequent and disjointed. Such changes are carefully planned and are high-profile 'showpiece' events. Senior leaders present their vision of the change process and the benefits of the change. Most often this type of change is driven by a desire to maintain an equilibrium state and as a result is a large-scale activity that has far-reaching consequences for the organization. Because of its scale and scope, episodic change is likely to be lengthy and protracted and may be both taxing and unsettling for employees. Weick and Quinn predict that organizations most likely to engage in change of this nature would be characterized by a focus upon efficiency; close connections between departments; entrenched and fixed organizational cultures; a drive to imitate others rather than develop innovative market-leading strategies and solutions; and a desire to respond to immediate challenges and events that currently exist in their operating environment.

Episodic change

In the latter part of the 20th century many organizations engaged in large-scale episodic change programmes because of rapidly changing market and economic conditions (eg expansion into emerging markets such as Eastern Europe and the Far East). For instance, one UK-based financial institution opted to change long-established operational practices. This involved altering the structure of the workforce, embracing fledgling technology and reviewing its portfolio of financial products. The new strategy was launched via a 'fanfare' presentation by the organization's senior management team from the company's London headquarters. The organization's staff were invited to view the presentation at a number of regional cinemas that had been hired to screen the event. The transformation process was scheduled to take place over a five-year period and would impact on every aspect of the organization's structure, processes and procedures. However, shortly after the change process had begun the realization dawned that even more radical change was necessary as the organization's operating environment became more complex and challenging. New competitors began to emerge and advances in technology meant that online commercial opportunities arose (eg enhanced customer advice and sales). As the full potential of the internet and e-commerce became apparent the company abandoned its original change programme part way through and opted to introduce another more radical change strategy that involved large-scale staff redundancies.

This case illustrates the way that episodic change is often experienced in organizations. Large-scale planned change is launched in high profile events but because the change is slow and complex to implement it is often insufficient and outdated before it has been completed – consequently further broad-ranging changes are required to respond to market and economic changes. In essence organizations engaging in this type of change often find that as soon as they have undergone one period of episodic change another equally disruptive and challenging change programme is necessary.

Continuous change

In contrast to episodic change, continuous change is an open-ended, developmental and cumulative process. It involves ongoing small-scale modifications which, when aggregated across departments and sub-units, result in significant change. The process does not tend to be planned and intentional; rather it is likely to be unpremeditated and improvised. Organizations engaging in continuous change view change differently from those that adopt episodic change in that they regard change as a constant that is to be embraced and accommodated. Change is not regarded as a high-profile event that is scheduled in advance; rather it is an ongoing pervasive pursuit that is a recognized feature of the organization's operations and activities. According to Weick and Quinn (1999) continuous change may be a useful precursor to a successful episodic change programme because the relatively small developmental changes involved can be used to prepare an organization for revolutionary planned change. In this way continuous change may act as a primer for more complex episodic change. For example, employees may be required to undertake regular skills updating in preparation for a large-scale radical organizational change programme that will require staff to be multiskilled and more flexible in their approach.

Categorizing change as either episodic or continuous raises an important question: 'Is change managed or led?' According to Landy and Conte (2010) episodic change is likely to involve management while continuous change is most likely to be driven by leadership. They argue that the planning and scheduling of episodic change lend themselves to being managed whilst the ongoing improvised characteristics of continuous change require effective leadership that demonstrates that constant incremental change is a way of being and operating.

One of the most challenging aspects of change is that there is no one universal solution to help those who are responsible for managing and leading organizations. Approaches to dealing with change are contingent upon the precise factors that are active in the environment and situation in which the organization operates (Norbäck *et al*, 2014). In practice, managers and leaders have to develop bespoke approaches that meet the unique challenges they face. As a result, although generic issues can be discussed, their implications and implementation will vary from organization to organization. The following section explores generic issues and challenges relating to leading and managing change in more detail.

Leading and managing change: challenges and issues

The key challenges and issues facing those responsible for leading and managing change in contemporary organizations include the following.

Generate a sense of urgency

Given the pace of change faced by most organizations it is essential that once the need for change is identified and agreed, action is taken and commitment secured. Merely identifying that change is necessary without taking appropriate action could jeopardize the future of an organization. Although the precise speed of change will vary it is essential that managers and leaders generate appropriate levels of urgency and maintain momentum to ensure that opportunities are not missed (Denning, 2010; Kotter, 2008).

Create an environment of trust

Managers and leaders need to communicate clearly and honestly to employees why the proposed change is necessary. Unless staff understand the reasons for change they may resist and mistrust those who are attempting to implement the change (Holt and Vardaman, 2013). To build trust it may be helpful to involve employees as early as possible in the change process. Genuine participation during the early stages can help to generate ownership and commitment. Furthermore, effective two-way communication with all affected parties can help to create new understandings and insights that may provide benefits before, during and after the change process takes place (Klonek *et al*, 2014).

Develop a team approach

Cooperation is a vital ingredient for the implementation of successful change (Pascale *et al*, 1997; Parish *et al*, 2008; Whelan-Berry and Somerville, 2010). Supportive relationships between all levels of staff are important because shared involvement can help to develop resilience that will enable employees to cope with the demands that change may bring. Allied to this is the concept of pluralistic leadership. According to Brooks (2003), in change situations leadership is often a shared or pluralistic undertaking and as a result should be viewed as a team activity. Moreover, Bate (1994) explains that most often it is networks of leadership, rather than individual leaders, that deliver the most effective change.

Create vision

It is essential that staff not only appreciate the benefits of change but also that they understand the processes and strategies that will be needed to deliver the change. Those charged with designing and implementing change need to be able to inspire, energize and empower colleagues to accept their vision of what can be if the change is successful (Galpin, 1996; Kotter, 2008, 2012; Waddell *et al*, 2004; Whelan-Berry and Somerville, 2010). This aspect is an important dimension of transformational leadership. Transformational leaders create compelling visions that appeal to the values of their followers and thereby create high levels of trust and loyalty.

Deliver 'quick' wins

If early on in the change process progress is seen to be occurring this will provide credibility, build confidence and maintain momentum. Acceptance of change can also be enhanced and improved by highlighting the potential benefits that may be achieved as a result of implementing the change and clearly identifying to whom the benefits will accrue (Moss *et al*, 2014). For example, organizations may offer incentives to staff as targets are achieved – this can be an effective way of demonstrating the benefits that are associated with the changes that are taking place and can act as a motivating factor for future change.

Make change 'stick'

Once change has been implemented it is crucial that staff do not return to the old ways of operating. It is likely that the change programme has required investment of key resources and consequently if regression to long-standing patterns, habits and approaches occurs, current and future organizational success may be jeopardized. For changes to stick it is likely that new shared values, group norms and other cultural aspects will need to be fostered and cultivated (Armenakis *et al*, 2000; Cummings and Worley, 2004; Kotter, 2012).

Use change as a political tool

Change can often be used a way for new managers or leaders to assert their power and authority. By changing aspects of the organization, new incumbents can demonstrate that they are in control, that 'old' long-established ways of functioning have passed and that a new era dawns. In extreme cases radical changes to the structure of an organization may be used by a new leader to remove troublesome or otherwise unwanted staff. Likewise leaders may seek opportunities to employ new staff to act as 'agents of change'. These individuals may have radical approaches and views and as a result may challenge prevailing attitudes and beliefs.

Activity – Problems and solutions?

ABC Group is a multidisciplinary design and manufacturing organization that aims to produce customized and technically advanced integrated systems that provide high-quality innovative solutions to a diverse range of clients. Founded 30 years ago the company has become established as a reliable SME that is well positioned in several domestic and international markets. The firm operates from one depot and employs 52 staff.

Over the last two years the senior management team have noticed that the company's markets are becoming more competitive and although the company has remained profitable it has failed to meet its annual gross profit target of 32 per cent. An initial investigation by a team of external consultants has indicated that the firm needs to identify which projects, products and customers are the most profitable so that the strategic direction of the company can be changed to maximize profitability and performance. The firm's senior management team has decided that to achieve this it is necessary to introduce a management information system (MIS).

Task: Prepare a presentation that the senior management team will deliver to the staff. The presentation must be persuasive and must clearly explain why the change is necessary and how the new MIS will be implemented.

Concluding thoughts

This chapter has explored the nature of change and its impact on the contemporary business environment. The key points can be summarized as follows:

- Change is a pervasive feature of 21st-century life.

- The factors that drive change are many and varied and can be categorized as either being internal or external to an organization.

- Resistance to change is common and can be caused by a range of both individual and organizational factors.

- There are various types of change including planned, unplanned, adaptive, fracturing, episodic and continuous.

- Leaders and managers face a range of challenges and issues as they attempt to deal with change.

Revision questions

1 What are the internal and external factors that drive change? Provide an example of each.

2 What are the barriers encountered by individuals as they attempt to deal with change?

3 What are the organizational barriers that can inhibit effective change?

4 Why is episodic change a challenge for many organizations and how can it be managed effectively?

5 Using examples to illustrate your answer, discuss the key challenges facing those responsible for leading and managing change.

Further study

There is a plethora of texts and articles that can assist in understanding the topics and issues discussed in this chapter. The titles listed below are indicative for the purposes of assisted development of your thinking.

Cameron, E and Green, M (2015) *Making Sense of Change of Management. A complete guide to the models, tools and techniques of organizational change*, 4th edn, Kogan Page, London

Kotter, J P (2012) *Leading Change*, Harvard Business Review Press, Boston, MA

Smith, R, King, D, Sidhu, R, Skelsey, D and APMG (2014) (eds) *The Effective Change Manager's Handbook: Essential guidance to the change management body of knowledge*, Kogan Page, London

References

Armenakis, A A, Harris, S G and Field, H S (2000) Making change permanent: A model for institutionalizing change interventions, *Research in Organizational Change and Development*, **12**, pp 97–128

Arnold, J (2005) *Work Psychology: Understanding human behaviour in the workplace*, 4th edn, FT-Prentice Hall, London

Bate, S P (1994) *Strategies for Cultural Change*, Butterworth-Heinemann, Oxford

BBC News (2015) Blockbuster goes into administration, retrieved on 23 January 2015 from http://www.bbc.co.uk/news/business-21047652

Brooks, I (2003) *Organisational Behaviour: Individuals, groups and organisation*, FT-Prentice Hall, London

Cullen, K L, Edwards, B D, Casper, W C and Gue, K R (2014) Employees' adaptability and perceptions of change-related uncertainty: Implications for perceived organizational support, job satisfaction and performance, *Journal of Business and Psychology*, **29** (2), pp 269–80

Cummings, T and Worley, C (2004) *Organizational Development and Change*, 7th edn, South-Western Publishing, Cincinnati, OH

Denning, S (2010) *The Leader's Guide to Radical Management: Reinventing the workplace for the 21st century*, John Wiley & Sons, Chichester

Frey, T (2011) 55 Jobs of the future, retrieved on 22 November 2014 from http://www.futuristspeaker.com/2011/11/55-jobs-of-the-future/

Galpin, T J (1996) *The Human Side of Change: A practical guide to organization redesign*, Jossey-Bass, San Francisco, CA

Holt, D T and Vardaman, J M (2013) Toward a comprehensive understanding of readiness for change: The case for an expanded conceptualization, *Journal of Change Management*, **13** (1), pp 9–18

Klonek, F E, Lehmann-Willenbrock, N and Kauffeld, S (2014) Dynamics of resistance to change: A sequential analysis of change agents in action, *Journal of Change Management*, pp 1–27

Kotter, J P (2008) *A Sense of Urgency*, Harvard Business Press, Boston, MA

Kotter, J P (2012) *Leading Change*, Harvard Business Press, Boston, MA

Landy, F J and Conte, J M (2010) Work in the 21st Century: An introduction to industrial and organizational psychology, John Wiley & Sons, Hoboken, NJ

Martin, J (2005) *Organizational Behaviour and Management*, 3rd edn, Thomson Learning, London

Moss, S A, Butar, I B, Hirst, G, Tice, M, Craner, M, Evans, J and Hartel, C E (2014) Leadership and strategy The vital but evasive role of cooperation and clarity of expectations during strategic change, *Journal of Leadership and Management*, **1** (1)

Mullins, L J (2010) *Management and Organisational Behaviour*, 9th edn, FT-Prentice Hall, London

Norbäck, M, Helin, J and Raviola, E (2014) Stabilizing movements: How television professionals use other people's voices to cope with new professional practices during times of change, *Journal of Change Management*, **14** (4), pp 434–52

Parish, J T, Cadwallader, S and Busch, P (2008) Want to, need to, ought to: Employee commitment to organizational change, *Journal of Organizational Change Management*, **21** (1), pp 32–52

Pascale, R, Millemann, M and Gioja, L (1997) Changing the way we change, *Harvard Business Review*, **75** (6), pp 127–39

Pettinger, R (2012) *Management: A concise introduction*, Palgrave Macmillan, New York

Sydow, J (2015) Networks, persistence and change: A path dependence perspective, in *Management of Permanent Change*, Springer Fachmedien, Wiesbaden, pp 89–101

Waddell, D, Cummings, T G and Worley, C G (2004) *Organisation Development and Change*, Thomson, London

Weick, K E and Quinn, R E (1999) Organizational change and development, *Annual Review of Psychology*, **50** (1), pp 361–86

Whelan-Berry, K S and Somerville, K A (2010) Linking change drivers and the organizational change process: A review and synthesis, *Journal of Change Management*, **10** (2), pp 175–93

Conclusion

This book has worked to highlight some of the prescient issues in contemporary organizational management. The early chapters provided an account which, while recognizing the value of normative leadership and management theory, also exposed its limitations in terms of its universal applicability. The concepts of organizational ambidexterity and talent management were introduced as a means of providing a fresh approach that might facilitate more agile and flexible stances and solutions in a rapidly changing world. These preliminary chapters also undertook the novel and valuable task of examining the historical philosophies and paradigms that underpin contemporary thinking on markets, management and organizations. If it is possible to reach back in time to better understand deep-rooted philosophies that exert strong influences over the ways in which management and organizations are perceived, we can then approach the world of work from a much more critical and enlightened perspective. More specifically, such responses might invoke approaches grounded in, for example, postmodernism, poststructuralism and critical realism.

Against this backdrop, subsequent chapters provided original insights into the recurrent and vital topics of, inter alia, team working, leadership, performance, the internet, management development and systems thinking. The composite effect of these chapters has provided the reader with useful insights and suggested actions and approaches in order to manage and work within the modern work environment. It is certain and inevitable that the evolving work environment will continue to call for various forms of complexity, agility, flexibility and adaptability. It is hoped that the materials within this book will have assisted and supported these ongoing transformations.

The editors:
Peter Stokes, Neil Moore, Simon M Smith,
Caroline Rowland and Peter Scott

INDEX

Note: The index is arranged in alphabetical, word-by-word order. The prefix 'Mc' and numbers in headings are filed as spelt out in full. Acronyms are filed as written. Page numbers in *italics* indicate a Figure or Table.

Emerging Markets:
Strategies for competing in the global value chain

The traditional dominance of international markets by companies from the US, Western Europe and Japan can no longer be taken for granted. Emerging market economies, from the powerhouse Chinese economy (set to pass the US in national income by 2020) to dynamic players such as Mexico, South Africa and Indonesia, are rapidly changing the competitive landscape. Companies that can successfully enter these emerging markets may reap rewards and benefits from cost reductions and market opportunities. By understanding their positioning in the global continuum of companies and customers – the global value chain – businesses can build their strategies for better competitiveness, more effective resource allocation and cost reduction, and heightened awareness of risks and benefits. And in each of these areas, companies can see how emerging markets fit into the total global strategy.

Packed with in-depth case studies of multinationals from both sides of emerging markets, including Accenture, Walmart, Google, Nike, Novartis, PetroChina, Embraer, Tata Group and FEMSA, *Emerging Markets* is essential reading for anyone wanting to understand the new competitive landscape and how to maximize their business opportunities there.

ISBN: 978 0 7494 7449 2
Published by Kogan Page

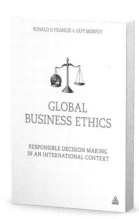

Global Business Ethics:
Responsible decision making in an international context

Corporate social responsibility, sustainability and acting ethically are all accepted business aims, but their meaning and implementation in a global context is far less clear-cut. *Global Business Ethics* cuts through the confusion to provide a coherent basis for ethical decision making within the complications of the international business landscape.

Underpinned by theory and including worked-through examples of ethical dilemmas and their solutions, this textbook will guide the reader beyond theory to real-world business decisions. Practical tools such as decision trees and suggested principles to apply in dilemma situations give readers the skills and confidence to tackle the ethical challenges they face, and a glossary of international codes related to ethics is provided for reference. Case studies include Walmart, Hershey's, Citibank, Ford, Nike, Johnson & Johnson, Harley-Davidson, The Body Shop and Procter & Gamble.

A chapter on the legal aspects of ethics provides clear guidance on the complex relationship between law and ethics in international business. The final part takes an in-depth look at the practical application of ethics in business life. Covering all the major theories of ethics, including an examination of the role of quantification of ethics, *Global Business Ethics* demonstrates how their principles can be applied to inform better business decisions.

ISBN: 978 0 7494 7395 2
Published by Kogan Page

Economics for Business: A guide to decision making in a complex global macroeconomy

Economics for Business is a thorough guide to key economic concepts and their applications in business. It provides readers with the economic tools and concepts to make decisions, sustain competitive advantage and confront the complexities of business head-on.

This comprehensive book covers the process of globalization and its implications for business, the role of the market and supply and demand, the impact of demand on branding and brand loyalty, and pricing strategies under various market structures. It explains the crucial importance of the financial system to individual businesses and the macroeconomy, allowing you to develop a clear understanding of the economic environment in which business takes place.

With specific business content integrated throughout and a global perspective on the current world of business, taking into account the financial crisis and its aftermath, *Economics for Business* is a streamlined and comprehensive introduction to economics for business students and a valuable resource for managers and executives who need a thorough grounding in economic concepts to grow their business.

ISBN: 978 0 7494 7019 7
Published by Kogan Page